KT-551-531

(1) MATT — DWK up CAPEX.

Ideal eh.

(2)

Investment in Manufacturing Technology

INVESTMENT IN MANUFACTURING TECHNOLOGY

Peter L. Primrose

Total Technology Department,
UMIST, Manchester

CHAPMAN & HALL
University and Professional Division
London · New York · Tokyo · Melbourne · Madras

Published by Chapman & Hall, 2–6 Boundary Row, London SE1 8HN

Chapman & Hall, 2–6 Boundary Row, London SE1 8HN, UK

Van Nostrand Reinhold Inc., 115 5th Avenue, New York NY10003, USA

Chapman & Hall Japan, Thomson Publishing Japan, Hirakawacho Nemoto Building, 7F, 1–7–11 Hirakawa-cho, Chiyoda-ku, Tokyo 102, Japan

Chapman & Hall Australia, Thomas Nelson Australia, 102 Dodds Street, South Melbourne, Victoria 3205, Australia

Chapman & Hall India, R. Seshadri, 32 Second Main Road, CIT East, Madras 600 035, India

First edition 1991

© 1991 Peter L. Primrose

Typeset in 10½/12 Times by
Mews Photosetting, Beckenham, Kent
Printed in Great Britain by
St. Edmundsbury Press, Bury St. Edmunds, Suffolk

ISBN 0 412 40920 8   0 442 31517 1 (USA)

Apart from any fair dealing for the purposes of research or private study, or criticism or review, as permitted under the UK Copyright Designs and Patents Act, 1988, this publication may not be reproduced, stored, or transmitted, in any form or by any means, without the prior permission in writing of the publishers, or in the case of reprographic reproduction only in accordance with the terms of the licences issued by the Copyright Licensing Agency in the UK, or in accordance with the terms of licences issued by the appropriate Reproduction Rights Organization outside the UK. Enquiries concerning reproduction outside the terms stated here should be sent to the publishers at the London address printed on this page.

The publisher makes no representation, express or implied, with regard to the accuracy of the information contained in this book and cannot accept any legal responsibility or liability for any errors or omissions that may be made.

A catalogue record for this book is available from the British Library

Library of Congress Cataloging-in-Publication data
Available

Printed on permanent acid-free text paper, manufactured in accordance with the proposed ANSI/NISO Z 39.48–199X and ANSI Z 39.48–1984

Contents

Acknowledgements   **viii**

Glossary   **ix**

1 Introduction   **1**

2 Investment appraisal   **6**
Appraisal techniques   8
Use of appraisal techniques   14
Replacement decisions   22

3 Identifying cash flow changes   **27**
Depreciation and overheads   29
Working life and resale value   33
Subsequent and delayed projects   40
Taxation and grants   44

4 Intangible benefits   **47**
Quantifying intangibles   49
Social costs   53
Non-existent benefits   55
Magnitude of benefits   58

5 Inventory savings   **65**
Valuation of inventory   66
Revaluation of inventory   72
The effect of inventory reduction   76

6 Costing systems   **80**
Standard costs   81
Cost allocation   83
Capacity constraints   88
Costing investment decisions   89

Machine utilization   91
Product life cycles   95

7 Risk and uncertainty   **100**
Technical risk   100
Commercial risk   101
Allowing for risk   101

8 Cost of capital   **107**
Inflation   111

9 Monitoring performance   **113**

10 Product quality   **115**

11 Just in Time (JIT)   **121**

12 Investment strategy   **127**

13 Industrial relations   **130**

14 Selecting technology   **135**

15 CNC machines   **138**
Batch quantities   139
Machine utilization   143
Scrap and rework   145
Start-up time   146
Component selection   147
Viability of CNC   149
Costs and savings of CNC   151

16 Flexible manufacturing   **153**
Machine utilization   155
Single-machine FMM   158
Multi-machine systems   163
Flexible transfer lines   168
Flexible factories   171
Selecting investment in FMS   172
FMS case study   178

17 MRP and MRPII   **183**
Costs and benefits of MRPII   184
MRPII case study   190

18 Computer aided design and manufacture (CAD/CAM) **195**
CAD   195
CAD/CAM   200
Process planning (CAPP)   202

CAD case study 1   204
CAD case study 2   206

19 Robots   **209**
Costs   210
Benefits   212

20 Computer integrated manufacture (CIM)   **215**
The scope of CIM   216
The extent of integration   218
Linking or integration   220
Transfer of data   221
CIM case study   224

21 Information technology (IT)   **228**

22 The future development of AMT   **232**

Index   **235**

Acknowledgements

This book is based on the work done in the Total Technology Department at the University of Manchester Institute of Science and Technology (UMIST). I would like to thank the head of the department, Dr Raymond Leonard, who provided enthusiastic support as the work progressed; and also Barry Harrison, who has helped transfer the results of my work to industry.

I should like to thank the research students in the department, who helped by trying out my ideas in the companies with which they were working. My thanks are also due to the Science and Engineering Research Council, who provided financial assistance for part of the work.

Peter L. Primrose
UMIST

Glossary

AA	Automated assembly
AGV	Automatic guided vehicle
AMT	Advanced manufacturing technology
ARR	Accounting rate of return
ASCII	American Standard Code for Information Interchange
CAD	Computer aided design
CAD/CAM	Computer aided design and manufacture
CAM	Computer aided manufacture
CAPM	Computer aided production management
CAPP	Computer aided process planing
CIM	Computer integrated manufacture
CNC	Computer numerical control
CPA	Critical path analysis
DCF	Discounted cash flow
DNC	Direct numerical control
DO	Design Office/Drawing Office
EBQ	Economic batch quantity
FIFO	First in first out
FM	Flexible manufacture
FMF	Flexible manufacturing factory
FMM	Flexible manufacturing module
FMS	Flexible manufacturing system
FP	'Family planning'
FTL	Flexible transfer line
GT	Group technology
IGES	Initial Graphics Exchange Standard
IRR	Internal rate of return
ILO	International Labour Office
IT	Information technology
JIT	Just in Time

LILO	Last in Last out
MAP	Manufacturing Automation Protocol
MBO	Management by Objectives
MIS	Management information system
MRP	Material requirement planning
MRPII	Manufacturing resources planning
NC	Numerical control
NPV	Net present value
OSI	Open systems interconnection
PCB	Printed circuit board
RGV	Rail guided vehicle
SA	Sensitivity analysis
SPC	Statistical process control
VA	Value analysis
VE	Value engineering
WIP	Work-in-progress

1 Introduction

Manufacturing companies are faced with a wide range of technology in which they can invest. Although this is generally referred to as **advanced manufacturing technology (AMT)**, the title is somewhat misleading because it can have an effect on the whole company, not just manufacturing. For convenience, however, the term AMT is used to refer to the whole range of technology now available to a manufacturing company. Not only are governments constantly trying to encourage industry to invest in order to remain competititve, the advocates of each aspect of AMT, such as vendors, consultants, academics and journalists, all have a vested interest in trying to convince companies that investment is essential.

The need always to be ahead of their rivals leads those advocates into promoting the latest developments in technology, even if some of the developments are 'technology for technology's sake', and may not provide as much benefit as less fashionable and cheaper alternatives. This leads to the proliferation of mnemonics (e.g. CAPM, CIM, CAD/CAM, JIT, GT, FMS, etc.) and the development of 'flavour of the month' technology.

Although companies could, in theory, find an application for each aspect of AMT, their first problem is to decide whether investment in AMT is really necessary, or whether they should concentrate their financial and management resources elsewhere, such as on changes in organization and management systems, design of new products or improved marketing and distribution.

The traditional attitude to investment appraisal has been that it is a final hurdle which has to be overcome in the investment process. Having spent considerable effort in selecting a technical specification, managers then have to try to get the investment past the accountants. The increasing difficulty of so doing, as technology becomes more complex and expensive, has helped develop the belief that existing accountancy procedures were inadequate when dealing with the complexities of AMT.

In fact investment appraisal must not be used as a technique whose aim is to give a final pass/fail verdict on projects, it must be treated as an aid to management decision-making and used as an integral part of the selection process. This process should start with identifying the areas in the company where resources need to be concentrated, and helping to select required technical specification, and then establishing the objectives and timetable for implementation.

There are two main problems associated with investment appraisal: one is ensuring that the correct appraisal techniques are used, the other is the need to overcome the widespread belief that some of the benefits of AMT are intangible and cannot therefore be included in a financial evaluation. Chapter 2 therefore describes the various appraisal techniques and their application, while Chapter 3 highlights the need to identify cash flow changes correctly.

The belief that some of the benefits of AMT are intangible is wrong and it can now be stated that:

There is no such thing as an intangible benefit, every benefit which can be identified can be redefined and quantified in financial terms and included in an investment appraisal. No benefit should ever be excluded on the grounds that it is intangible.

While they believe there are benefits which cannot be included in an investment appraisal, managers have an excuse for making investments without a financial evaluation. As a result, investment policy within a company becomes highly subjective and decisions are biased by personalities.

The ability to quantify all potential benefits shows that the magnitude of some of the benefits which were previously being excluded as intangible can be far larger that the direct savings which managers have traditionally concentrated on. At the same time, some of the benefits previously claimed for AMT are seen to be of little value and are, in some cases, non-existent. The importance of quantifying intangible benefits is that investment in much of AMT will only make financial sense when the aim is to achieve these benefits.

Much of the literature about AMT and Just in Time (JIT) puts considerable emphasis on the need to reduce inventory. However, Chapter 5 shows that the way in which inventory changes are valued is complex and reductions can have a major, and negative, effect on reported profits. It can be seen that in the majority of companies the magnitude of benefits resulting from inventory reduction are likely to be much smaller than those obtainable from other changes.

One of the reasons why the concept of intangible benefits developed is that they do not appear in the department where the investment is made, but appear elsewhere in the company. However large the benefits are going to be, if they have not been quantified in an initial evaluation, they will appear as unexplained variances and not be attributed to the project. However, even if the benefits have not been quantified, all the costs will still be known (because the bills have to be paid) and will be included in the company's costing system.

Thus the result is that any investment which is made without a financial evaluation must appear in the costing system to have increased the cost of manufacture. The previous inability to quantify many of the perceived benefits of AMT therefore has led not only to the belief that there was something wrong with investment appraisal, but also that there was something wrong with cost accounting.

It has seemed logical that if investing in AMT was the right thing to do, and the company's costing system has shown that this was not the case, then there must be something wrong with cost accounting. However, it is a fact that the benefits of AMT were described in terms such as better-quality products, increased flexibility of production, improved inventory performance, etc., which meant that accountants were unable to measure the performance of AMT in financial terms.

Another reason for the development of the intangible benefit concept is that there is not a direct link between cause and effect and the magnitude of the benefit has to be estimated rather than calculated. For example, with a new machine tool which can produce as much as two old machines, the number of operators required will be halved. On the other hand, with a **flexible manufacturing system (FMS)** which can improve delivery and thereby result in increased sales, the relationship between delivery improvement and sales increase is indirect and can only be estimated.

The result is that projects aimed at achieving indirect savings are perceived to have a much higher level of risk. However, not only are there techniques which can be used to reduce the level of perceived risk, but the potential magnitude of indirect savings can be so large that they may more than compensate for any element of risk.

When investment appraisal was used only to give a final pass/fail verdict on projects, considerable efforts were made to calculate the optimum value of the cost of capital which was used for making this yes/no decision. However, when investment appraisal is correctly used as an aid to decision-making, it can be seen that calculating an accurate cost of capital is no longer important.

The ability to quantify all the costs and benefits of AMT in financial terms means that they can be reflected in costing systems, and such systems can then be used to monitor and control performance. The ability to do this results in a considerable change in attitude towards post-audits, whose aim has often been seen as trying to apportion blame for a project's failure.

Because attempts to improve product quality have normally concentrated on efforts to reduce the cost of scrap, rework, etc., quality-related investments have tended to be defensive in nature, with their justification being based on cost reduction. The ability to quantify the benefits of 'better-quality products' shows that by far the largest benefit comes from the potential increase in sales volume. Not only does this mean that investments to improve product quality can be highly profitable, but also that there has to be a fundamental change in the way that companies approach quality improvement.

The introduction of JIT is not normally seen as an investment decision. However (like any other investment), JIT involves considerable expenditure and can produce financial savings, and as such it can be evaluated in the same way as any other AMT project. The ability to evaluate JIT in financial terms shows that many of the benefits claimed for JIT can be very small in relation to the costs of obtaining them.

As a result, companies that are considering the introduction of JIT, or have already introduced it, need to re-examine their objectives. Because the use of JIT has not been evaluated, it has not been possible to reflect the costs and benefits of JIT in costing systems. This has helped to encourage the belief that cost accounting was inadequate for controlling a 'JIT environment'.

In the past, most AMT investments have been aimed at improving departmental performance. This has meant that, in most companies, technical innovation was expected to be initiated by the departments which would be most affected. As AMT has changed, it can now affect the total company, with the major benefits no longer occurring in the department where the investment is made. As a result, a change in approach is needed towards identifying potential areas for investment, and managers throughout the company must become aware of the potential benefits of AMT.

The investment appraisal techniques used in the past have over-emphasized the benefits of reducing direct labour. The result has been that much of AMT has been aimed at labour-saving and therefore is seen as a threat to jobs, resulting in industrial relations problems. The changes in objectives from reducing costs to increasing competitive ability and profitability means that investing in AMT can help to increase job security. The result can be a much more enthusiastic and effective implementation.

The change in financial objectives means that there has to be a major change in the technology selected which, in turn, will affect the way in which AMT is developed in the future. By identifying the costs and benefits of the main areas of AMT it can be seen how these can be related to selecting the required technical specification.

Several case studies are included in this book in order to demonstrate the importance of including company-wide benefits in an evaluation. In addition, the case studies help to illustrate how companies can evaluate projects which involve replacing an earlier AMT investment and how to tackle projects where there is a choice between alternative levels of technical sophistication.

In the past, there was a universal belief that existing accountancy procedures were inadequate when dealing with the complexities of AMT. Fortunately, it can now be seen that the problems of evaluating and costing AMT have been the result of a mutual lack of understanding between accountants and non-financial managers, resulting in their inability to relate technology to accountancy.

While there was a belief that something was wrong with accountancy, companies refrained from changing their systems because they did not know what was the right thing to do. In fact there is nothing wrong with accountancy principles, for the problem has been the failure of companies to update their procedures to reflect the way that AMT is changing the company organization.

Although investment in AMT can be highly expensive, it can also be most profitable. For many companies, investing in AMT may be essential for their long-term viability. By helping to overcome the communication problems between managers of different disciplines, and by describing the relationship between AMT and accountancy, the aim of this book is to help companies re-examine their investment needs and increase the rate at which manufacturing industry is introducing new technology.

Chapter

2 Investment appraisal

The traditional view of investment appraisal has been that the sole reason for its use has been to give a final yes/no–pass/fail verdict on a project. The result was that when managers were trying to persuade their company to invest in a project which they were convinced for technical reasons was essential, they saw the use of investment appraisal as a hurdle that had to be overcome, not as a technique for evaluating the project's worth or comparing it with alternative projects.

The emphasis, then, was on trying to justify a decision which had already been taken, rather than the evaluation of alternatives. The attitude of managers was 'how big a value of savings do I need to get it past the accountants?'. This approach therefore has encouraged managers to try to estimate the maximum possible savings and the minimum possible costs.

Because managers may have spent much time and effort investigating the technical aspects of a particular project, they become committed to the belief that it is essential. As a result, they can be more easily susceptible to persuasion by vendors, consultants, etc. and prepared to accept untypical demonstrations which may show unrealistically high levels of saving. When evaluating investments, managers tend to concentrate their efforts on trying to identify and estimate savings. However, when a company is considering an investment in an aspect of technology where it has little or no experience, it is easy to make the investment decision without being aware of the full cost implications.

The need to identify all of those cost implications is especially important in the case of computer systems, such as CAD or MRPII, which have extremely high running costs. The failure so to do, when combined with the use of over-optimistic forecasts of savings in projects which can take several years to achieve the level of full savings, leads to a situation where it is highly unlikely that the forecast return on investment will ever be achieved. The result is that AMT is concluded to be a failure.

6

Any investment decision must be based on assumptions made about future events, and because of this, the result must be inexact and subject to error. Investment appraisal cannot give an exact verdict on any project, it is only an aid to management decision-making, and as such the result will only be as good as the assumptions that are used in the evaluation. However, investment appraisal must be used for much more than just giving a final pass/fail verdict; it must be used from the start of a project as an integral part of the selection process.

Manufacturing companies have a very wide range of technology in which they can invest. The manager in charge of almost every department in the company will be able to make out a case for investment in some aspect of AMT to improve operating efficiency. The first problem which has to be tackled, then, is to identify the areas of the company where resources should be concentrated. Using investment appraisal to help make that choice allows the conflicting claims to managers to be compared in an objective way.

Having identified the area for investment, the company will then be faced with the problem of selecting the required technical specification and the supplier. The range of possible options is likely to be extremely large, for example, in the UK there are over 200 different CAD systems available and over a hundred MRPII systems to choose from; and, in addition, the suppliers of each of these systems will be able to present reasons why their particular system should be chosen.

Having selected the supplier and defined the required specification, the next stage of the investment process is to establish clearly defined and measurable objectives and a timetable for implementation. The aim in doing this is not just to be able to monitor progress in order to take corrective action quickly if anything starts to go wrong. It is also to ensure that the rate at which the most important objectives are achieved is optimized. One of the main reasons why AMT has often been reported as a financial failure is that companies have been unable to reflect the investment correctly in their financial systems: it is only by quantifying all the costs and all the benefits in financial terms during the initial investment appraisal that this can be done.

The aim in selecting investments therefore is not just to get more than the minimum required rate of return, for this could be achieved by selecting projects which will do little more than provide this minimum return. The aim must be to try to identify the most profitable way that a company can invest its financial and management resources. Investment appraisal is a management tool which helps companies to do this, its objectives being as follows:

1. To help select the most important areas of the company where initial investment in AMT should be concentrated.
2. To help choose the correct technical specification and supplier.
3. To help establish the objectives and timetable for implementation.

4. To quantify all costs and savings, so that the investment is correctly reflected in the company's costing system and balance sheet.
5. To ensure that the investment will be profitable.

The way that money is raised for an investment programme varies between companies, as does the cost of such finance. When the money has to be borrowed from outside (e.g. banks or shareholders), the company will have to pay interest on the outstanding value of the loan until the total has been repaid. When the money is obtained from the company's own resources, its cost will be not just the value of the investment, but also the loss of the interest which could have been obtained if the money had been lent elsewhere.

Although there are different ways of raising money, the only effect this has on an investment appraisal is the magnitude of the value used by the company for the cost of capital. Whichever way the money to finance investments is raised, projects must produce sufficient savings in order to achieve the following:

1. Repaying the initial loan.
2. Paying for running costs.
3. Paying interest on money borrowed.
4. Making sufficient profit to compensate for any element of risk in the project.

Because these costs represent cash payments, it is important that all the savings also represent cash values; and, as a result, one of the biggest problems encountered by non-financial managers is the need correctly to identify cash flow changes. Unfortunately, much of the financial information available to managers is that contained in their company's costing system – but the information in such systems is based on the allocation of depreciation and overhead costs and does not represent cash flows.

The aim in an investment appraisal is to identify all the additional cash flows (both costs and savings) which will result from making the investment. An evaluation must compare the cash flows that will happen if the investment is made with those which will happen if it is not made, in order to identify the changes in cash flows. When there are a number of alternative options, such as comparing several different technical specifications which could result in different levels of costs and savings, care must be taken not only to avoid any double counting, but it is also important to ensure that no values are left out of the evaluation.

APPRAISAL TECHNIQUES

Four main techniques qre used in industry:

1. Payback.
2. Accounting rate of return (ARR).
3. Internal rate of return (IRR).
4. Net present value (NPV).

The last two are based on the use of **discounted cash flow** (DCF); each of the above techniques has advantages and disadvantages when applied in practice, but before considering these, it is necessary to look at the techniques themselves.

PAYBACK

This is the most commonly used technique, mainly because it is the simplest to understand and use. It is the calculation of the payback period required to recover the initial cost of a project and uses the simple formula:

$$\text{Payback period} = \frac{\text{Capital cost}}{\text{Annual savings} - \text{Annual costs}}$$

For example, a project that has an initial capital cost of £120 000 and annual running costs of £10 000 would have a two-year payback period if annual savings were £70 000:

	Year 0 £	*Year 1* £	*Year 2* £
Capital cost	−120 000		
Running cost		−10 000	−10 000
Savings		−70 000	+70 000
Cash flows	−120 000	+60 000	+60 000

In all examples given here, the standard accountancy convention is used, that investment takes place at the end of year 0 and operation starts at the beginning of year 1. Although running costs and savings can occur throughout each year of the project life from the beginning of year 1, the convention assumes that they will occur at the end of each year.

Doing this may slightly understate the return on investment, but it will never be possible in an evaluation to predict the timing of cash flows with any accuracy. As with most accountancy conventions, it is based on using conservative estimates when there is an element of uncertainty.

The understatement of return caused by taking savings as if they occurred at the end of each year, instead of throughout the year, can be partly offset by the assumption that initial expenditure takes place at the end of year 0.

In practice, most capital purchases are not ordered and installed within a few days; it may take several months from the time of placing an order until the equipment becomes fully operational, and this may have involved several payments over that period.

Typical stage payments can be 30% of price with order, 60% prior to despatch and the final 10% after commissioning and acceptance. Because the discounting process makes early cash flows worth more than later ones, the error involved in assuming payment is at the end of year 0 may offset the error in taking savings at year-ends.

A further factor which can help reduce the importance of the error caused by these assumptions is that for many projects, especially large computer systems, the build up of savings will start at zero at the beginning of year 1 and gradually build up to the full level, possibly after two or three years. Not only will the savings be greater towards the end of each year than at the beginning, but unlike savings, the running costs will probably be at a reasonably constant level throughout each year.

If, in the above example, the annual savings were only £50 000, rather than £70 000, the figures would be:

	Year 0 £	Year 1 £	Year 2 £	Year 3 £
Capital cost	− 120 000			
Running cost		− 10 000	− 10 000	− 10 000
Savings		+ 50 000	+ 50 000	+ 50 000
Cash flows	− 120 000	+ 40 000	+ 40 000	+ 40 000

This would now give a three-year payback period.

ACCOUNTING RATE OF RETURN (ARR)

This can be defined as the average annual profit (after depreciation) as a percentage of the capital outlay. A simple formula for this is:

$$\text{ARR} = \frac{\text{Annual revenue} - \text{Accounting depreciation}}{\text{Capital cost}} \times 100\%$$

annual revenue being the difference between annual savings and annual costs. The above formula becomes much more complex if factors such as capital grants and taxation are included in the calculation.

DISCOUNTED CASH FLOW (DCF)

Calculating the repayment of house-purchase loans or bank overdrafts is based on the fact that when money is borrowed interest has to be paid on the total amount outstanding until both the loan and the interest are repaid; for example:

Year	Loan outstanding, 1 January £	Annual interest at 10% £	Loan outstanding 31 December £	Repayment made 31 December £
1	1000	100	1100	0
2	1100	110	1210	610
3	600	60	660	660
Total		270		1270

This is the basis of compound interest, with interest being added to the loan at the end of each year. If, for example, £100 is lent for two years at 10% interest, its value at the end of the second year will be:

$$£100 \times (1 + 0.1) \times (1 + 0.1) = £121$$

If the loan had been for three years and interest 20%, the value would be:

$$£100 \times (1 + 0.2) \times (1 + 0.2) \times (1 + 0.2) = £172.80$$

Receiving £100 today is worth more than receiving £100 in a year's time, because the money received today could be invested to obtain interest. Conversely, £100 to be received in a year's time is worth less than £100 today. If £100 is invested at 10% for two years, it will be worth £121 at the end of that time; if, however, the loan had been at 10% for three years, the initial £100 would be worth £133.10.

This means that for a company looking for investments which would give a return of 10%, it may be worth investing £100 if this would result in a benefit of over £121 in two years time. It would not be worth investing if it were to be three years before the benefit of £121 would occur.

With an investment where one has to spend money today, the value of future savings must be adjusted for the fact that the longer it will be before they are received, the less will be their worth in repaying the initial investment. With compounding, the aim is to calculate the future value of an investment, while discounting is the converse.

With discounting, one is trying to calculate the value today of benefits which will be received in the future. Thus £121 to be received in two years time, and discounted at 10% for two years, is worth £100 today. This *opportunity cost* of waiting for money to be received is perceived as interest forgone from other opportunities during the waiting period.

NET PRESENT VALUE (NPV)

Net present value is a discounting technique which considers not only the magnitude of cash flows for expenditure and savings, but also the timings of these cash flows. It discounts all of a project's cash flows back to the time of the start of the project, year 0.

The discount rate which is used is the minimum rate of return required for the type of project contemplated, including an allowance for any perceived risks. If the NPV is positive, the project would be acceptable because the expected return will be higher than the minimum required. Take as an example a project with the following cash flows:

Year	Cash flows £	Discount factor 12%	Present value £
0	− 1000	−	− 1000
1	+ 250	0.8929	+ 233.23
2	+ 350	0.7972	+ 279.02
3	+ 400	0.7118	+ 284.72
4	+ 400	0.6353	− 254.20
5	+ 350	0.5674	+ 198.59
NPV			= + 239.76

Using 12% as the minimum acceptable rate of return for this type of project, the NPV calculation shows that the project would be acceptable because the NPV value is positive.

In the past, the way to calculate NPV was to look up the discount factors in discount tables. Such tables give the appropriate factor for each combination of year and interest rate (i.e. for a 12% cost of capital the factor for cash flows in year 1 would be 0.8929). The calculation was then carried out, as in the above example; doing this, even using a calculator, can be time-consuming and prone to error – fortunately the latest computer programs do all the calculations automatically.

The formula for NPV is:

$$NPV = C_0 + \frac{C_1}{(1 + r)^1} + \frac{C_2}{(1 + r)^2} + \frac{C_3}{(1 + r)^3} + \ldots + \frac{C_n}{(1 + r)^n}$$

where C_n is the total cash flow in year n, and r is the discount rate.

For example, using a 10% discount factor, a project costing £1000 in year 0 and producing savings of £300 a year for five years would give:

$$NPV = -1000 + \frac{300}{(1 + 0.1)} + \frac{300}{(1 + 0.1)^2} + \frac{300}{(1 + 0.1)^3} + \frac{300}{(1 + 0.1)^4} + \frac{300}{(1 + 0.1)^5}$$

thus NPV $= -1000 + (300 \times 0.9091) + (300 \times 0.8264) + (300 \times 0.7513)$
$+ (300 \times 0.6830) + (300 \times 0.6209)$

NPV $= -1000 + 272.73 + 247.93 + 225.39 + 204.90 + 186.28$
NPV $= 137.23$

INTERNAL RATE OF RETURN (IRR)

Internal rate of return is the rate of return which will make the NPV of the project equal to zero. Because it can be likened to a home loan, and its use shows a specific return from an investment, it is usually easier for non-financial managers to understand when comparing projects since they are more used to thinking in terms of 'rates of return' than positive or negative present values.

Using discount tables to calculate IRR requires an element of trial and error as one has to discover the discount rate which will make NPV $= 0$. This involves doing NPV calculations for a range of values; for example:

Year	Cash flow £	NPV =	Present value (20%)	NPV =	Present value (21%)
0	−1000		−1000		−1000
1	+250		+208.33		+206.60
2	+350		+243.04		+239.60
3	+400		+231.48		+225.80
4	+400		+192.92		+186.60
5	+350		+140.67		+134.93
		NPV =	+£16.44	NPV =	−£7.02

This example shows that the discount rate which makes NPV $= 0$ lies between 20% and 21%; further calculation would bring this to 20.7%. Calculating IRR using discount tables is an even more time-consuming and error-prone process than is NPV.

However, for a manager without accountancy training it is more meaningful to say that a project will give a return of 20.7% than to say it has an NPV of +£239.76. Ideally, an evaluation should provide the results in terms of both IRR and NPV as the first is normally more easily understood by non-financial managers, while the second would be preferred by accountants for use in comparing projects.

With a loan for house purchase, where one knows the value of the amount borrowed, the number of years over which repayments will be made and the current rate of interest, it is the size of the repayments which is calculated. With IRR, where the amount invested, the life of the project and repayments (savings) are known, the rate of interest (rate of return) is calculated.

USE OF APPRAISAL TECHNIQUES

Each of the four techniques described have limitations in normal use, and the problems that these limitations cause are increased when the techniques are applied to complex investment projects such as CAD, FMS and MRPII. In considering the problems associated with using the various techniques the characteristics of the projects to be evaluated have to be understood, the main ones being:

1. In some cases, it may be several years from starting to spend money on a project until it is fully installed and operational. This is particularly true with systems such as MRPII which can be installed in a series of modules.
2. It may take several years before the full level of savings is being achieved. With CAD systems, for example, draughtsmen are more productive when modifying existing drawings than when creating new ones but, initially, they spend all their time creating new drawings.
3. In evaluating a project a large number of factors may have to be included (20–30 being typical); as a result, the pattern of cash flows over the project life can be highly complex.
4. The way capital grants and taxation will affect a project can be complex and it may also have a major effect on profitability.
5. Over the working lives of many computer systems the total running costs can be greater than the initial capital and installation costs.
6. Because any evaluation must be based on assumptions about future events, they are subject to uncertainty. The complexity of AMT projects appears to increase this uncertainty, so that an evaluation must be able to compare a range of likely outcomes.

The problems of using each of the four appraisal techniques has to be considered in relation to each of the above characteristics. However, despite the problems associated with their use, all four techniques are nevertheless widely used. A survey of 100 major companies in the UK, published by the Institute of Cost and Management Accountants in 1988, showed that most companies used more than one technique. Table 2.1 shows their relative use. The primary technique employed is shown in Table 2.2 (some companies quoted two primary methods).

Table 2.1 Use of appraisal techniques

Technique	Percentage of companies
Payback	92
ARR	56
NPV	68
IRR	75

Table 2.2 Primary appraisal techniques

Technique	Percentage of companies
Payback	47
ARR	18
NPV	23
IRR	42

PAYBACK

Despite the large number of companies that use payback, it is normally condemned in accountancy literature because it has two major limitations, namely:

1. It takes no account of the timing of cash flows.
2. It ignores what happens after the payback period.

These limitations can be illustrated by considering three simple projects:

	Year 0	Year 1	Year 2	Year 3	Year 4	Year 5
	£	£	£	£	£	£
A	−1000	+500	+500	0	0	0
B	−1000	+200	+300	+500	0	0
C	−1000	+200	+300	+400	+500	+600

A company looking for projects with a two-year payback period would accept A but would reject B and C. A company looking for projects with a three-year payback would accept A and B but would still reject C.

While A and B provide a three-year payback, neither generate sufficient savings to pay interest, let alone make a profit. If the projects are compared using DCF, the IRR is :

$$A = 0\%$$
$$B = 0\%$$
$$C = 23.2\%$$

The use of payback can result in incorrect decisions being made, as in the following simple example:

	Year 0	Year 1	Year 2	Year 3
	£	£	£	£
Capital cost	−120 000			
Running costs		−10 000	−10 000	−10 000
Savings		+90 000	+50 000	0
Annual cash flow	−120 000	+80 000	+40 000	−10 000

In theory, this project could be accepted by a company looking for projects that give a two-year payback. Although a decision to accept the project obviously would be wrong, projects such as this may often be accepted in cases where the person doing the evaluation excludes from the calculation all cash flows beyond the end of the required payback period.

The normal assumption that is made when using payback is that, as illustrated in Fig. 2.1, there is a point in time (the end of year 0) when the investment is made, the old process stops, the new one begins and the full level of savings is achieved from the start of year 1. When technology was relatively simple and companies normally invested in manually operated machine tools, not CNC, the errors resulting from using this assumption were

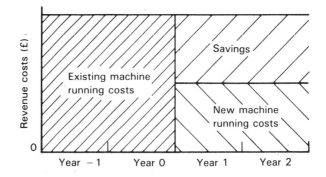

Fig. 2.1 Traditional assumption made with payback.

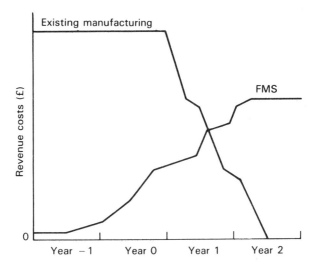

Fig. 2.2 Build-up and run-down of revenue expenditure.

not too great. As technology has become more complex, the initial cash flows can be spread over several years. For example, the introduction of FMS, as shown in Fig. 2.2, may involve expenditure on fixtures, tooling, programming, training, etc. for a long time before the system is installed.

Even after installation, there may be another extended period during which output is increased such as from one shift to two or even three. With many projects, such as FMS, revenue expenditure must be started well before capital; and even after the capital expenditure, there may be a long delay before the project is fully operational and the full level of savings starts to be achieved. At the same time as revenue expenditure is increasing for the new project, the running costs for the old process may be declining, as shown in Fig. 2.2. In such cases, the problem arises of where does the payback period start from?

As well as having to allow for initial costs being spread over several years, another problem is the time taken to achieve the full level of savings. Taking the example of a CAD system, where it is assumed that it will be two years before full savings are being obtained, a very simplified view of the build up of savings may be that shown in Fig. 2.3. Savings are assumed to have reached 50% of the full level by the end of the first year, and they will reach 100% by the end of the second year.

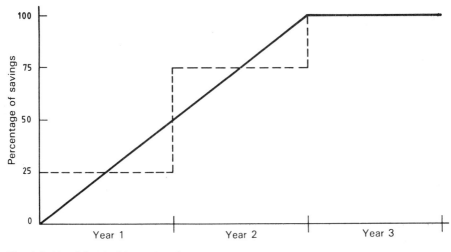

Fig. 2.3 Simplified build-up of savings

Although the level of savings at the end of the first year is 50%, the average for the first year is only 25%. Similarly, the average for the second year is 75%. Taking as an example an investment of £100 000 with running costs of £10 000 a year, in a company which requires a two-year payback to justify expenditure, the cash flows needed using the traditional assumption in Fig. 2.1 would be:

	Year 0	Year 1	Year 2	Year 3	Year 4
	£	£	£	£	£
Capital	− 100 000				
Running		− 10 000	− 10 000	− 10 000	− 10 000
Savings		+ 60 000	+ 60 000	+ 60 000	+ 60 000
Cash flows	− 100 000	+ 50 000	+ 50 000	+ 50 000	+ 50 000

If, however, the build up of savings was as shown in Fig. 2.3, the figures would be:

	Year 0	Year 1	Year 2	Year 3	Year 4
	£	£	£	£	£
Capital	− 100 000				
Running		− 10 000	− 10 000	− 10 000	− 10 000
Savings		+ 15 000	+ 45 000	+ 60 000	+ 60 000
Cash flows	− 100 000	+ 5 000	+ 35 000	+ 50 000	+ 50 000

Although the long-term level of savings would be £60 000 a year, these would be insufficient to provide even a three-year payback. However, if the life of the project is assumed to be ten years, it would provide a 33.1% IRR (ignoring taxation). If a two-year payback was required, the cash flows would need to be:

	Year 0	Year 1	Year 2	Year 3	Year 4
	£	£	£	£	£
Capital	− 100 000				
Running		− 10 000	− 10 000	− 10 000	− 10 000
Savings		+ 30 000	+ 90 000	+ 120 000	+ 120 000
Cash flows	− 100 000	+ 20 000	+ 80 000	+ 110 000	+ 110 00

where the savings in years 1 and 2 represent 25% and 75% of the savings in year 3 onwards.

This raises the problem of how companies decide the length of the payback period that they require. The criteria used in selecting this period – one or two years being common – is often highly arbitrary. In companies that use both payback and DCF the criteria for setting the required payback period may well be different to that used in setting the required DCF rate of return.

Taking a project with a constant level of savings over a ten-year life, it is shown in Fig. 2.4 how as the level of saving increases, IRR compares with the payback period. Thus companies seeking a payback of two or three years may look for projects which will give a return of approx. 50% and 30%

IRR respectively. This compares with a more usual 10%–15% after tax cost of capital that companies would use with DCF techniques. The result of using both payback and DCF at the same time is that attractive long-term investments, possibly giving over 50% IRR, and which may be vital for the company's viability in the long term, can be rejected because they do not provide the required short-term payback.

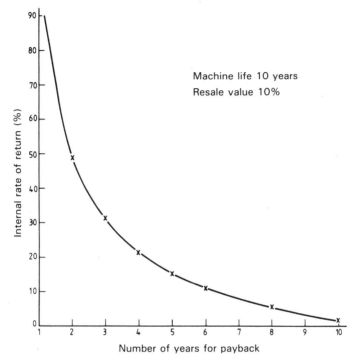

Fig. 2.4 How IRR varies with payback period.

Using payback can result in incorrect investment decisions being made. For example, a manager investigating the purchase of a CNC machine tool may start by specifying a good-quality machine which could be expected to have a working life of at least ten years. It is assumed that the machine would be able to produce components to the required quality standards and cycle times throughout its working life.

However, if the manager was unable to show that the machine would provide a return within the required payback period, the technical specification may be reduced, so that a cheaper machine – with a much shorter working life – would then be considered. A simple example is provided by the following.

The machine originally specified would cost £100 000 and have a working life of ten years; the machine would generate savings of £25 000 a year throughout its life. If the company's requirement was that projects must provide a three-year payback, this machine would be rejected. An alternative machine could be specified, costing £75 000. However, although still generating savings of £25 000 a year, and providing a three-year payback, the working life is expected to be only four years. Using DCF, the returns are:

Capital cost	Working life	Annual savings	Payback period	IRR
−£100 000	10	£25 000	4 years	21.4%
−£75 000	4	£25 000	3 years	12.5%

The first machine would probably be rejected using payback, as would the second using DCF.

One of the most commonly quoted benefits of AMT is *inventory reduction*, but as described in a later chapter, this will provide only a one-off saving. Although many projects, such as the introduction of Just in Time (JIT), are aimed at inventory reduction, high stock levels are normally only a symptom of other problems in the company. If the underlying cause of these problems is not identified and solved, the short-term benefit of reducing stocks may create additional long-term problems elsewhere in the company.

For example, a company may invest in a project which results in a stock reduction, but as a result of reducing stock levels, the company's ability to respond to fluctuations in customer order intake may be reduced, leading to a reduction in orders. Evaluating the project using payback would include the one-off value of the inventory saving, but it would not include the cost of the long-term loss of orders, even if this had been identified.

ACCOUNTING RATE OF RETURN (ARR)

This technique is used to show the profitability of an investment in a company's accounts. However, the method used for calculating ARR depends on which of the many accounting conventions the company uses to calculate earnings and capital employed. One of the failings of ARR is that it is dependent on the use of depreciation. However, depreciation does not represent changes in cash flows, rather it is a set of artificial values used for product costing and reporting profits in the company's annual accounts. The methods used to calculate depreciation are highly arbitrary and its use in ARR normally results in the profitability of investments being understated.

Although it is relatively easy to use and understand, ARR suffers from the same problems as payback relating to the timing of cash flows because it assumes that £1 now is worth the same as £1 in the future. ARR only seeks to measure the impact of a project on the company's Profit & Loss account and does not measure the economic value of a project. Although it is widely used, it has even more disadvantages than payback if used for investment appraisal.

DCF TECHNIQUES (NPV AND IRR)

Although most accountancy literature recommends the use of DCF and condemns the use of payback and ARR, it should be realized that until recently, DCF techniques were difficult to understand and use. Traditionally the calculation of NPV and IRR employed discount tables which are both difficult to use and time-consuming, especially in the case of IRR which requires a process of iteration.

This is especially so with complex projects which can have different cash flow values for each year of a project's life. The problems of using discount tables for DCF calculations, without the probability of error, discouraged non-financial managers from using them. This reinforced the belief that investment appraisal involved estimating a single, most optimistic set of values which were then submitted to the accountants for them to pronounce a 'yes'/'no' verdict on a project. Needless to say, a 'no' verdict helped to reinforce the traditional engineer–accountant conflict.

It is only since computer programs were developed, allowing non-financial managers to evaluate any investment project without the need of financial training, that the practical problems of using DCF have been overcome. The criteria for such programs should be as follows:

1. It can be used by managers without the need for financial training.
2. It can be used to evaluate and compare any investment project using the same criteria.
3. An evaluation must be able to include *all* the factors affected by the investment, including capital allowances, grants, taxation, etc.
4. An evaluation must adhere strictly to established accountancy principles, so that the results can be checked by, and be acceptable to, accountants and financial managers.

The concept of IRR is doubtless easier to grasp than NPV because it can be compared to a normal loan. However, NPV is a better method technically, especially when trying to choose between a number of mutually exclusive projects where the acceptance of one will prevent the acceptance of the others. Ideally, an appraisal should provide the result in terms of both NPV and IRR.

Probably the first computer program to meet these criteria and which has been used widely in industry is IVAN, which was developed at UMIST. It was during the development of IVAN that it was first shown how every factor affected by an investment project could be defined in financial terms and therefore be included in an investment appraisal. It was only in the late 1960s that DCF started to be widely employed for investment appraisal. Up to that time, most of the investments being evaluated, such as manually operated machine tools were relatively simple, so that the errors resulting from the use of payback were not seen as significant.

In most manufacturing companies the change from being labour intensive to being capital intensive has been a gradual process. At the same time, the increase in technical complexity of investments has also tended to be gradual. Because of this, the problems caused by the continuing use of payback are only now obvious, with the benefit of hindsight.

Although payback should never be used for investment appraisal, because its use will result in companies making the wrong investment decisions, many companies use payback still. This helps to illustrate the fact that the problems of evaluating and costing AMT projects are caused by the use of outdated and incorrect procedures rather than by any failings in basic accountancy principles.

REPLACEMENT DECISIONS

A large body of knowledge exists on the subject of evaluating investment projects and few accountancy books fail to include a section on the subject; however, the treatment normally concentrates on the following areas:

1. Advantages of DCF over payback.
2. Comparison between NPV and IRR.
3. Analysis of risk in projects.
4. Cost of capital

Only a very small proportion of the extensive body of literature deals with the problems of practical applications, the main emphasis being on the theory which underlies the measurement of investment return and the treatment of risk. Even when practical examples are provided, these are normally investments for new 'green-field site' projects or for expansion projects. The examples are such that no account needs to be taken of how the investment will affect existing conditions.

In practice, the majority of investment decisions taken in industry involve replacement of existing facilities. In some cases, the replacement element may be obvious such as simply replacing an old machine by a new one, or less obvious such as replacing drawing-boards by CAD. Even in most expansion situations, the investment in increased capacity is likely to involve the replacement of some of the existing equipment.

In any investment decision the reason for an evaluation is to compare what will happen if the investment is made with which will probably happen if it is not. Even in the case of a new project, where no existing facilities will be affected, the evaluation is between leaving the money in the bank (or not borrowing it) and making the investment. In such cases, the cash flows of the project have to be evaluated to ensure that they will provide a greater return than the 'do nothing' alternative. The 'do nothing' assumption is that the company can always invest the money in an alternative project, or lend it, to obtain the minimum return required in an evaluation. Any investment therefore must provide a greater return than that which can be achieved from the 'do nothing' option.

With 'green-field' projects, it is necessary only to consider the cash flows created by the project. The reason that evaluating replacement decisions can be much more complicated is that the cash flows created by the investment must be compared with the cash flows that will occur if the investment is not made. In many cases, the consquence of not making the investment can be the continued deterioration of existing facilities. This means, then, that in carrying out an evaluation one has to estimate two separate sets of cash flow.

In any evaluation the costs of the investment are all those costs which will be incurred if the investment is made, *less* those costs which would be incurred if the investment is not made, but which would be avoided by making the investment. In the same way, the savings are those which will result from the investment *less* those which would occur without the investment. Care must be taken to avoid either double counting or leaving out any factors, both for costs and savings.

For example, in evaluating a CNC machine to replace conventional old machines, the alternative could be to replace them with new conventional machines (assuming that doing nothing was not a viable alternative). Investing in CNC would avoid the cost of replacement by new conventional machines and an allowance for this would have to be included. If this is the case, an allowance could not be included for the savings, such as a reduced level of scrap and rework or lower maintenance costs, if these savings would have been obtained not only from the CNC machine, but also from installing the new conventional ones.

With replacement decisions, there are usually several alternatives which can be considered, such as:

1. Do nothing.
2. Replace 'like with like'.
3. Invest in more sophisticated technology.

The 'do nothing' alternative is normally a decision to postpone replacement for a year, with the project then being re-examined to see whether, because of changed circumstances, the potential savings have increased, or the costs decreased. When considering replacement with more sophisticated technology, it may be that there are several levels of sophistication and cost which could be considered.

Where there are alternative levels of sophistication, it is important to start by evaluating first, the lowest cost option, because it may be possible to obtain many of the benefits from that level of investment. Even if the more expensive option could be justified, in comparison with the existing situation, it may be that the extra costs involved do not produce any significant benefits in addition to those which can be obtained from the cheaper option.

The procedure that has to be adopted is first to evaluate the cheapest option. Having done that, the next evaluation is to compare the additional costs against the additional benefits of the next cheapest option.

It is only if investment in the cheapest alternative is not financially viable that the more expensive option should be compared with the existing situation. The object of such evaluations is to identify the most profitable investment. It is not to try to justify investment in the most sophisticated technology possible, unless of course that happens to be the most profitable choice. The following, highly simplified, example illustrates the process; for clarity the effect of taxation has been excluded:

A company has two manual lathes which are old and in poor condition, and the machines are operated on two shifts. The decision is whether to replace them with two new manual lathes, with one new CNC or with a **flexible manufacturing module (FMM)**, each option would have the same equivalent capacity; the costs are;

manual lathes	£20 000 each;
CNC lathe	£80 000;
FMM	£150 000.

All three alternatives are assumed to have a working life of ten years.

At present, the cost of maintenance is £2000 a year for each machine; in addition, the cost of scrap is £3000 a year for each machine. If the existing machines are not replaced, these costs will continue.

Comparing the alternative of doing nothing with investing in two manual machines gives the following cash flows:

	Year 0 £	Year 1 £	Year 2 £	Years 3–10 £
Capital cost	−40 000			
Savings		+10 000	+10 000	+10 000
Cash flows	−40 000	+10 000	+10 000	+10 000

This would provide an IRR of 21.4%, so investment would be justified.

Investing in a CNC lathe, instead of two manual lathes, would cost £80 000 but would avoid the expenditure of £40 000. Only two operators would be needed instead of the four required for the new manual machines, giving an annual saving of £10 000 per operator. Because the existing costs of maintenance and scrap would be avoided by investing in manual machines, these costs would not be claimed as an additional saving for CNC. For the second evaluation the cash flows are;

	Year 0 £	Year 1 £	Year 2 £	Years 3–10 £
Capital cost	−80 000			
Capital avoided	+40 000			
Savings		+20 000	+20 000	+20 000
Cash flows	−40 000	+20 000	+20 000	+20 000

This would provide an IRR of 49.0%, so the additional investment would be justified.

The third alternative of investing in a FMM would cost £150 000 but would avoid expenditure of £80 000 on CNC. The FMM would have the ability to run for long periods without an operator, so it is assumed that only one operator would be needed to produce the same output as the CNC lathe and therefore saving an additional £10 000 a year. For the third evaluation the cash flows are:

	Year 0 £	Year 1 £	Year 2 £	Years 3–10 £
Capital cost	−150 000			
Capital avoided	+80 000			
Savings		+10 000	+10 000	+10 000
Cash flows	−70 000	+10 000	+10 000	+10 000

This would only provide an IRR of 7.0%, so the additional investment would not be justified.

In the above example, investing in CNC compared with the manual machines would provide a higher return than investing in the cheaper alternative. However, even if the return from CNC had been lower than that from investing in manual machines, the investment could still have been justified, provided the return was above the company's required minimum.

Carrying out the evaluation in the above way shows that the company should invest in CNC and not FMM. If the first two stages had been omitted, the evaluation of FMM against the existing situation would compare a capital cost of £150 000 against annual savings of £40 000 and thereby show that FMM was viable.

If investment in manual machines had not been viable, investment in CNC should have been compared with the existing situation. In the same way, it is only if the investment in CNC had not been justified that the FMM should have been evaluated against investing in the manual machines.

3 Identifying cash flow changes

Most of the accountancy literature dealing with investment appraisal concentrates on the techniques used for DCF calculation such as a comparison between NPV and IRR. However, in the practical use of appraisal techniques the main problem encountered is the need to identify correctly all the cash flows which will be affected by the project. All cash flow changes have to be identified in such a way that they can be included in an evaluation; there are three elements which have to be considered.

1. The nature of the cash flow changes.
2. The magnitude of the changes.
3. The timing of the changes.

Because most investment projects in industry involve replacement decisions, it is normal for the new investment to be seen as a way of improving efficiency and reducing costs, especially if the project being considered is more sophisticated than the equipment that is being replaced.

Most manufacturing companies have an **absorption costing system** for internal cost control, the objective of the system being to ensure that all costs of manufacture are absorbed in selling prices. In order to do this, all the costs within a company are forecast and then allocated to products.

The costing system then measures all costs as they occur in order to identify any positive or negative variances from the original forecasts. The allocation of costs between products is done by creating a *standard cost* for every component and then adding up the cost of all components in each product. The standard costs are based on the allocation of allowances for depreciation and overheads.

Because these costing systems exist, they provide a convenient way of measuring the performance of departments. Managers who are trying to improve the efficiency of their department aim to achieve positive variances against standard. This objective can be reinforced by **management by objectives (MBO)** schemes, which can reward the achievement of such positive variances.

Managers often see reducing standard costs as being one of their primary objectives. As a result, much of the literature describing new technology emphasizes its ability to reduce costs, such as labour and operating expenses, and is portrayed to managers as a means by which they can improve their department's efficiency. The emphasis on the need to reduce costs, and the fact that costs are measured by the costing system, means that managers try to justify investment aimed at cost reduction by using data from the costing system. Unfortunately, the changes in standard costs which they achieve may only represent changes in depreciation and allocated overheads and do not represent changes in cash flows.

A simplified example of an absorption costing system is that of a machine shop where a £120 000 machine has been bought. The standard cost would be made up of four main elements:

1. Labour.
2. Operating expenses.
3. Machine depreciation.
4. An allocation of fixed overheads (e.g. rent, rates, administration, etc.).

It is estimated that the machine will have a life of ten years and will be used for 3000 hours a year. The rate per hour for depreciation will be:

$$\frac{£120\ 000}{30\ 000} = £4.00$$

The standard cost will comprise the following:

	£
Labour	4.00
Operating expenses	2.00
Depreciation	4.00
Fixed overhead	10.00
Rate per hour	20.00

Of this rate, only labour and operating expenses represent cash flow expenditure, the remainder being unaffected by variations in the number of hours worked on the machine.

Problems arise when this information is used to make decisions for which the data was never intended, a typical decision is: 'we decided not to replace that machine as it would cost £20 per hour to make the parts here and we can subcontract them for £15/h'. If it is decided that components will be subcontracted for £15/h, instead of being made in-house for £20/h, the depreciation rate would have to be recalculated. If 1500 hours' work a year was going to be sent out, the machine would now be used for only 1500 hours instead of 3000. The depreciation rate would be recalculated as £8/h.

The fixed overhead costs will not be reduced by the decision to subcontract. Thus the £10 × 1500 h would have to be redistributed over all the remaining in-house work, thereby marginally increasing all the other standard costs.

The effect that subcontracting would have on cash flows would be a saving of £4/h labour and £2/h operating expenses. Because this would be at a cost of £15/h, the net result is an increase in cash flow expenditure of £9/h. The apparent saving of £5/h according to the costing system would, in reality be a loss of £9/h.

Although this means that subcontracting work which could be done in-house may not be as attractive as the costing system shows, it also means that an investment aimed at reducing the amount of work currently being subcontracted can be highly profitable. For example, if 3000 h/year of work can be brought in-house by investing in a new machine tool costing £120 000, the cash flows would be:

	Year 0 £	Years 1–10 £
Capital cost	− 120 000	
Labour cost (3000 × £4)		− 12 000
Operating expenses (300 × £2)		− 6 000
Reduced subcontract (3000 × £15)		+ 45 000
Annual cash flows	− 120 000	+ 27 000

This would give an IRR of 18.3%.

DEPRECIATION AND OVERHEADS

DEPRECIATION

An examination of the literature advocating investment in CNC machines has shown that when examples were given to demonstrate the advantages of CNC, the method used to calculate the savings is invariably the same. The technique used is to select a representative component, or group of components, and then to calculate the costs of manufacture using the existing method and the proposed method. The difference between the two costs is used as a saving which is extrapolated to give the total saving. This value is then employed to calculate a return on investment.

Unfortunately, the principle used to calculate the component cost by the two methods of manufacture is the same as that used in absorption costing. As a result, the costs include an allowance for depreciation and quite often

Table 3.1 Component costs including depreciation (in pounds)

Machine costs	Existing method	CNC
Capital cost/machine	20 000	100 000
Cost per year (10 years)	2 000	10 000
Cost per hour (depreciation)	1.00	5.00
Cost per component		
Component time	2 h	1 h
Labour cost @ £4/h	8.00	4.00
Operating expenses @ £2/h	4.00	2.00
Depreciation	2.00	5.00
Component cost	14.00	11.00

unaffected overheads. The result of using this technique has been that the benefits of CNC have been consistently understated. The following example shows the technique that is used.

A company is considering buying a CNC machine for £100 000 to replace two old, manual machines, which originally cost £20 000 each, both types of machine having an expected working life of ten years when working 2000 h/year on a single shift. A sample component is selected as being representative of the total load, and it is calculated that it will take 1 h to machine on CNC compared with 2 h on the existing machines. The cost of labour is £4/h and operating expenses (variable overhead) is £2/h. The costs are as shown in Table 3.1. As 2000 components a year can be produced on the proposed machine using single-shift working, the savings are shown to be:

$$£3.00 \times 2000 = £6000/\text{year}$$

This £6000/year saving would then be used to calculate the return on the investment of £100 000. However, depreciation has been included in the evaluation. Not only does this not represent a cash flow change, but its use in this context amounts to double counting. Because the capital cost is already included in the appraisal as the initial expenditure which has to be justified, it cannot be used again to calculate savings. If depreciation is not included, the component costs are as shown in Table 3.2.

The savings now become:

$$£6.00 \times 2000 = £12\ 000/\text{year}$$

Including depreciation has resulted in the savings being considerably understated. The problem is made much worse if it is assumed that the existing machines have got to the stage where they are over ten years old and their depreciation value is zero.

Table 3.2 Costs excluding depreciation (in pounds)

Cost per component	Existing method	CNC
Component time	2 h	1 h
Labour cost @ £4/h	8.00	4.00
Operating expenses @ £2/h	4.00	2.00
Component cost	12.00	6.00

Using the figures in Table 3.1 would still give a component cost of £11 for CNC, but if the value of the machines were zero the cost of the existing method would reduce to £12, suggesting that there was a negligible saving from using CNC. The result of using this method to calculate savings is that the older the existing machines get, then the smaller the savings from replacing them become.

Considering cash flows only, the evaluation should be:

	Year 0 £	Year 1 £	Year 2 £	Years 3–10 £
Capital cost	− 100 000			
Labour saving		+8 000	+8 000	+8 000
Operating cost saving		+4 000	+4 000	+4 000
Cash flows	− 100 000	+ 12 000	+ 12 000	+ 12 000

Not only would this level of savings justify the investment, but if the manual machines had got to the stage where they were becoming unreliable and replacement was essential, the investment in CNC would also avoid spending £40 000 on manual machines and the project would become even more viable. If fixed overheads which will be unaffected by the proposed investment are included, the evaluation can be distorted in other directions.

OVERHEADS

To illustrate the consequences of including unaltered overheads an example is taken of a company that is considering replacing two manual machines, which originally cost £30 000 each, by a CNC machine which would cost £150 000. The existing machines, still only a few years old, are in good condition. Both types of machine would be depreciated over ten years, and each with an estimated usage of 3000 h/year; the standard costs are as follows:

	Manual	CNC
	£	£
Labour per hour	4.00	4.00
Operating expenses per hour	2.00	3.00
Depreciation (3000 h/10 years)	1.00	5.00
Fixed overheads per hour	10.00	10.00
Standard cost per hour	17.00	22.00

Assuming that the proposed CNC machine was capable of doing the work of the two manual machines, this would give:

Cost of existing method   = 2 × 3000 × £17.00 = £102 000/year
Cost of proposed method = 1 × 3000 × £22.00 =   £66 000/year

This would show a saving of £36 000 a year. If this was used to calculate the return on investment in the CNC machine, it would give an IRR of 20.1%, suggesting that the investment would be viable.

If only cash flow values are used, the figures become:

	Manual	CNC
	£	£
Labour/h	4.00	4.00
Operating expenses/h	2.00	3.00
Cost per hour	6.00	7.00

Cost of existing method on two machines   = 2 × 3000 × £6.00 = £36 000
Cost of proposed method on one machine = 1 × 3000 × £7.00 = £21 000

The annual saving now becomes £15 000, which would give a zero IRR.

Unlike the earlier example of the effects of including depreciation, which resulted in the benefits of CNC being understated, the effect of including both depreciation and overheads has been to overstate the case for CNC. However, both methods give the wrong results. With one method companies will refrain from making profitable investments, and with the other they will make unprofitable ones.

The complexity of AMT projects is such that a considerable number of factors may need to be included in an investment appraisal, not all of which need to be dealt with in the same way. When non-accountants use spreadsheet-type programs, they tend to oversimplify evaluations by excluding some of the factors and invariably understate the profitability of the investment. Managers who do not use spreadsheets for investment appraisal on a regular basis, and who are not familiar with the way that the various cost and savings factors need to be dealt with, can easily make major errors in their use. It may be all too easy for managers to be misled by spreadsheets, and although accountants will probably point out any errors when evaluations are eventually submitted to them, they will not see the preliminary evaluations which may result in a manager deciding to stop investigating a particular project.

One of the advantages of a dedicated computer program for investment appraisal, such as IVAN, is that the person using it does not actually need to apprehend any of the accountancy rules involved. At the same time, the format of the data input is designed to prevent the use of non cash flow information such as depreciation and unaltered overheads. Because users cannot alter the rules built into the program, all the arguments and uncertainties associated with setting up spreadsheets are thus eliminated.

WORKING LIFE AND RESALE VALUE

WORKING LIFE

With capital equipment, there are three different types of lives which require to be considered; it is possible for all three of these to be of different lengths:

1. Physical working life.
2. Depreciation life.
3. Life for capital tax allowances.

The period over which capital assets are depreciated in a company's accounts is determined by the accounting conventions used within the company. Depreciation life is normally determined by rules such as: 'all machine tools are depreciated over ten years.' As a result, this life may not be the same as the physical life of an asset.

Because the depreciation life is decided when an asset is acquired, and the physical life is only known when it is eventually decided to dispose of the asset, it has to be assumed that the two lives will be different. Companies tend to use a common life to depreciate all assets of a similar type. For example, many companies depreciate their machine tools over ten years and computers over five years.

However, before the widespread introduction of CNC, the *average* age of machine tools in many companies was over twenty years. Consequently, the majority of machines, being older than their depreciation life, would have a zero book value. This would not be a true reflection of the condition of the machines or their physical value, or of how many more years' working life the machines had remaining.

Table 3.3 How IRR changes with working life

Working life (years)	IRR %	Working life (years)	IRR %
4	0	13	23.4
5	7.9	14	23.7
6	12.9	15	24.0
7	16.3	16	24.2
8	18.6	17	24.4
9	20.2	18	24.5
10	21.4	19	24.6
11	22.3	20	24.7
12	22.9	–	–

The third life is the period over which an investment is offset against taxation and this will vary according to the type of asset and the current tax legislation. The effect of tax life in an evaluation is dealt with later in this chapter. Although the life for taxation purposes may also be different from the physical life, unlike depreciation it can have an important effect on cash flows, therefore allowance must be made for it in an investment appraisal. The most important life is the physical working life of an asset because this determines the number of years during which there will be cash flow changes which have to be included in an evaluation.

A number of mathematical techniques have been developed to try to predict the future life of assets, based on the use of statistical probability. Unfortunately, any such method is only going to provide a meaningful answer if the life of a sufficiently large number of similar products is already known.

This means that because a large number of similar machines may have already reached the end of their working lives, the expected life of conventional manual machine tools could be calculated. When considering new technology, however, the new machines will be unlike those which are reaching the end of their working lives. Consequently, there is unlikely to be sufficient data to use mathematical techniques and expected life has to be estimated rather than calculated. In estimating the probable life several factors need to be considered; for instance:

1. How well proven and established is the chosen make and specification?
2. How rapidly is the current state of technology changing?
3. Is the investment for long-term general use, or short term for a specific project?
4. How hostile an environment will the equipment be working in?
5. What percentage of available time will the equipment be utilized?
6. What is the quality of the equipment in relation to the required application?
7. How long will the supplier provide spares and service?

Before looking at these factors in more detail, it is first necessary to consider whether or not working life is important, and how much effort should be devoted to its estimation. To illustrate this, an example is taken of an investment costing £10 000 which generates net cash flow savings of £2500 a year. The IRR is calculated for a working life which varies from four to twenty years; the results are shown in Table 3.3 and illustrated in Fig. 3.1.

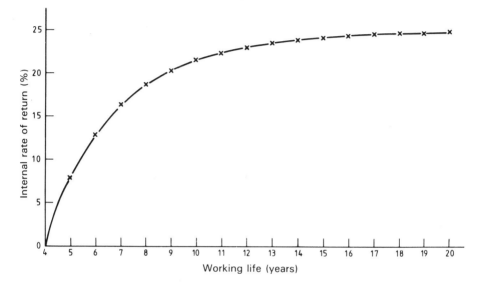

Fig. 3.1 How IRR changes with working life.

This suggests that if the life of the investment is going to be ten years or over, as would be the case with conventional manual machine tools, any errors in estimating the expected life will not have a significant effect on the return calculated. However, for investments whose life is likely to be less than ten years any errors in estimation become increasingly important as the expected life reduces.

Table 3.3 helps to illustrate one of the dangers of using payback with its emphasis on short-term returns. The project used in the example, costing £10 000, would provide a four-year payback and IRR of 21.4% from annual savings of £2500 if the life was to be ten years. If the life was only to be four years, it would still give a four-year payback but the IRR would now be 0%.

Until the advent of computer technology, the rate of change in machine tools was extremely slow, so that when companies were replacing conventional machines – even ones that were twenty years old – the specification of the replacement machine could be somewhat similar to that of the old one. This means that not only were there comparable machines to use as a yard-stick for estimating expected life, but the life would normally be so long that the accuracy of the estimate was not important.

As depreciation life of machine tools was often ten years, any error in an evaluation caused by using the depreciation life for the working life was not usually significant. It is only now, when working life is much shorter, that using depreciation life in an investment appraisal can be seen to cause problems.

In the early days of computer technology there was little or no practical experience to use as a guide to expected life. In addition, because of the rapid rate of change, it was likely that plant was being replaced because it had become obsolete, as more sophisticated technology became available, rather than replaced because it was worn out and incapable of performing to specification. Although some areas of technology are still highly original, with a rapid rate of innovation, there is now sufficient experience of computer technology to enable realistic assessments to be made about the future.

In the early 1960s numerical control (NC) machine tools started to be introduced into industry. Although today's CNC machines are very different to those early machines in terms of basic design configuration, control system capability, performance and general reliability, much of the change took place in the early years. While manufacturers continue to develop new features, the rate of change is sufficiently slow that most companies buying CNC machines today will do so with the intention of keeping them until they are worn out and unreliable, rather than having to replace them in a few years with a new design in order to gain the advantages of the latest technology.

As CNC technology has developed, the machines and their control systems have become increasingly reliable. While they may not yet have reached the same level of reliability as manual machines, which are often still capable of producing components within specification after twenty years, many of the CNC machines currently being installed could be expected to have a working life of about ten years.

The expected life of machines will be reduced by such factors as operating in a hostile environment, or being expected to perform continuously on the limit of their capability. In some cases, CNC machines may have to be replaced not because they are worn out and beyond repair, but rather that the manufacturer will no longer provide spares and service. However, although it is a factor which has to be considered, it is not as critical today as it was in the early days of CNC machines because most manufacturers are now well-established companies with a proven track record.

This is not the case, however, with computer systems. The ease with which computer companies can be set up, combined with the rapid development and expansion of the computer industry, means that many potential suppliers will be unable to demonstrate their ability to provide long-term support for the systems they are selling.

Trying to chose between a major well established supplier with an expensive product and a small new company with an equally good, but cheaper, product is difficult. However, it is possible to evaluate the difference in order to obtain some measure of whether the risks involved are justified.

As an example, a company has a choice between buying a computer system from a large, long-established company for £150 000 and one from a small, new company for £100 000. The performance of the two systems is assumed to be the same, both generating savings of £30 000 a year. However, it is assumed that the major supplier would be able to offer support for at least ten years, while support from the other supplier may not be available after five years. Evaluating the two options gives:

Major supplier	*Year 0*	*Years 1–10*
	£	£
Capital cost	− 150 000	
Savings		+30 000

Small supplier	*Year 0*	*Years 1–5*
Capital cost	− 100 000	
Savings		+30 000

The first gives an IRR of 15.0%, while the second gives 15.2%. In this case, there is little to choose between the two options. However, the assumption of five-year system support from the small company is critical; if instead of five years it might only be three or four, the investment would be wrong. The potential long-term viability of suppliers therefore needs close examination.

In practice, the comparison may be more complex than the above example indicates because the system from the small company may be technically superior. In that case, there would be a difference not only in costs and life, but also in savings, to be included in an evaluation. In the 1960s, when computers started to be widely used in industry, one of the most common early applications was **stock control**. This used to be a highly labour-intensive function, which had a simple set of rules and therefore lent itself to application on the early data-processing machines. Since those early applications, stock control has become more sophisticated, with the emphasis now being placed on planning rather than just recording stock levels. This is reflected in the change of name to **material control**, and the computer packages known as **material requirement planning (MRP)**; and MRP is now well established for the traditional stock control function. The MRP computer systems are being extended to embrace **production control**, with emphasis now on **manufacturing resource planning (MRPII)**. MRPII systems are relatively new, with a considerable amount of technical development still taking place, and there is little successful long-term operating experience yet available.

Whereas machine tools are seen always as having a finite life, the installation of MRP/MRPII may be seen as being a 'permanent' feature in the company where it can have an indefinite life. This view is reinforced by the cost of installing such systems. It will normally take several years from making the initial investment until the system is fully implemented. During this period of introduction the labour needed to enter into the computer the large amount of data required to run the system is a major cost factor.

The installation and running of MRPII can represent a major commitment both of financial and management resources – so when the computer hardware starts to become unreliable and has to be replaced, the cost of replacing the whole MRPII system with a different system can be enormous. Thus the replacement of the hardware will probably be by the latest model of the same make, or a compatible 'clone'.

Although the hardware may be replaced, the software would normally be retained, the original software being enhanced with extra features that require a larger computer to run them. Because of this, there is no obvious point in time which could be regarded as the end of the system's life.

The term **computer aided design (CAD)** can be traced back to about 1960, but the early systems were developed by companies for their own in-house use. It was not until the early 1970s that today's turnkey-type package systems started to become available, with the real growth of CAD starting in the late 1970s. Because of the rapid rate of technical improvement of CAD in the 1970s and early 1980s, companies which bought the early systems usually considered their replacement because much more efficient systems were now available rather than because the old system was worn out.

Although technical improvements are continuing still, the rate of change has slowed such that companies buying CAD today are likely to retain their system for its full working life, possibly amounting to ten or more years. Even then, that replacement may be simply the hardware and updating the existing software. As with MRPII, the major cost of a CAD system is the labour required to enter all the data; this means, then, that an investment in CAD must also be seen as a permanent or long-term commitment.

RESALE VALUE

One of the cash flows which has to be included in an evaluation is the resale value of the investment at the end of its working life. With projects such as robots or machine tools, it is often assumed that it will be possible to sell the equipment as a going concern, for use secondhand or for reconditioning. As such, a nominal value of 10% is commonly used. With computer systems, which are likely to be obsolete when replaced, the resale value may be negligible and a 0% value assumed.

As with working life, it is necessary to consider how much effort should be devoted to estimating resale value, and how much effect a variation in the assumed value will have on the calculated return on investment. To illustrate this, two examples are taken: one is an investment costing £10 000 which produces savings of £2000 a year for ten years; the other also costs £10 000 but produces savings of £3000 for five years. In both cases, the IRR is calculated using a resale value in the final year, which varies from 0% to 50% of the original value. The results are shown in Table 3.4 and illustrated in Fig. 3.2.

Table 3.4 How IRR changes with resale value

Resale value (percentage of original)	Five-year life IRR %	Ten-year life IRR %
0	15.2	15.0
10	17.2	15.7
20	19.0	16.3
30	20.7	16.8
40	22.2	17.3
50	23.7	17.8

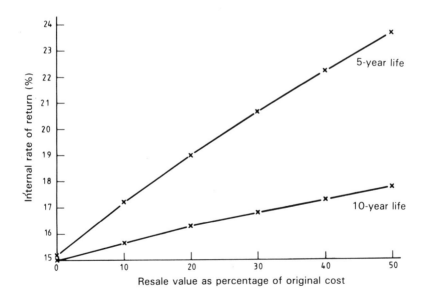

Fig. 3.2 How IRR changes with resale value.

Fortunately, the effect of errors in estimating the resale value of projects is not likely to be significant, provided that the working life is reasonably long. Even for projects with a short life, the size of the error made in estimating the resale value is likely to be assuming 10% rather than 20%, or 10% instead of 0% – not 0% instead of 50%. The magnitude of the effect on the IRR is such that reasonable care in estimating is needed, rather than considerable detailed investigation.

SUBSEQUENT AND DELAYED PROJECTS

SUBSEQUENT PROJECTS

There is normally an implicit assumption when making investments that the company is a going concern and has a long-term future. This means that unless an investment is for a specific project which will have a finite life, it is assumed that the investment is the first of a series. At the end of the life of the current investment, it will be replaced in turn by another which will be similar, or better.

When there is a rapid rate of technical innovation, such as in the early years of a new technology, there should be plenty of additional savings to justify the 'second-generation' replacement. The problem is what happens when the rate of innovation slows and then stops. To illustrate what does happen, an example is taken of a project costing £10 000 which generates savings of £3000 for five years, the cash flows being:

	Year 0 £	Years 1–5 £
Capital cost	− 10 000	
Savings		+3 000

This will give an IRR of 15.2%.

If it is assumed that at the end of five years the investment is replaced by another which is identical, the cash flows now become:

	Year 0 £	Years 1–4 £	Year 5 £	Years 6–10 £
Capital costs	− 10 000		− 10 000	
Savings		+3 000	+3 000	+3 000

This also gives an IRR of 15.2%.

The assumption usually made in an investment appraisal is that at the end of the life of the project being evaluated, if it is not to be replaced by equivalent or better equipment, conditions will revert to those which existed when the original evaluation was made. If conditions did revert back to the original, then an evaluation at that time would produce a case for a replacement which was equally good as that for the original investment.

When considering replacement of existing equipment, it is important to take into account both the additional savings that could be obtained from investing in the latest technology and the savings which arise from avoiding the 'do nothing' alternative. For example, a company that has invested in CAD will eventually be faced with the alternative of replacement with a new CAD system or reverting to manual procedures. When technical innovation is still taking place, the additional capability may provide savings which will help justify a replacement. If these are significant, they may justify investment in a replacement before the existing equipment has reached the end of its useful life.

If, in the above example, instead of waiting until the end of the fifth year when replacement would have to be made, an investigation in the third year showed that new equipment was now available which would produce additional savings of £2000 a year. The question is whether to invest in year 3 or wait until year 5. The easiest way to evaluate this choice would seem to be to compare the investment in year 3 with the existing equipment. This would give the following cash flows:

	Year 3 £	Years 4–5 £	Years 6–8 £
Capital cost	−10 000		
New savings		+2 000	+2 000
Existing savings			+3 000

The savings of £3000 a year have not been included in years 4 and 5 because they would still be obtained if the investment was not made.

Doing the evaluation this way shows an IRR of 21.3% and suggests that the investment should be made. However, the evaluation does not allow for the fact that making the investment in year 3 avoids an essential replacement in year 5. The replacement in year 5 would also allow the full £5000 a year saving to be made from year 6 onwards.

To get the correct answer it is necessary to compare cash flows over a longer period, thus the investment in year 3 will generate the following cash flows:

	Year 3 £	Years 4 and 5 £	Years 6 and 7 £	Year 8 £	Years 9–13 £
Capital	−10 000			−10 000	
Savings		+2 000	+5 000	+5 000	+5 000

Delaying investment till year 5, which is the 'do nothing' alternative against which the above must be compared, would give:

	Year 5	Years 6–9	Year 10	Years 11–15
	£	£	£	£
Capital	− 10 000		− 10 000	
Savings		+5 000	+5 000	+5 000

The difference between the two sets of cash flows, which is the comparison between investment in year 3 and the 'do nothing' alternative, is:

	Year 3	Year 4	Year 5	Year 8	Year 10
	£	£	£	£	
Capital	− 10 000		+ 10 000	− 10 000	+ 10 000
Savings		+2 000	+ 2 000		

Bringing the capital expenditure forward by two years only produces additional savings of £2000 for two years and provides an IRR of 12.9%.

In textbook examples of projects which include changes in working capital (i.e. raw material, WIP, finished stock, etc.), the projects are normally presented as a stand-alone investment rather than as the first of a series. In addition, the investments invariably involve increasing, rather than reducing, stock levels. Because of this, the change in inventory at the start of the project life, which, in the examples, is normally investment in the additional working capital required to run the project, is reflected by an equal reduction at the end of the project's life.

In practice, most investments involving changes in working capital are those where the objective is inventory reduction. Additionally, the investment will normally be the first of a series, so that the initial inventory reduction will not be replaced by increasing stock levels at the end of the project life. This means that the evaluation of the initial investment should include the value of the inventory reduction at the start, but it should not include a value for the replacement of inventory at the end of the project life.

In evaluating the investment that will be needed as a replacement at the end of the first project's life the evaluation would include, as a saving, avoiding the cost of restoring the inventory to its original level. This would normally be of equal value to the saving produced by the first project, thus making the cash flows for subsequent projects the same as those of the first one.

DELAYED PROJECTS

The above examples considered the case where a replacement decision could be brought forward because of the current availability of new technology. However, an alternative situation may exist where the new technology is not yet available and the decision which has to be made is whether or not to delay making an investment. Although it may be possible to justify investment today, the objective in delaying investment would be to obtain the additional savings which can be achieved from the expected developments in technology which will soon be available.

The technology in all areas of AMT is still being developed, and although progress is faster in some areas than in others, manufacturers will always be promising improvements in the near future. In some cases, this will not present a problem because it may be possible to invest in existing technology, with the assurance from the manufacturer that it can be upgraded as the expected developments become available.

A problem arises, however, when there is a choice between investing now, obtaining immediate benefits or delaying investment in the hope of obtaining even larger benefits in the future. It is important that the nature of the expected additional benefits are clearly defined. Both the additional costs which will be incurred and the additional savings have to be quantified and the expected timing of cash flows estimated. It is necessary to make an accurate assessment of the length of delay before the new technology will become available. This should include any allowances required for delays in commissioning the new, possibly prototype, equipment, as compared with the time needed to install existing and proven technology.

To illustrate this, an example is taken of a choice between two investments. One investment is of £10 000 in technology which is available now, and which will produce savings of £2000 a year for at least ten years. The alternative is to delay investment for two years, at which time the cost will be £15 000 but the savings will be £4000 a year, again for at least ten years. It would not be worth investing £10 000 now and then replacing it in two years time at an additional cost of £15 000.

The cash flows for investing now, as compared with doing nothing, will be:

	Year 0 £	Years 1–10 £
Capital	− 10 000	
Savings		+2 000

This would give an IRR of 15.0%.

The cash flows for investing in two years time, again compared with doing nothing, will be:

	Year 2 £	Years 3–12 £
Capital	− 15 000	
Savings		+4 000

This would give an IRR of 23.4% and provide a better return than investing now in existing technology. In both cases, the evaluation is done against the alternative of doing nothing rather than evaluating the two options against each other. If the expected life of the investment was to be much shorter, the evaluations would need to include the subsequent replacement investments because the timing of these cash flows could have a significant effect on the result.

TAXATION AND GRANTS

TAXATION

Because tax rules change as government policy changes, any book about investment appraisal can become quickly out of date if it is based on the tax rules current at the time of writing. However, taxation does not apply equally to both costs and savings and it can have a significant effect on the viability of projects; therefore, it cannot be ignored.

Although tax rates and their application are subject to change, the basic principles tend to remain unchanged; for example, taxation does not apply equally to all cash flows and its application to each of the following may be different.

1. Capital expenditure.
2. Revenue costs and savings.
3. Grants.
4. Changes in inventory levels.

The effect that taxation has on the way inventory changes are valued is highly complex and is dealt with in a later chapter.

Any cash flow changes in revenue – i.e. savings, installation costs and running costs – are reflected in the company's accounts at the end of the year during which the cash flow changes occurred and are reported as an increase or a decrease in profits. This, in turn, produces an increase or decrease in the amount of corporation tax which has to be paid.

The normal convention in investment appraisal is that tax will be payable in the year following that in which the revenue cash flow change occurs. With capital expenditure, there are a variety of ways in which capital can be offset against corporation tax; usually these are:

1. 100% of capital cost is allowed to be offset in the first year.
2. An initial percentage is offset in the first year with the remaining balance offset on a 'straight line' basis. An equal annual allowance is used until the total value has been offset.

3. An initial percentage in the first year with the remaining balance offset on a reducing basis. The following example shows a 25% initial allowance and a reducing balance allowance of 25%.

	Year 0 £	Year 1 £	Year 2 £	Year 3 £	Year 4 £	Year 5 £
Capital	−10 000					
Initial 25%		2500				
25% of remaining			1875	1406	1055	791
Remaining balance		7500	5625	4219	3164	2373
Tax at 35% rate		+875	+656	+492	+369	+277

Tax at a 35% rate is reclaimed in the first year on the 25% initial allowance ($2500 \times 0.35 = £875$). In the next year tax is reclaimed on 25% of the balance of £7500 which is remaining, thus:

$$(£7500 \times 0.25) \times 0.35 = £1875 \times 0.35 = £656$$

Further complications can arise from the fact that different types of capital investments can be subject to different capital allowance rules. For example, land and buildings, which are regarded as long-term assets, are often treated differently to plant and machinery, thus the percentage used may be 10% rather than 25%.

Where the reducing balance method is used, and an asset is sold at the end of its working life, the remaining balance is normally reduced by the amount of the selling price. If the selling price is less than the remaining balance, the new reduced balance will continue to be offset. The life for tax purposes will therefore be different to the physical life. In some cases, such as assets with a very short life, the tax rules may allow the whole of the remaining balance, less the selling price, to be offset at the time the asset is sold. Hence asset life and physical life will be the same.

For many investments, the process of offsetting the reducing balance will continue after the asset has reached the end of its working life and been disposed of. Fortunately, the value of the remaining balance, as a percentage of the initial capital cost, will be sufficiently small after ten years that ignoring it in the evaluation will produce a very small error. In the above example, the value of tax in year 11 would be only £49.

To illustrate the application of taxation, an example is taken of an investment of £10 000 which will produce savings of £2000 a year for ten years. The corporation tax rate is taken as 35% and capital allowance of 25% in the first year with the balance being reduced by 25% each year; the cash flows are:

	Year 0	Year 1	Year 2	Year 3	Year 10	Year 11
	£	£	£	£	£	£
Capital	−10 000					
Capital tax		+875	+656	+492	+66	+49
Savings		+2000	+2000	+2000	+2000	
Revenue tax			−700	−700	−700	−700
Net cash flow	−10 000	+2875	+1956	+1792	+1366	−651

This would give an IRR of 12.3%, compared with 15% if tax was excluded, as would be the case if a company was not making sufficient profit to be liable for payment of corporation tax.

GRANTS

There are a variety of different grants available in the UK but the rules which govern eligibility keep changing. The availability of grants may be dependent on the area of the country where the investment is to be made, or on the type of technology. Grants may be available for help not only with capital investment, but also with consultancy costs which may, or may not, be associated with a capital project.

In the past, these grants have been tax free in the UK. Also they have not reduced the value which could be offset against corporation tax; the following example shows what can happen:

	£
Consultancy cost	−10 000
Tax allowance (35%)	+3 500
Grant (at 50% of cost)	+5 000
Net cost to company	−1 500

The way that taxation affects grants can be very favourable, so that in considering any investment project not only should availability of grants be investigated, but where a grant is available, the effect on tax liability should also be examined.

4 Intangible benefits

In the early days of computers their use in industry tended to be for office applications such as payroll, stock control and costing, or on the shopfloor for **numerical control (NC)** machine tools. These early uses were aimed at improving efficiency of departments that were labour intensive and their financial justification, based on reducing manning levels, was relatively simple. Here the emphasis was on the automation of clerical and manual functions, and with little change in the functions being performed.

Although these early systems were expensive when originally installed, the labour savings available were great. As technology has developed, the originally available savings in labour and operating expenses largely have been achieved, so that scope for further improvements in departmental efficiency are limited. Fortunately, modern technology is no longer simply aimed at automating manual tasks; it has been realized that AMT can have a much greater effect on a company than just improving the efficiency of the department where it may be installed. People advocating investment in AMT have made considerable efforts to identify the company-wide benefits which it can produce, but describe these benefits always in generalized terms, such as the following:

1. Increased flexibility of production.
2. Better-quality products.
3. Improved documentation.
4. Ability to respond to market needs.
5. Need to keep up with competition.
6. Improved company image.
7. Better management control.
8. Obtaining experience of new technology.

Usually managers would start with the belief that a particular aspect of AMT could be used in their department and they would select an application which was aimed at improving operating efficiency. Having defined the required specification, they would then try to justify the expenditure. In so doing they would attempt to identify the benefits.

Although there were some benefits which could be easily quantified, such as labour and operating expenses, others could not. The way in which these benefits have been described has meant that they always seemed to be incapable of quantification, even in technical terms, let alone in financial ones.

With the **flexible manufacturing system (FMS)**, for example, the cost of the early systems was so great that it was not possible to justify them using direct savings alone. However, it was realized that FMS would provide 'increased flexibility of production', as well as reducing labour costs, but there seemed to be no way in which this benefit could be included in the financial justification. Considerable efforts were then made to try to develop a method of quantifying the flexibility of FMS, the aim being to provide a measure, such as the percentage of flexibility, which any particular FMS may have.

Because these benefits could not be quantified, then, they have tended to be treated as a rather abstract concept, or simply an interesting phenomenon. As such, they are referred to as 'intangible', and as a result of their difficulty in justifying investments in financial terms, managers have had to fall back on the argument that there are a lot of unquantifiable intangible benefits, producing lists such as the one above. Their inability to justify investments, which were seen as essential, on the basis of quantified benefits, has meant that managers have faced several options.

1. Overrule the advice of the accountants and invest as an 'act of faith' in the hope that the intangible benefits will somehow help the company.
2. Use unrealistically high estimates of direct savings in the hope that it would not matter because there would be other benefits which would appear and compensate.
3. Refrain from making investments which could have been vital for the company's future.

As well as the obvious problem that act of faith investments may not be profitable, such investments cannot be correctly included in absorption costing systems. As described in a later chapter – and however good the investment may be – the intangible benefits will not be attributed to it in the costing system. This has led to the belief – possibly wrong – that the investment is a failure.

With any investment project, it is necessary to define the optimum specification. One of the reasons for using investment appraisal is to define the objectives of the investment in such a way that the investments can be compared with the cost of the technology required to achieve them.

If benefits have to be excluded from an evaluation because they are thought to be intangible, there is a danger that the ability to achieve the benefits may require an increase in investment cost, without providing the quantifiable benefits to justify the increase.

Another reason for conducting an investment appraisal is to provide quantified objectives for monitoring the performance of implementation. If there is only one objective for an investment the implementation can be directed towards its achievement, but where there may be several different benefits the need is to identify the most important ones. Thus the aim is to concentrate resources on ensuring that these are the first to be achieved.

Because the nature of intangible benefits was not originally well understood, there was the general belief that they would somehow automatically appear once an investment had been made. However, many of the benefits of AMT do not automatically appear, rather their achievement has to be planned.

With AMT, there are a variety of benefits which may appear elsewhere in the company than the department responsible for installing the project. Although these may have been identified, once the investment decision has been made, the motivation of managers in charge of projects is likely to be aimed at improving their department's efficiency, rather than achieving benefits elsewhere in the company for which they may get no credit. Even if the selected technology makes it possible to obtain the intangible benefits, if their achievement has been excluded from the objectives set for implementation it is quite possible that the benefits may not be achieved or at best, achievement is long delayed.

The concept of intangible factors applies only to benefits, not to costs, because once a cost has been identified it can be estimated. The problem with costs is not an inability to estimate them – as happens with intangible benefits – but rather that companies may fail to identify that a cost factor exists. This is especially true in the case of companies investing in an area of technology where they have no previous experience.

QUANTIFYING INTANGIBLES

Work done at UMIST showed in 1985, for the first time, that there should be no such thing as an intangible benefit. But identifying the nature of intangibles it was possible to show that every benefit could be quantified. Since that time, no one has described a benefit that could not be redefined into quantifiable terms.

While technology was simple, and aimed solely at departmental efficiency, it was possible for managers to measure existing costs and then calculate the expected saving. When cause and effect can be directly related, it is usually possible to calculate the magnitude of the benefit. For example, if a **computer numerical control (CNC)** machine can produce components in half the time take by manual machines, only half the previous labour may be required.

The nature of intangible benefits is such that they do not appear in the department where the investment is made, but occur elsewhere in the company. In addition, the relationship between cause and effect is indirect, so that their magnitude has to be estimated rather than directly calculated.

Using investment appraisal to do no more than provide a final 'yes'/'no' verdict on a project means that a single set of figures has to be calculated; but with intangible benefits, it is not realistic to do this. For example, an FMS which reduced manufacturing lead time could improve delivery performance, resulting in an increase in sales. However, it would not be possible to calculate the magnitude of the sales increase as a direct relationship, the value could only be estimated. This has led people to confuse their inability to put benefits into quantifiable terms, with the accuracy with which their value can be estimated. In fact there are two distinct problems and these must be dealt with separately, namely:

1. The form in which the benefit is quantified.
2. Estimating the magnitude of the benefit.

The approach which was adopted at UMIST was to study in turn each area of AMT, making a complete list of all the intangible benefits that others had previously identified. Each one of these was then investigated in order to identify what these generalized statements really meant; by doing this it was possible to show that each could be redefined into terms which were quantifiable.

It was found that one of the reasons why intangible benefits presented problems in the past had been that a single generalized statement can often refer to several quantifiable benefits. For example, the statement 'better-quality products' can mean some or all of the following, each of which can be quantified:

1. Reduced scrap.
2. Reduced rework.
3. Reduced disruption of production caused by scrap and rework.
4. Reduced warranty and service costs.
5. Reduced cost of inspection and quality assurance.
6. Reduced cost of concessions and design changes.
7. Reduced cost of documentation and change control.
8. Reduced need for safety stocks.
9. Increased sales of better-quality products.

In the case of the 'increased flexibility of production' of FMS, it was possible to identify at least twenty-five different aspects of flexibility, which are discussed in detail in a later chapter. It was found, however, that in every case the flexibility was part of the technical specification. What had to be quantified in financial terms was not the flexibility, but the benefits, such as increased sales or reduced stock levels, which resulted from having the flexibility.

Having redefined the list of intangibles, it was then possible to compile them into lists of quantifiable factors. The lists were then improved on the basis of experience gained from evaluating actual projects . These lists are given in later chapters. Great care is needed in redefining intangibles to ensure that not only are all potential benefits included, but any duplication is avoided. Thus, while a single item, such as 'better-quality products', can result in savings in a number of areas (as in the above list), several items can produce benefits in the same area. For example, both improved product quality and reduced delivery time can result in increased sales. To try to avoid duplication, the lists which were produced were divided up into the areas of saving rather than the cause of the saving.

One of the problems encountered in correctly identifying benefits is that while the majority may be obvious, there may also be secondary, less obvious ones. For example, the introduction of **manufacturing resources planning (MRPII)** can result directly in improving delivery performance and reduced disruption of production. By so doing, foremen may then spend less time acting as progress chasers and more time concentrating on improving the efficiency of their department, thus producing additional savings.

Another example of secondary benefits was a company that had acquired a reputation for good quality by having its installation engineers spend a long time in the customer's factory, commissioning the machinery and staying on until all the teething problems had been resolved. Ensuring that the product was correct before despatch not only reduced the installation costs, but the much shorter commissioning period meant that payment could be obtained much earlier, thus improving cash flow timing and reducing bank overdraft costs.

While it is possible in evaluating a project to start with a checklist of potential quantifiable benefits, such as those which were developed, and use this to identify the ones which may be relevant, there is always a danger that there can be areas of benefit which are not on the list. Benefits are usually perceived as being intangible when a manager has started by finding an application for AMT and then tries to identify the benefits. Starting by identifying the required benefits before selecting the technology helps to overcome the problem. When it is not possible to do this, the following procedure can be used to identify and quantify potential benefits:

1. Identify that a benefit may exist and describe it in general terms.
2. Redefine into quantifiable terms.
3. Estimate the approximate magnitude of the value.
4. Carry out evaluation using budget estimates for costs and savings.
5. Determine if the benefit will have a significant effect on the profitability of the project.

6. If significant, improve the accuracy of the estimate.
7. Ensure that the technical specification will allow the benefit to be achieved.
8. Carry out final evaluation.

The nature of intangibles is such that they will not occur in the department where the project is being investigated, but arise elsewhere in the company. As a result, it is important that the effect of the investment is defined in terms which will be understandable to those people, probably from a different management discipline, who are being asked to produce estimates; for example:

1. Poor delivery performance is thought to be causing a loss of sales.
2. FMS is identified as a way to improve delivery performance.
3. Existing performance is measured (12 weeks is presently being quoted).
4. The key components which affect product delivery are identified.
5. An FMS is designed that can produce all of these components.
6. The new improved delivery is calculated (this will be 6 weeks).
7. Marketing are asked: 'will a reduction from 12 to 6 weeks have an effect on sales volume [either increasing it or preventing its decline]?'
8. If 'yes', Marketing are asked to estimate the percentage improvement.

In situations such as this, it would be unrealistic to expect Marketing to produce a single estimated value. They would normally want to provide a range of pessimistic and optimistic and most likely values – e.g. 'At least 5%, at the most 15%. but most likely about 10%'.

Once a range of estimates has been obtained, an evaluation can be carried out which gives a range of values of IRR and NPV. These values can then be related to the assumptions made about the project. This will allow the directors, when deciding whether or not to approve the project, to consider factors such as the following:

1. Will the FMS reduce delivery lead time by the estimated amount?
2. If so, will this affect sales volume?
3. How realistic are the estimates from Marketing?
4. How likely do you think it is that the estimated DCF returns will be achieved?

One of the dangers with the traditional approach of selecting technology, and then trying to justify it, is illustrated by the above example. If the decision to invest in FMS had been initiated, as is common, with the attitude that 'everyone is saying that FMS is essential, let's see if we can find an application', then it is likely that the design of the FMS – and the components planned for it – would have been selected for technical reasons.

Attempting to identify benefits to justify the investment would be done after the design was finished. If the initial motivation had not been to improve product delivery, it is probable that the FMS which was selected would not be able to produce *all* of the key components which were affecting product delivery. Therefore, although the FMS might improve the delivery of individual components, it would not improve product delivery. Thus it would fail to achieve the most important and largest potential saving, namely the increase in sales.

In the past, before it was realized that all benefits could be quantified, an alternative approach for dealing with intangibles had been suggested. This was to start by carrying out an evaluation which included all the direct savings which could be quantified. If the DCF return was below the value required for acceptance (the shortfall being represented by the negative value of NPV), a decision could be made as to whether or not the value of the identified intangibles was likely to be greater than this negative NPV.

Unfortunately, this approach reinforced the view that investment appraisal was just a technique for giving a pass/fail verdict on a project, and helped to encourage the attitude, 'How big a value do I need to get it past the accountants?' Using this approach does not allow investment appraisal to be used for comparing investment in alternative areas of technology, selecting between different specifications or identifying the objectives for implementation.

Once it has been shown that intangible benefits could be quantified, experience of evaluating a wide range of projects in companies showed that these savings can be much greater than traditional direct savings. In fact much of AMT only make financial sense when it is aimed at achieving the benefits which were previously thought to be intangible.

The fact that intangible benefits are the most important results in a major change in the objectives of investment; and this, in turn, means that the nature of the technology chosen has to change. One of the dangers of the approach suggested in the past is that the importance of intangibles is not identified, nor is the need for a change in objectives and technology.

As an illustration of the importance of intangibles, it has been discovered that in many engineering companies the cost of running the Drawing Office (DO) is less than 1% of the cost of sales. If, by investing in **computer aided design (CAD)**, the company could increase sales by only 1%, the extra profit generated from the contribution to overhead recovery would be greater than any saving which could be realistically made by reducing the cost of running the DO.

Unfortunately, most companies which have invested in CAD have tried to justify the cost on the basis of quantifiable DO savings, and this has then been reflected in the type of CAD system selected. The effects of CAD outside the DO (e.g. on sales) always have been seen as intangible.

SOCIAL COSTS

Companies are commercial organizations whose aim is to make a profit from the funds which the owners have invested in the company. The *raison d'être* of new investments therefore is to help improve profitability and long-term competitive ability. The investments may be defensive such as preventing loss of market share, or expansionist such as increasing short- or long-term profitability. In either case, the investment will be aimed at achieving financial objectives, hence the benefits can be defined in financial terms.

However, in addition to these financial objectives, a company has also to satisfy its responsibilities to society and fulfil its legal obligations. Some projects therefore may not have commercial objectives, but be aimed at fulfilling these responsibilities. If an investment's sole objective is to satisfy a social or legal requirement, such as installing equipment to avoid emission of hazardous and illegal waste material, the decision to invest is purely a policy decision if there are no additional financial benefits. The decision, then, is: 'do we spend £x to satisfy our obligations', and investment appraisal would not be used in such circumstances.

However, in many cases the investment can provide financial benefits in addition to satisfying the company's social responsibility. For example, the investment in a robot to perform a hazardous task may not only eliminate a safety problem, but also save the cost of an operator. Consequently the company may be faced with a choice; for instance, does it spend £50 000 and eliminate only the safety hazard, or does it spend £75 000 and save the cost of the operator as well.

Trying to estimate the financial value of being able to fulfil the company's social responsibilities, so that a figure can be included in an investment appraisal, would thus be highly subjective. Such an approach may well be open to criticism, including the accusation of trying to put a value on human life. Fortunately, alternative approaches are possible.

One approach is to start by identifying the potential benefits of an investment, the value of any commercial benefits are then estimated and an investment appraisal carried out. If the DCF return is below the cost of capital, the shortfall – represented by the negative NPV – is the cost of fulfilling the company's social obligation. A policy decision can then be made whether or not to pay the identified cost of satisfying the company's responsibilities.

For example, a company may consider investing in a robot at a cost of £75 000 to perform the task which is a safety hazard. Doing this will save the £10 000 a year cost of the existing operator, as well as eliminating the hazard. An evaluation based on a ten-year working life, and using 15% as the cost of capital, gives an NPV of −£24,812. Then the policy decision is: 'do we spend £24,812 to eliminate the hazard?'

In some cases, there can be alternative ways of satisfying the social responsibility. Here investment appraisals can be carried out to help determine the most cost-effective way of fulfilling the responsibility. The evaluations will include, as a financial benefit, the cost saving of not having to satisfy the obligation by an alternative method.

For example, a company has a press which has been condemned as unsafe by the Health and Safety Inspectorate. The company has to choose between investing in new controls and guards at a cost of £30 000 or to invest in a new press. The new press would cost £100 000, but in addition to eliminating the hazard, would produce operating savings of £15 000 a year.

Assuming that both the existing press with new controls and the new press itself would have working lives of at least ten years, the evaluation of the new press would produce the following figures:

	Year 0 £	*Years 1–10* £
Capital cost	− 100 000	
Cost avoided	+ 30 000	
Savings		+ 15 000

Investing in the new press would give an IRR of 16.9%, in addition to eliminating the safety hazard. The comparison is between the new press and the cheapest alternative method of eliminating the hazard because 'doing nothing' is not an acceptable option.

When the aim of an investment is to obtain commercial benefits, the objective of investment appraisal is to maximize the value of the benefit. When the aim of the investment is to fulfil the company's social and legal obligations, the objective of investment appraisal is to minimize the cost of fulfilling those obligations. The aim is not to try to find ways of avoiding these obligations.

NON-EXISTENT BENEFITS

When companies start to investigate a project by trying to identify an application for the technology, rather than investigating ways to solve a specific problem, they produce a list of various intangible benefits which seem applicable. However, a benefit is only a benefit if it can produce a genuine saving, whereas several of the intangible benefits often quoted for AMT may not always result in a cash flow saving. In some cases, the benefits quoted actually represent costs.

One of the dangers of making an investment without a financial evaluation, on the grounds that the benefits are intangible, is that the value of the benefits may be negligible.(*Note*: no benefit should ever be excluded from a financial evaluation on the grounds that it is intangible. Benefits should only be omitted because their financial value is insignificant.)

One of the benefits often quoted for FMS is that it will save floor space. A common approach in trying to quantify this is to calculate the reduction in required area, and then include this in an evaluation using a value for pounds per square foot. This value would be based on the total cost of the factory building, including factors such as rates, heating, lighting, building maintenance, etc. This total cost is then divided by the total floor area, as is done in an absorption costing system, to find the cost per square foot.

Although an FMS may occupy less floor area than the machines it replaces, this may not in many cases represent a cash flow saving because – as Parkinson's Law suggests – other activities will just expand to fill the space available. What has to be investigated is not only the reduction in the area required, but what will happen to the space vacated.

The following are some of the ways in which saving floor space may result in a cash flow saving:

1. It avoids construction of a new building or extension.
2. A vacated building can be sold or demolished, giving savings in rates, heat, light, etc.
3. It provides the space for work to be bought back from outside contractors.
4. It provides space for expansion of production which otherwise would not be possible.

In each of these examples, the saving would not be quantified by using a standard rate per square foot because not all the factors used to produce such a rate may be affected. The need is to start by defining what will happen as a result of reducing floor areas. Having done this, one then identifies the specific cash flow changes which will take place as a result.

In some cases, the installation of FMS may require more, rather than less, floorspace. Although FMS technology is now becoming proven and standard systems can be purchased, most companies will plan to install the FMS and have it fully operational before starting to dispose of their existing plant. This will mean that additional floorspace is needed for the initial installation, and providing this may involve cash flow expenditure. The space vacated by the subsequent disposal of plant may, or may not, result in a cash flow saving. Although the final result of installing FMS may be a reduction in the floor area required, this may represent a cost increase rather than a saving.

A similar problem arises in the way that some companies evaluate reductions in inventory where they include not only the value of the inventory itself, but an additional figure for the reduced cost of storing inventory. This may be a percentage of inventory value, based on a standard rate which has been calculated from the total value of inventory and the total cost of running the stores function.

While reducing the level of inventory will produce a cash flow saving from the value of the inventory reduction, there may not be any saving in the cost of storekeeping. There will only be a saving in storage costs if the stock reduction is going to be sufficiently large that there will be changes in the storage and work-handling operations; for example:

1. Reduced labour – e.g. storekeepers, work movers, Material Control Staff.
2. Reduced operating costs – e.g. less use of lift trucks.
3. Avoids costs such as a planned stores expansion.
4. Vacates space which, as discussed above, results in a cash flow saving.

Small reductions in inventory levels may not result in any savings in stores and work-moving costs, but large reductions may result in changes such as being able to close down a complete store. As with floorspace, the need is to define what changes the inventory reduction will cause and then to identify any specific cash flow savings.

One of the reasons often suggested for investing in AMT is that companies need to invest to obtain experience of new technology, obtaining such experience being quoted as an intangible benefit, is something which only large companies could afford to consider.

If a company feels that it needs to gain experience in any specific aspect of AMT, it must be because it is envisaged that the company will have a lot of applications for the technology. This means, then, that if a company is sufficiently large to be able to consider an investment to obtain experience, it should also be able to identify several applications where the initial investment in the new technology might be viable.

If this is not the case, the best application should be selected and a financial evaluation carried out, including all the quantifiable factors. The negative NPV then represents the cost of obtaining the experience. The decision to invest is thus a policy decision, based on an examination of the need to obtain the experience and whether the cost of so doing is justified. In such an evaluation, the factor of gaining experience should be dealt with as a cost rather than a benefit.

One of the consequences of managers using absorption cost data on a regular basis is that it encourages the attitude that there should be a rate per hour which can be used in an evaluation, even if the rate used is not a standard cost rate. For example, savings in labour are often included on the basis if number of hours × cost per hour, even if this cost is only based on wage rates plus direct employment costs.

An example of this is an investment in an office computer system which will cost £5000 and is expected to save 5 hours' work per week for 45 weeks per year. The saving is then calculated on the basis of £8000/year salary, plus direct employment costs, which divided by total hours a year gives a rate of £7/hour:

Saving = (£7/h) × (5 h/week) × (45 weeks/year) = £1575/year

Assuming that the office computer will have a life of five years, the saving of £1575 a year would give an IRR of 17.3%.

The problem with this method is that if there are only a few people in the department, the 5 hour per week reduction in work content may not result in a reduction in the number of hours worked. The consequence may be that the existing remaining work, or even non-work activities, will just expand to fill the time available and there will be no cash flow saving, although there would still be a cash flow expenditure.

In a large department, such as a machine shop or assembly shop, when there is flexibility of labour to move between jobs as work content changes, it is normally assumed that because there is a regular turnover in the labour-force any small reduction in the numbers employed, as a result of investment projects, can be made by avoiding replacement of people leaving.

It is normally assumed that any specific investment or cost reduction project is only one of several. As a result, while a project in itself may not lead to a specific, named individual leaving, without being replaced, it will still be expected to create a cash flow saving because the project when combined with others will lead to an overall reduction in employment levels.

An alternative situation can arise with project costs. For example, if a project involves training the existing workforce, the cost of running the training course, plus the costs such as overtime or subcontract of making up the time spent on the training course, would represent cash flow expenditure. However, the wages of people sent on the course should not be included in an evaluation as these will still have to be paid if the training were not done.

MAGNITUDE OF BENEFITS

Although every company perceives itself as being unique, the nature of the problems it is faced with is not. Thus all companies have problems of delivery performance, product cost, excess inventory, obsolete designs, product specification, product quality, etc. What is unique within any particular company is the relative importance of each of these problems. Two companies of the same size, and operating in the same market, may perceive a different set of problems as being the most important; for example, one may be concerned with delivery performance and obsolete products, while the other may regard manufacturing costs and quality as the most important.

Once all the benefits of AMT have been redefined into quantifiable terms, they can be summarized into a number of general headings; thus:

1. Reduced operating costs, including labour.
2. Reduced level of inventory.
3. Reduced material costs: raw material and bought-out content.
4. Increased sales volume, or preventing sales being lost.
5. Increased sales margin: ability to charge more for the same cost, or eliminating unprofitable orders.

To illustrate the relative importance of the various types of benefit, an example is taken of a company with an annual turnover of £1.3 million, made up as follows:

	£
Material costs	400 000
Labour costs	100 000
Variable operating expenses	100 000
Manufacturing overhead	400 000
Cost of manufacture	1000 000
Administrative overhead and profit (30%)	300 000
Sales revenue	1300 000

Assuming that total inventory levels represent the equivalent of a five times a year stock turnover, the value of inventory will be £260 000.

Figure 4.1 shows the cost of manufacture and is typical of diagrams used by those writing about **Just in Time (JIT)** to illustrate the declining importance of direct labour-savings. An argument that is often put forward in trying to justify the need for JIT is that companies concentrated their efforts in the past on reducing direct labour because this was their largest item of cost. Having succeeded in this they now have to look elsewhere for further areas of saving, and because material costs are now the largest factor, efforts should be concentrated on reducing inventory. The assumption that is made is that reducing inventory (by the use of JIT) will reduce material costs, which is not the case. The value of a 10% change in annual values will be as follows:

	£
10% reduction in material costs	40 000
10% reduction in labour costs	10 000
10% reduction in operating expenses	10 000
10% increase in sales volume	70 000
10% increase in selling price	130 000
10% reduction in inventory	26 000

Although there is a tax advantage in inventory reduction, it provides only a one-off saving, while the others represent annual values. As a result, the 10% inventory reduction may produce the smallest benefit.

Taking projects with an expected life of ten years, to compare the value of annual savings with one-time inventory savings, Fig. 4.2 shows the relative magnitude of some of the financial benefits. Although this provides some indication of the possible relative importance of benefits, it is necessary to relate these values to the probability of being able to achieve them.

The largest benefit would result from making a 10% increase in selling price, such as by a considerable improvement in delivery performance or product quality, without increasing the cost of the product and, at the same

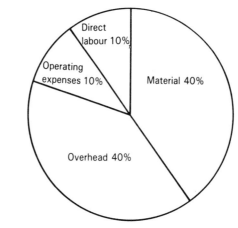

Fig. 4.1 Cost of manufacture.

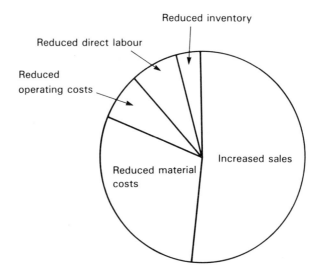

Fig. 4.2 Relative magnitude of benefits.

time, without any loss of sales volume. However, it is probably much less easy to achieve this than a 10% increase in sales volume, assuming that the selling price was correct in the first place. Because managers have concentrated on improving operating efficiency in the past, and most of the obvious cost reduction projects have already been implemented, it is probably easier to identify investments which will increase sales by 10% than ones which would reduce *total* direct labour costs or operating expenses by 10%.

Obviously the above example is highly simplistic, and the relative magnitude of all the cost factors will vary considerably between companies – as will the possibility of making changes. In order to help identify the areas of the company where resources need to be concentrated, it would be possible to carry out an analysis such as that above and then list the potential benefits which can be obtained from AMT in declining order of magnitude and feasibility. Usually such a list would consist of the following:

1. Increasing sales volume, or preventing sales being lost, by making products more competitive (e.g. delivery, price, quality, product specification, etc.).
2. Increasing selling price, without a corresponding increase in product cost or loss of sales (e.g. charging a premium price for improved delivery).
3. Eliminating unprofitable orders (e.g. by improving quotation system).
4. Reduced cost of material content in products.
5. Reduced operating costs (e.g. labour).
6. Reduced inventory levels.

The financial advantage of increasing sales volume is that in order to produce the additional products needed for extra sales, only expenditure on the variable cost elements – e.g. material, direct labour, operating expenses, etc. – will be required. All the cost factors included in the fixed overheads, including depreciation and indirect labour, will remain unchanged. In the case of large changes in sales volume, some of the fixed overheads will become variable, such as would be the case if extra machine tools have to be purchased to provide extra capacity. However, the aim of carrying out the above analysis is only to help identify areas for further investigation, not to produce exact figures.

In the past, when the companies tended to be labour intensive, with a simple management structure and low capital costs, a high proportion of product cost was variable. As a result, the contribution to recovery of fixed overheads from additional sales would be relatively small. However, companies have been investing in increasingly complex and expensive technology and, at the same time, reducing the number of direct workers while increasing the number of indirect staff. This means that an increasingly large percentage of selling price is represented by fixed costs which will remain unchanged as sales volume increases.

The consequence of this is that as companies respond to pressures to invest in new technology, the financial advantages of increased sales volume will continue to become more attractive and the importance of projects aimed at increasing sales will become greater. With some capital-intensive companies, almost all the costs incurred in producing additional products to satisfy an increase in sales may be the cost of raw materials. The difference between the selling price and the raw material cost of additional sales is almost all profit.

Reducing the cost of the material content in products can provide two types of benefit. If the selling price of products is unchanged, the saving will be the reduction in material cost. If, however, the selling price is reduced in line with the lower cost, the benefit will come from the effect on sales volume and its contribution to overhead recovery.

Making a list as the above helps to identify the need to change the objectives for investments away from the traditional objectives that managers have concentrated on in the past. Managers must now consider the types of project which have been ignored in the past because of difficulties faced by managers when trying to show that such investments could be profitable.

The traditional attitude towards investment appraisal was that of a final pass/fail hurdle to be overcome. This meant that in carrying out an evaluation a single value had to be calculated for each cost and saving factor. The inability – or possibly just reluctance – of departments such as Marketing to commit themselves to single value for savings has helped to reinforce the belief that indirect benefits could not be included in an evaluation.

Unfortunately, experience now shows that when managers were trying to calculate the value of savings in factors which would seem to lend themselves to exact calculation, they could make major errors. An example of this can be seen in the case of CAD. The literature describing the application of CAD shows that most of the companies which have attempted a financial justification have done so on the basis of savings in Drawing Office (DO) labour.

The early use of CAD was for applications, such as printed circuit board design, which gave a very considerable increase in productivity. For a long time it was assumed that the introduction of CAD in engineering companies would also give large productivity improvements, and ratios of at least 3 : 1, or even 4 : 1, were widely quoted, the assumption being that once CAD was fully operational, two-thirds to three-quarters of the original DO labourforce would be needed no longer.

While it would seem to be feasible to carry out trials in order to confirm these productivity gains, there appears to be no factual evidence to support them in a scientific manner. In fact the available evidence now suggests that the original estimates were completely unrealistic, and that for most companies an overall productivity improvement of 1.5 : 1 would be a more realistic assumption, although even this might be over-optimistic.

Although one would assume that they would calculate the value of savings exactly, managers have consistently predicted savings which were more than twice the level achieved in practice. The consequences of this are not just a failure to achieve the forecast return on investment. If a CAD system has been purchased on the assumption that 3 : 1 productivity improvements were possible, the size of the system purchased and the number of terminals would probably be only half that needed if the ratio in practice was 1.5 : 1.

For some purposes, it is necessary to have a single estimated value of future sales volume, such as is required to calculate future production capacity, or for establishing standard cost rates. The fact that a single value for forecast sales is produced, and then rarely if ever exactly achieved in practice, helps to reinforce the belief among engineers that marketing managers can never forecast sales with any degree of accuracy.

When engineers try to get marketing managers to estimate the effect of a project on sales, they have not only to describe the consequences of the investment in an understandable manner, but also they need to realize that marketing managers will be unable to forecast a single value with a great degree of accuracy. It is unrealistic to expect anyone to forecast accurately the level of future sales because there are far too many variable factors which can influence the market-place (many of them being completely unpredictable). The problem is made worse if forecasts are needed not just for a single standard product, but for a range of different products, each of which can be sold in variable form. The problem of obtaining estimates is made worse if the original motivation for a project was 'let's see if we can find an application for this new technology'. In such cases, it is probable that the nature of benefits will not be clearly defined.

However, AMT only makes real financial sense if the motivation is: 'we have a problem, let us see if this new technology can help solve it.' Using this approach means not only that the benefits will be genuine, and potentially large, but there is the added advantage that the objective of the investment is one which everyone can understand.

The widespread belief among engineers that marketing managers cannot produce realistic estimates of future sales must be wrong. However, a distinction should be drawn between realistic estimates and exact estimates. The nature of estimates made about future sales means that it is unreasonable to expect anyone to be able to produce an exact figure.

If marketing managers are incapable of relating changes in products, such as improved delivery performance or improved quality, to the needs of the market, and the effect this will have on sales volume, the question must be asked: 'how does the company ever decide what products to make?' Also, if marketing managers do not know the needs of the company's market for product specification, delivery, price, sales volume, and so on, how shall engineers know what products to design, what manufacturing facilities are needed and how much production capacity has to be provided?

Thus, when marketing managers are unable to estimate the effect which an investment will have on sales not as a single value, but a range of likely outcomes (e.g. optimistic, pessimistic and most likely), then the reason is probably one of the following:

1. The problem is not aimed at solving a genuine marketing problem.
2. The effect of the project has not been presented in understandable form.
3. Marketing managers do not understand the nature of the company's business.

When managers are investigating a project which is aimed at improving the efficiency of their own department, their motivation would be to submit their most optimistic estimates of saving. As was found in the example of CAD, managers can allow themselves to be persuaded, often by untypical demonstrations, to accept unrealistically high estimates of savings, which are unlikely to be achieved in practice. Again, when managers in a different department to that investigating a project are asked to provide estimates, their motivation is likely to be the opposite. They will be reluctant to commit themselves to any figures which they are not confident of achieving. This is especially so in Marketing, where payment by results schemes are common and managers would expect to see their estimates reflected in revised sales targets.

The result is that any project which is designed to have a genuine impact on sales has two advantages, the first one being that the forecast sales improvements are likely to be more realistic than forecasts of direct cost savings. Secondly, as shown earlier, the value of increased sales can be much greater than other types of saving.

5 Inventory savings

Inventory reduction is often portrayed as a major reason for investment in AMT. Unfortunately, much that is written about changing inventory levels can be misleading because it is based on over-simplified assumptions. Any consideration of inventory changes must take into account the following factors:

1. The way that inventory changes are valued.
2. The nature of the inventory.
3. The effect that changing the levels of inventory can have on the operation of the company.

Authors often confuse the high, ongoing cost of the material content in products with the cost of carrying inventory, the implication being that reducing inventory will reduce material costs. While reducing material costs will reduce the value of inventory, reducing inventory levels will have little or no effect on the cost of material content.

Although inventory reduction is portrayed as being 'a good thing', in practice a reduction can result in serious problems if the full implications are not fully understood and examined before any changes are made. Within a manufacturing company there are two major types of inventory, namely:

1. Consumable supplies such as tooling, welding materials and gases, maintenance spares, heat treatment chemicals, paints, etc.
2. Materials, components and products intended for sale.

The line between these categories may not be completely clear-cut; for example, paint may be thought of as either a consumable or as part of the final product. However, for simplicity only the problems of evaluating changes in the second category will be dealt with.

Textbook examples normally deal with new or the expansionary type of projects which require additional working capital for inventory at the start of the project, the examples normally proferred showing an equal value being returned at the end of the project life. In practice, most projects will be aimed at trying to reduce the levels of inventory. Unfortunately, the way that reduction in inventory is valued is much more complex than addition, therefore this chapter will concentrate on the problems of inventory reduction.

In any project involving inventory reduction it is important to differentiate between the value of an asset and the cost of physically holding it in stock. This arises not just because the changes have to be costed in a rather different way, but the way in which the changes are made is also different.

Physical storage costs include factors such as the use of lift trucks, the number of storekeepers, work-movers and clerical staff, etc. Reductions in these costs must be included in an evaluation as separate cash flow savings and not included in any changes in the value of inventory. Not only are they valued in a different way, but changes in the physical costs of holding stock may not be in proportion to changes in the value of inventory. For instance, a 10% reduction in inventory levels may not reduce the physical storage costs by 10%.

One aspect of physical holding cost is deterioration in the quality of stock. If this is a problem, it may be possible to deal with it by improving housekeeping, such as the use of **first in first out (FIFO)** procedures, rather than trying to solve it by reducing stock levels which may well create problems elsewhere in the company. Additional problems such as a high rate of stock obsolescence may be caused by faults in the material control system, or ineffective design change control procedures. The cost of obsolescence, as with quality deterioration, is part of the physical holding cost.

If problems such as these are not recognized as separate from the problem of inventory levels, it is possible that efforts to eliminate obsolescence will start by trying to reduce stock levels in the hope that this will cure the problem. Not only can this be the wrong approach, but because the real cause of the problem may well not have been identified it may not be solved.

The value of inventory is dependant on two separate elements: one is the quantity of the stock being held; and the other is the book value of the individual components and products. The objective in inventory reduction is to reduce the total value, and this may be achieved by reducing either or both of these two elements. Attempts to reduce inventory must not just be aimed at quantity reduction, value reduction may be just as important, for example, by holding stocks of raw material rather than finished components.

VALUATION OF INVENTORY

Inventory can exist in several forms within a manufacturing company; for example:

1. Raw material (e.g. bar, plate, castings, forgings, etc.).
2. Work-in-progress (WIP).

3. Finished components, manufactured in house.
4. Finished components, bought in complete.
5. Finished product awaiting sale.

The way in which each of these can be valued in a company's accounts can vary slightly and is dependent on the book-keeping rules used by the company. For example, the way in which WIP is increased in value as it progresses will vary between companies because this depends on the stages at which costs are allocated. Although the basic principles employed will be standard, it is important to find out the rules being used within a company when first considering any project aimed at inventory reduction.

Investments in AMT which are aimed at reducing inventory are often just concerned with WIP, but WIP may represent a small proportion of total stock value, possibly only 15%–20%. At the same time, the investment may only affect part of the total WIP. For example, changes which affect component manufacture WIP may not alter assembly WIP.

Although component manufacture lead times are normally much longer than assembly lead times, this can be offset by the higher book value of components in assembly which will comprise both finished components and bought-in items. Consequently, the value of WIP in assembly may well be similar to that in component manufacture.

To illustrate the way in which inventory is valued, an example is taken of a component which has a selling price of £130, made up as follows:

	£
Raw material cost	40.00
Labour cost	10.00
Operating expenses	10.00
Manufacturing overhead (including depreciation)	40.00
Cost of manufacture	100.00
Administration overhead and profit	30.00
Selling price	130.00

The raw material is taken from stores and is passed through three manufacturing operations of equal length. Figure 5.1 shows how the value of the component increases at each stage until it is put into the stores as a finished component with a book value of £100, this representing the total manufacturing cost. Although the component will eventually be sold for £130, the normal conservative accountancy convention is that stock is valued at cost, rather than sale price, except where for some reason (such as with obsolete stock) the selling price will be less than the purchase or manufacturing price.

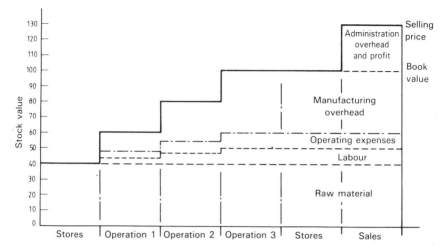

Fig. 5.1 Increase in component value during manufacture.

In terms of cash flow expenditure, the manufacture of the component has only cost £60, that is £40 for material and £20 for labour and operating expenses. The remaining £40 of book value represents the allocation of overheads which will be unaffected by changes in the number of components produced.

Relatively small changes in manufacturing throughput, especially if only temporary change to reduce inventory levels, will not alter expenditure on the factors included in fixed overheads such as supervision, maintenance, rates, heating, lighting, depreciation allocation and inspection. Although major changes in volume can result in changes in overhead factors, meaning that more factors will be classed as variable overhead rather than fixed, most projects aimed at inventory reduction will not involve such changes unless included as a saving elsewhere in the evaluation.

Figure 5.2 shows the assumption which is normally made about batch manufacture, namely that stock is being replenished at regular periods as each batch of components is completed. The objective, then, is to time the completion of a batch to coincide with the stock level reaching the planned minimum safety stock level.

There are two ways in which a reduction of finished component inventory is normally brought about: one way is to reduce the minimum level of safety stock; and the other is to reduce batch ordering quantities, as shown in Figure 5.3, and thereby reduce the average stock level. It is of course possible to have a combination of the two methods. WIP can also be reduced by having shorter lead times, thereby delaying the start of batches. These reductions are not achieved by increasing sales for a short period of time in order

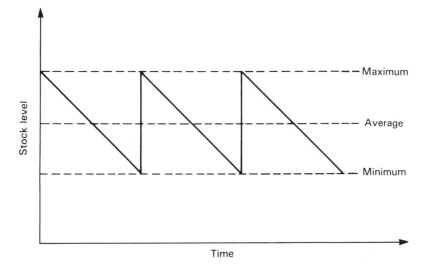

Fig. 5.2 Traditional concept of batch manufacture.

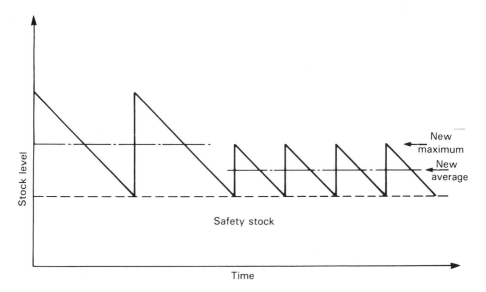

Fig. 5.3 The effect on stock levels of reducing batch sizes.

to sell off the excess stock, rather they are achieved by restricting the supply process until the stock has been consumed and it has been reduced to the new level.

Figure 5.4 shows how the pattern of manufacture may be changed in order

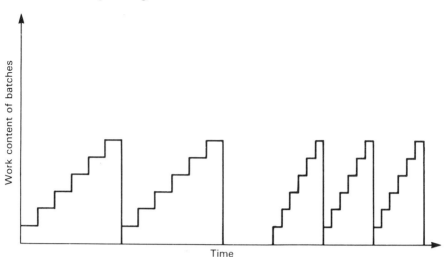

Fig. 5.4 Introduction of smaller batch sizes.

to introduce smaller, and more frequent, batch quantities while, at the same time, reducing stock levels. Even if the reduction in stock levels was planned to coincide with the start of a period of sales growth, the benefit of increased sales would be included separately in an evaluation (assuming the increase was going to be caused by the project). In addition, the reduction in the required stock levels would still be achieved, either by a temporary restriction in the supply process or, if production was planned to increase to suit the new sales level, the stock reduction would be achieved by delaying the start of the production increase.

The importance of this is that in valuing a reduction in stock levels, the valuation is based on the restriction of the supply process and not the sales value of the stock. Only in the case of selling off obsolete stock is this not so because once the obsolete stock has been sold, it would not be replaced, and also there is no replacement supply process to restrict.

Care is needed in valuing the sale of obsolete stock. It is first necessary to identify the stock which will only be sold as a direct result of the project being evaluated (and which otherwise would not be sold at all). The second problem is to compare the expected selling price with the value of the stock in the company's accounts because selling obsolete stock for less than book value may create problems in the balance sheet.

Take as an example the component quoted earlier, which has a book value of £100. The cash flow saving which results from restricting the supply process in order to avoid making components, and thereby allowing stock levels to decrease, is:

	£
Material	40.00
Labour	10.00
Operating expenses	10.00
Cash flow saving	60.00

Except for very large changes in stock levels, the factors comprising the £40 manufacturing overhead element will be unchanged by a temporary restriction in the supply process.

The majority of companies use double-entry book-keeping systems for their accounts, and because of the way such systems operate, the £60 cash flow saving in material, labour and expenses is recorded as an increase in cash and an equal reduction in stock value. The result is that there is no change in the total value of assets. This means, then, that it is treated in a different manner from operating savings which are recorded in the accounts as a reduction in the cost of manufacture. A reduction in the cost of manufacture produces a corresponding increase in profit which, in turn, increases the liability for taxation. However, the cash flow element in stock reduction is not reported as an increase in profits and therefore does not incur tax liability.

At the end of the financial year in which the stock reduction was made, the annual stock check will record the reduction in stock levels. Both the new stock level and the previous level will be valued in the company's accounts at the full book value, not just the cash flow value.

With the example component, the £60 cash flow element of the stock reduction already will have been recorded in the accounts, but the remaining £40 portion, representing the allocation of fixed overheads, is now recorded as a reduction in assets. Unlike the cash flow portion, the reduction in the ovehead element is recorded in the accounts as a corresponding reduction in profits. Although this reduction of the overhead element does not itself represent any change in cash flows, the reduction in reported profits results in a corresponding reduction in tax liability which does represent a cash flow saving; the total effect is:

	£
Cash flow saving (no tax liability)	60.00
Reduction in asset value	40.00
Book value of component	100.00
Reduction in reported profits (from reduction in asset value)	40.00
Reduction in tax liability (from reduction in reported profits) (£40.00 × 35%)	14.00

Total cash flow saving	£
Cash flow saving	60.00
Saving in tax liability	14.00
Total cash flow saving	74.00

The proportion of book value representing the cash flow element and the overhead allocation element will not only vary between different companies, but between different types of stock within the same company. For example, raw materials and bought-in complete components will normally have a very low overhead element, possibly only a nominal amount to cover the costs of ordering, inspection, handling and storage. On the other hand, WIP and components manufactured in house will have a much higher element representing the allocation of manufacturing overheads and depreciation. As a result, changes in the levels of different types of stock will not have the same effect in the company's accounts.

REVALUATION OF INVENTORY

If a project involves a cost reduction, not only does this result in a cost saving which is included in the investment appraisal, it will also be reflected in the fact that the book value of the components produced after the cost reduction is implemented will be reduced when standard costs are next revalued.

This means that any of the components affected by the cost reduction which are being held as stock (including WIP) at the time of the next annual stock check will have a lower asset value. As a result, the value of assets in the company's accounts will be reduced. This reduction in the value of assets will happen, even if there is no reduction in stock levels. If the cost reduction takes place at the same time as a stock reduction, the change will be additional to any changes in asset values caused by changes in stock levels.

A reduction in book value caused by revaluation will appear in the accounts as a reduction in assets, and also as a corresponding reduction in profits. Although this reduction in book value does not itself represent a change in cash flow, the reduction in reported profits represents a reduction in tax liability which does provide a cash flow gain.

Take as an example a component which used to have a book value of £100 and which has been reduced to £75, as follows:

	Old costs	New costs
	£	£
Material	40.00	30.00
Labour and variable cost	20.00	15.00
Manufacturing overhead	40.00	30.00
Book value	100.00	75.00

The effect will be:

	£
Reduction in asset value	25.00
Corresponding reduction in reported profit	25.00
Saving in tax liability (resulting from reduced reported profit) (25.00 × 35%)	8.75

The stock revaluation happens as the result of a change in the standard cost of components, not from a reduction in stock levels. Thus, for a project which involves a reduction in both the value and the quantity of stock there are four elements to be considered:

1. Once-off cash flow saving from curtailing the supply process in order to reduce the quantity of stock.
2. Once-off reduction in tax liability resulting from having a lower quantity of stock at annual stock check.
3. Ongoing cashflow savings resulting from the reduction in cost of manufacture or purchase.
4. Reduction in tax liability as a result of stock having a lower book value at annual stock check.

However, if a project involves both a major cost reduction and a major reduction in stock levels, care must be taken in deciding how the reduction in stock levels is going to be valued.

It is necessary to decide whether the cash flow element (e.g. material, labour and expenses) in the saving resulting from reduced stock quantities is to be valued on the basis of the old method of manufacture, or the new method. Two different situations may exist (as illustrated in Fig. 5.5).

1. Little risk is perceived in the introduction of the new process, so that stocks are allowed to run down before the new process is fully commissioned. In this case, it is the old supply process which is curtailed and savings would be valued using the old costs.

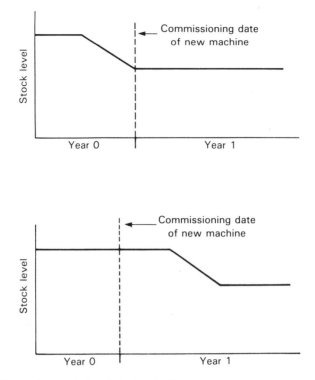

Fig. 5.5 Alternative methods of stock reduction.

2. Where there is a risk or uncertainty regarding the new process, it may be decided to have it fully commissioned before starting to run down stock levels, full production would be achieved before being reduced to consume stocks. In this case, the savings would be valued using the new costs.

Because the saving comes from curtailing the supply process for both material purchase and manufacture, rather than from the sale of the excess stock, the valuation of the cash flow element of inventory reduction must be based on whether it will be the old or the new process which will be curtailed.

Although this cash flow saving from inventory reduction will occur at the time when the supply process is curtailed, the reduction in asset value in the company accounts may not be reported until the stock level check at the end of the financial year. By this time, the inventory may already have been revalued on the basis of the new cost of manufacture.

Two examples will illustrate this: one is where the inventory reduction is costed on the basis on the old method of manufacture, with a subsequent revaluation to calculate the reduction in stock value; and the other is where the inventory reduction is costed on the basis of the new method of manufacture:

Component costs are: Old book value £100.00 New book value £75.00
Stock levels are   Before change, 200 off   After change, 150 off

Based on the reductions being made while the old method of manufacture is still used, the savings are as follows:

	£
Cash flow savings (£60.00 × 50 off)	= 3 000
Reduced tax liability (£40.00 × 50 off @ 35%)	= 700
Initial saving from stock reduction	3 700

150 components are revalued (from £100.00 to £75.00)

Reduced tax liability as result of revaluation (£25.00 × 150 off @ 35%)	= 1 312.50
Total cash saving	5 012.50

Assuming the revaluation is done after the reduction in stock levels has been recorded, and the reductions are made after the new method of manufacture has been introduced, the savings are as follows:

	£
Cash flow savings (£45.00 × 50 off)	= 2 250.00
Reduced tax liability (£55.00 x 50 off @ 35%)	= 962.50
Initial saving from stock reduction	3 212.50

150 components are revalued (from £100.00 to £75.00)

Reduced tax liability as result of revaluation (£25.00 × 150 off @ 35%)	= 1 312.50
Total cash saving	4 525.00

The reduction in stock levels (e.g. 50 off) is only recorded in the accounts at the end of year stock check, if the stock has not yet been revalued at that time, the reduction in assets recorded will be 50 off at £100 each. As this stock would have been produced using the new method, only £45 would have been already recorded as a change from stock to cash, the remaining £55 would now be reported as a reduction in assets.

In the above example, it was assumed that the revaluation is done after the reduction in stock levels was recorded. However, if the revaluation is carried out before the stock check, the total cash saving will not change. The values will be:

Cash flow savings (£45.00 × 50 off)	= 2250
Revaluation of 200 components (£25.00 × 200 @ 35%)	= 1750
Reduction in book value of 50 components	
(£30.00 × 50 @ 35%)	= 525
Total cash saving	= 4525

The importance of inventory revaluation will be dependant on the magnitude both of the stock reduction and the cost reduction. The way that any evaluation is done will depend on the nature of the project, the timing of the changes and the way that the company records any changes in inventory levels and book values.

In any project where a reduction in inventory levels or a change in the value of inventory is going to be a major factor, it is essential to investigate in detail how the changes will be costed, and what effect any changes in the value of assets will have on the company's balance sheet.

THE EFFECT OF INVENTORY REDUCTION

Any reduction in inventory values in a company's accounts will not only produce a cash flow saving, but also a change in asset values. This change in asset values will be reported as a reduction in profits. This results in a paradox that while inventory reduction is portrayed always as an ideal objective, achieving the reduction may appear to have had exactly the opposite result to the one originally intended. Because of this, any project involving a planned change in inventory values must take into consideration the effect on the company's management of having to report to shareholders an apparent failure to meet profit forecasts.

Although high inventory levels are always portrayed as being a symptom of inefficiency, there is no such thing as a correct level of inventory. The optimum required level is something which is dependant on many different factors such as market requirements, manufacturing facilities and product design. Thus two companies of the same size, competing in the same market, may have very different optimum stock levels because their products are of different designs.

High inventory levels are themselves not a problem, they are only a symptom of other problems. There is a danger that if the real reason why the inventory is there is not understood, then any action taken to reduce stock may not be solving the correct problem. It is important to start by identifying the basic reasons why inventory is there, and changing the need for inventory. Only then should stock levels be reduced.

Carrying stock is an integral part of a company's manufacturing operation, and it is there to help iron out problems both in the supply process and the sales function. Supply problems may be due to the length and uncertainty of the process, or the inflexibility and unreliability of the ordering and scheduling procedures, while sales problems can be caused by fluctuations in sales volume and product mix.

The combination of the problems being that the production process can be too long and inflexible to satisfy the market requirements for variations in product specification. To help overcome these problems companies hold stock at various stages in the manufacturing process. The different types of inventory can be there for different reasons.

The need to have high levels of WIP may be a result of having long lead times and uncertainty of supply. These problems can be caused by the difficulty of scheduling work in a batch manufacturing environment, where there is the possibility of scrap and rework if the manufacturing process is not completely reliable.

Stocks of finished components and finished product may be held to overcome supply problems and also to help smooth out the short-term fluctuations in sales volume and product mix. Figure 5.6 is based on actual figures

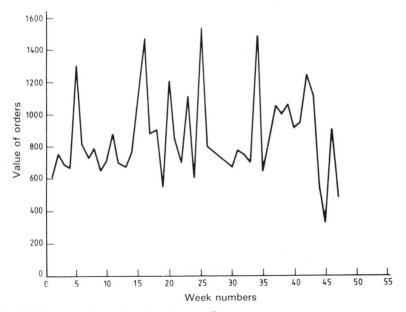

Fig. 5.6 The way that receipt of orders can fluctuate.

from a company and shows the way that receipt of customers' orders can fluctuate. The company concerned had a four-week manufacturing lead time.

When the receipt of orders can fluctuate in this way, it is unrealistic to expect Marketing to be able to forecast short-term order input with the accuracy which would be required by manufacturing in order to plan a uniform throughput. Therefore, to obtain orders companies may either have to carry finished or semi-finished stocks or change their manufacturing process to provide the flexibility which would be needed to quickly change output to respond to fluctuations in customers' needs.

Changing the manufacturing process in order to reduce the need for stock will not in itself bring about a change in stock levels. To make a permanent change in stock levels requires a change in the way that the stock is ordered in the material control system.

While large, sophisticated MRP packages may contain a number of different sets of ordering rules, which can be used simultaneously for different components, some MRP packages may have little flexibility for rule changing. If the change in the manufacturing process that is needed to reduce stock levels is such that the ordering rules within an MRP package need to be altered, it may not be worth while making the change, unless there is going to be a major saving in inventory value.

For example, inventory reduction is often portrayed as an objective for investing in CNC machining centres because the number of operations can be reduced. However, the introduction of a single machine may only affect a small percentage of components. Without a change in ordering rules, all that will happen is that lead times will be reduced and finished components put into stores at an earlier date. The reduction in the level of WIP is the same as the increase in the level of finished components and, in effect, increases the value of inventory.

In evaluating the benefits of inventory reduction it is important to identify the way in which the supply process will be curtailed in order to bring about the stock reduction. In reducing bought-in components, and the raw material content of WIP, it is likely that material purchases will be reduced or stopped for a short time in order to use up existing stocks.

In order to reduce WIP the manufacturing process will only be restricted for a short period of time. As a result, there is a danger that the labour element will not be curtailed because, unlike material purchases, labour cannot be easily turned off and then back on again.

It is unlikely that operators' wages will be stopped, so that unless specific plans are made which identify how the labour-saving is to be implemented, it is likely that Parkinson's Law will operate, with work expanding to use the labour available. Consequently, there may be no cash flow saving at all.

If the planned labour saving does not occur, the forecast cash flow element will be reduced. Also both the reduction in asset values and corresponding profit reduction will be increased.

A commonly suggested method of reducing inventory is to reduce ordering quantities and thereby have a larger number of smaller batches. This will be economical only if changes can be made which will reduce the cost penalties of having smaller batch sizes such as batch set-up times. However, consideration must also be given to other problems which can arise from an increase in the number of batches.

Even if there are no direct cost penalties, such as premiums for ordering smaller quantities, or loss of quantity discounts, there may be less obvious penalties. An increased number of batches may require increased work moving facilities or lead to increased production-control problems as a result of the larger number of orders which need to be monitored and progressed.

The nature and potential magnitude of savings from inventory reduction means that there is a danger that the one-off savings in inventory value may not offset the additional long-term costs. While it may be possible to change the manufacturing process or ordering system in order to reduce the size of batches, and thereby reduce the level of inventory, the savings may be less than the cost of increasing the number of batches which will have to be produced. The need is to compare the short-term savings from inventory reduction with the potential long-term cost increases, thereby emphasizing the need to evaluate long-term changes in cash flows, rather than looking only at short-term payback.

While it is important that companies keep trying to reduce all their costs, including inventory, projects whose principal objective is inventory reduction may not be very profitable in comparison with other projects which are aimed at solving problems in manufacturing or sales.

Chapter ▰▰▰▰▰▰▰▰▰▰▰▰▰▰▰▰▰▰▰▰▰▰▰

6 Costing systems

Non-financial managers often believe that accounting is an exact science, a view that is encouraged by the need for a company to have a highly accurate book-keeping system which records all cash receipts and payments throughout the company, however small the sum. The need to record all cash transactions is not just because management is responsible to the company's owners, and has to show how the owners' money has been spent, but also because the company is required to produce annual accounts which are subject to an independent audit. Because these accounts are used for such purposes as determining tax liability, the way the accounts are kept is governed by rigid accountancy rules and legislation. The nature of these systems is such that not only do they have to be extremely accurate, but they are also extremely inflexible.

In addition to its book-keeping systems, many companies also have an internal cost accounting system for product costing which, by contrast, is both inexact and highly flexible. The rules for such systems can be varied to suit a company's own needs.

The difference between these systems is such that there are two separate accountancy disciplines, each with its own professional institution. **Financial accounting** is concerned with the book-keeping and auditing role, while **management accounting** is concerned with the company's internal costing system. In some companies the gulf between the accounting disciplines is similar to that which exists between design and production engineers.

The original purpose of these internal costing systems was to try to ensure that all the costs of manufacture were absorbed into the product selling price, thus *absorption costing*. When a company is producing only one standard product, it may not need an absorption cost system because all the costs of running the company and producing the product can be allocated to the one selling price.

With one product, the only complexity that arises is the division between those costs which are fixed, irrespective of sales volume, and those which will vary with changes of volume. However, the majority of companies make more than one product or, even if only making one product, produce variations of it which require different manufacturing resources.

Product costing and the establishment of selling prices is not an exact science because the price which customers are asked to pay will depend as much on external market forces as on internal manufacturing costs. Prices can only be established after comparison with competitors' products and prices.

Selling prices are often determined by an assessment of 'what the market will bear'. However, in establishing selling prices, it is essential to make sure that products are never, unknowingly, sold at a loss. The emphasis in costing systems is often just ensuring that the total of all costs is recovered in total sales receipts.

Costing information is widely available within a company and is used to monitor the actual cost of manufacture against the forecast. As a result, non-financial managers often use the information for purposes for which it was never originally intended, but without realizing the implications of what they are doing. In fact many of the reported problems with costing systems are the result of just that.

STANDARD COSTS

At the time when the early cost systems were being developed, engineering companies were usually labour intensive, with direct labour often being the largest single cost factor. As a result, cost systems were developed which used direct labour as the basis for measurement. All other costs were then apportioned to this to establish a labour/hour rate, such that:

$$\text{Labour/hour rate} = \frac{\text{Total of all manufacturing costs including depreciation}}{\text{Total hours worked by all direct workers}}$$

This labour rate is then used to produce a standard cost for each component and product, such that:

Standard cost = Material Cost + sum of (operation times × labour rate)

It is much easier to calculate the standard costs if a single labour/hour rate is used for all direct workers, but although some companies still use a single rate for all direct workers, irrespective of their jobs, most companies will now have several different rates. In order to establish these rates the factory is divided into a number of different cost centres, for example, assembly workers would be costed at a different rate to machine operators, and different types of machine would also be in different cost centres.

Having a single rate which is the same for all direct workers means that some workers, such as in assembly or operating machines with a low capital cost, will have their time costed at an excessively high rate. On the other hand, the operators of large, expensive machines will have a rate which is too low. Using such a single cost rate will mean that complex products, which require the use of expensive machinery, will have their cost of manufacture understated, while simple products will have their cost overstated.

Because customers are likely to buy products where the selling price has been underquoted compared with the true cost, and will rarely buy products whose price is overquoted, the use of a single cost rate will tend to increase the proportion of low profit or unprofitable orders. Here, then, there are no 'swings and roundabouts'. The result is that such companies will tend to keep designing products which are more and more complex, because these are the easiest to sell while, at the same time, the company becomes less and less profitable. Although so doing is obviously wrong, the costing system will continue to suggest that it is the correct thing to do and the company may be unaware of the problem.

Another problem which results from the use of a single labour/hour rate for all direct workers is that companies will send simple work out for subcontract. Companies will send out operations, such as on pillar drills or capstan lathes, because they can easily find other companies which will produce at less than a standard cost rate which is too high.

At the same time, the company could be taking in subcontract work for their large and expensive machines such as multi-axis machining centres. Other companies would be quite happy to pay the standard cost rate to have work done on machines where the cost was too low.

A similar type of problem arises in companies that use the same cost rate for several different types of machine. Production engineers will try to plan components for the machine which will give the lowest standard cost for the component. This leads to all components being planned for the most expensive, high-technology machines because these will provide the shortest operation times, but without the standard cost reflecting the high capital costs involved.

This will result in the expensive machines being overloaded and will, in turn, lead to pressure for investment in more machines. If the procedures for investment appraisal are inadequate and do not identify what is happening, the company may end up making unnecessary, and expensive, investments.

In order to avoid the problem the costing system should be modified such that the rate/hour reflects the capital cost, operating costs and supporting services such as programming. The way that components are planned for machines can be distorted by inaccuracies in the cost system, therefore when there is pressure to invest in new machines in order to create additional capacity, it is important that the total load be checked to see if there are alternative types of machine that could be used if their cost rate were altered.

As computer technology has developed, companies have invested in increasingly sophisticated manufacturing technology. At the same time, they have also been reducing the relative size of their direct labourforce. As a result, many companies have changed from being labour intensive to being capital intensive, but because the change has normally been a gradual one, they have not changed the basis of their cost system. Making such a change can involve a major investment in new computer systems for cost accounting, plus a considerable amount of cost and disruption in changing all the data on the old system. Because of this, companies have been reluctant to update their cost system.

This reluctance has been reinforced by a widespread belief that there is something wrong with conventional accountancy principles when applied to AMT and that a new type of costing system had to be developed. While companies may have recognized that there are failings in their existing procedures, they have not wanted to commit themselves to an expensive change which may only be for a short term.

COST ALLOCATION

The advent of FMS has highlighted the problems of costing procedures. The FMS have the ability to operate in such a way that the activity of the system is independent from the activity of the human operators. As a result, manning levels can vary between shifts, and the system can be left running unmanned between shifts and during meal-breaks.

Companies which have a costing system which is based on labour/hour rates find that, according to the rules of their cost system, the FMS may be producing components at different costs on each shift. During the periods of unmanned running, the FMS will be reported as producing components without any cost at all. This has often been quoted as proof that there is something wrong with cost systems.

In fact the only problem is that the company concerned has not updated its procedures to reflect the change from being labour intensive to being capital intensive and started to use a more appropriate basis for cost such as machine/hour rates. Again, the problems are not in the basic accountancy principles, but in the use of outdated procedures.

As well as labour/hour or machine/hour rates, there are a number of other bases for cost allocation, and care is needed in their selection and application. One method of allocating costs is on the basis of material costs, where material represents a major percentage of total cost. However, the following example shows the difficulty of doing this correctly.

Company A makes a product for the construction industry which is made from steel strip. The product is made in two lengths, 10 ft and 20 ft, the manufacturing process is to punch holes in the strip and then cut off to length. The equipment used and time taken are the same for both lengths. The cost of material is £8/ft.

It is estimated that the market for the next year is 1000 of each size. The total cost of punching and cutting off 2000 items a year is estimated at £60 000. If costs are allocated on the basis of material cost, the selling price would be based on the following:

Company A	10 ft length £	20 ft length £
Material cost	80.00	160.00
Process cost	20.00	40.00
Total cost	100.00	200.00

As the processing cost should be the same for both, the 10 ft length would be underpriced while the 20 ft length overpriced.

Company B, with identical plant, also expected to sell 2000 items, but had allocated their processing cost equally to both lengths. They would have calculated the total cost to be:

Company B	10 ft length £	20 ft length £
Material cost	80.00	160.00
Process cost	30.00	30.00
Total cost	110.00	190.00

If price was the only factor affecting sales, the result would be that Company A might sell 2000 of the 10 ft length, but none of the 20 ft, while company B would only sell 20 ft lengths. In both cases, the companies would recover the total material costs, but the recovery of processing costs would be:

Company A 2000 units × £20.00 = £40 000
Company B 2000 units × £30.00 = £60 000

Processing costs are not in proportion to material costs and, as a result of the incorrect allocation of processing costs, Company A has made a loss of £20 000, even though it has sold 2000 units as forecast, and the costing system appears to show that all costs have been absorbed.

Although a company may use DCF techniques for evaluating investment in capital plant, it is probable that decisions about minor non-capital expenditure will be based on the use of standard cost data, especially where the decisions are made at plant level.

To illustrate what happens in such cases, an example is taken of a company where the cost of labour is £5/h and where, for CNC machine tools, the cost system adds 400% overhead (including depreciation), giving a rate of £25/h.

The company can invest in quick change tooling to reduce set-up times on two machines. For both machines the cost of the tooling would be £10 000, but on machine A the saving would be 4 h/week, while on machine B it would be 8 h/week. The savings would be calculated as:

Machine A = 4 h/week × 50 weeks × £25/h = £5 000/year
Machine B = 8 h/week × 50 weeks × £25/h = £10 000/year

Based on these figures, tooling for machine B would seem to be the best investment. However, closer examination may show that the existing set-ups on machine B do not produce any scrap or rework and the machine is not operating to its full potential capacity. Reducing the set-up time would not affect the component-ordering process, therefore the only saving will be the labour costs and the cash flow savings will be:

Machine B = 8 h/week × 50 weeks × £5.00/h = £2 000/year

Machine A on the other hand is overloaded and surplus work is having to be subcontracted at £30/h. Reducing the set-up times by 200 h/year will reduce subcontract by 200 h. The saving, however, is not in labour or machine costs because the hours worked by the machine and operator will be unchanged, it is only the work content which changes. The saving is the reduction in subcontract costs and will be:

Machine A = 4 h/week × 50 weeks × £30.00/h = £6 000/year

The use of standard cost data would have resulted in the wrong decision being made. Not only would the company have made an investment which was not financially viable, but by spending the money on tooling for machine B, they may have refrained from spending it on machine A.

The use of standard cost data based on labour/hour rates suggests that cost reduction projects aimed at labour-saving can be very attractive. For example, if labour costs £5/h and 400% is then added for overhead allocation, giving a rate of £25/h, saving a worker would appear to save £25/h. In reality, the saving may only be £5/h, the remainder representing allocation of overheads and depreciation which are unaffected by the project.

The use of standard cost information in cost reduction projects may overstate the savings by several hundred per cent. The availability of cost data has led managers to invest in plant and equipment where they have justified cash flow expenditure on the basis of standard cost savings. Although such projects may be reported in the cost system as a cost reduction, thus reinforcing the manager's belief that they were doing the right thing, in cash flow terms the investment may not be viable.

Because the use of standard data has over-emphasized the advantages of labour savings, companies may in the past have concentrated too much effort on reducing the size of their direct labourforce. While it is important to reduce all costs as much as possible, cost reduction involves managerial and financial resources, and by concentrating on labour-savings, other more profitable areas of cost reduction may have been ignored.

The use of standard cost data for decision-making in cost reduction projects will invariably result in incorrect decisions being made. In some cases, the value of projects will be overstated because the apparent saving will include a large element of the allocation of overheads and depreciation which will not be changed by the project.

In other cases, however, the use of standard cost data to compare bought-out against made-in costs will consistently bias the decision against in-house manufacture. This will be the case with decisions about whether to make components in-house or to buy them outside, and with decisions about sub-contracting work.

For example, a component whose standard cost for manufacture in the company is calculated at £100 each may be available bought-in at £90, the obvious decision would be to buy the component complete. However, a detailed breakdown of the costs may be:

	Made-in costs £	Bought-in costs £
Material cost	20.00	20.00
Variable costs	20.00	
Overhead allocation	60.00	60.00
Bought-in cost		70.00
Total cost	100.00	150.00

Because the in-house overheads will still exist whichever way the component is produced, they must not be attributed to only one of the alternatives.

Although a company may use DCF for its formal investment appraisal procedures, it is quite easy for production engineers to be making *negative* investment decisions using standard cost data without being aware of it. For example, they may decide not to investigate the replacement of machine tools, or investment in additional plant capacity, because according to cost data it is cheaper to use outside suppliers.

It is possible that the decision made by many companies to concentrate on making those complex components which require considerable technical expertise in-house, and subcontracting all their simpler components, may have been made as a result of the incorrect use of standard cost data. Because standard cost data can be misleading when used for decisions such as 'make or buy', the concept of variable costing was developed, the aim being to identify those cost factors which will vary as the result of any planned changes in the company's operation. Unfortunately, many of the managers who are responsible for the 'make or buy' decisions in companies are probably unaware of the difference between standard and variable cost, while the accountants who do understand the difference may not be involved in making the decisions.

Components will normally be planned for production on the machines which result in the lowest standard cost. As a result, if work has to be re-routed to alternative machines because of production capacity overload, a higher component cost is produced. This will appear to have increased the cost of manufacture by creating an operating variance, and this may be reported as a reduction in departmental performance. Because of this, Production Managers may be reluctant to transfer work and instead allow the workload to build up on the overloaded machines.

Although re-routing work, such as from CNC to manual machines, may result in an increase in costs, the real increase will be much lower than that shown by the cost system. It will normally be only the cost of additional labour and operating expenses such as electricity and tooling. Depreciation and overhead allocation, which represent the major proportion of standard costs, will be unaffected.

One of the reasons why standard costs can never be accurate is that they are compiled on the basis of a sales forecast which predicts a single value for the sales volume of each product. Overheads are then allocated on the basis of the forecast load for all the machine tools and plant required to produce the forecast sales.

With standard costing, a single set of values is usually calculated once a year, and these values remain unchanged unless there are major variations in sales compared with the forecast. However, actual sales volume will inevitably be different to the forecast and, as a result, machine loads will be different from those calculated. This means that the allocated overhead costs will be either over- or under-absorbed. One of the uses of variable costing is to evaluate the effect of changes in sales volume and selling price away from those forecast.

However, the nature of variable costs is such that they are never constant. The dividing-line between a cost factor being fixed and its being variable will alter, depending on the nature of the changes being considered. For example, minor changes in inventory levels might have no effect on the cost of the storekeeping function, and this cost could be classed as a fixed overhead. However, increasingly large changes in inventory levels would start to affect such factors as the number of storekeepers and may lead to changes in the size and number of stores required.

CAPACITY CONSTRAINTS

Although standard costs are used for product costing, the relationship is not always direct because selling prices are influenced by market forces. If a company is in a situation where because of capacity constraints it could sell more than it could manufacture, it would probably increase the selling price in order both to increase profit and curtail demand.

Doing this may disguise from production engineers the benefits of future investment to increase capacity because the potential for increasing sales at these higher prices would seem to be unlimited. Efforts would instead be concentrated on trying to determine the optimum mix of products to provide the maximum profit.

When sales are being restricted by a capacity constraint, the company may not want to invest in plant to increase capacity because it is thought that the constraint is of a temporary nature. This would be the case if new products were being designed which would reduce the load on the bottleneck, or if future sales were expected to decline due to market changes. Where the constraint is a permanent one, it is important to identify its true nature and the effect which eliminating it will have.

In many companies Production Managers spend their lives trying to remove production bottlenecks and are often faced with the phenomenon of 'galloping bottlenecks'. As soon as they identify one bottleneck and eliminate it, they find that the bottleneck has moved elsewhere. Care must be taken when investing in plant to eliminate a permanent bottleneck because its removal may only result in the appearance of another bottleneck which limits the hoped for increase in capacity.

Evaluating possible investments to increase capacity should include the option of reducing selling price in order to increase sales volume, thereby increasing the overall contribution to overhead recovery. Variable cost data should be used to assess the cash flow value of the increased overhead recovery which would result in changes in sales volume and price.

When there is a production constraint which is restricting sales volume, variable cost rather than standard cost should be used to determine the optimum and most profitable product mix. However, the actual product mix will not just be based on profitability; it will also be determined by such factors as the need to retain customer goodwill.

While it is important that products are never sold unknowingly for less than their cost, as can happen if the costing and estimating systems are inaccurate, a company may still accept a selling price lower than standard cost as part of a policy of trying to increase sales volume. Again, variable rather than standard cost should be used to calculate the overall effect on overhead recovery and profitability from increased sales volume.

When a new machine is purchased, there can be pressure to get it fully utilized as soon as possible. This pressure can be increased if the costing system appears to show that the new machine provides a cost reduction compared with the old methods. The result may be that some components are planned for the machine because of the pressure to increase utilization quickly.

However, when the new machine does become fully utilized, there can be pressure to invest in additional machine capacity because of a work overload. When this happens, it is important to investigate the total load to ensure that it does not contain components which the cost system appears to show provide a saving but, in practice, do not represent any significant cash flow saving.

Not only should the cost system be able to provide the data to make decisions about which products should be produced if total output is restricted, it should also be able to supply data for making decisions about the value of providing short-term capacity increases, such as transferring work between load centres, subcontracting or hire of plant.

Although the cost of increasing capacity by alternative methods may be greater than the standard cost, the need is to determine whether the contribution to overhead recovery from the increased output will compensate for the increase in manufacturing costs.

COSTING INVESTMENT DECISIONS

Managers are often persuaded by the advocates of AMT that investment is essential for the future of their company, but because they are unable to quantify the benefits, the company goes ahead and makes the investment without a financial evaluation. Having done so, they find that once the machinery or computer system has been installed and is fully operational, their costing system shows that the investment has increased the cost of manufacture.

The conclusion here is that either investing in AMT was the wrong thing to have done or there is something wrong with the costing system. The size of the problem is such that surveys suggest that about 50% of AMT investment has been unprofitable, although it is impossible to obtain any accurate figures because of the nature of the problem.

In some cases, the company will have invested in the wrong technology or have the wrong specification, or may have been unable to get the technology to operate correctly. Although some of the perceived failure of AMT may be due to such reasons, the problems of this nature are such that investigation would normally identify what had gone wrong and, in many cases, the faults could be corrected.

There is, however, a more fundamental problem which has only become obvious with the benefit of hindsight, and which helps to explain the majority of cases where AMT appears to have been a financial failure. The problem originates from the difficulties that companies have had in the past when trying to justify investment in complex, new technology projects.

The universal belief that many of the benefits of AMT were intangible has meant that companies which could not justify the investment on the basis of direct savings either had to refrain from investing or had to make the investment decision as an act of faith. If savings had been quantified which were going to be greater than costs, there would have been no need to make the investment decision without an evaluation.

For any investment, whether it is evaluated or not, all the capital, installation and running costs will be known and quantified because the bills have to be paid. Any unplanned or unforeseen costs would have to be quantified when they occurred and costs which were originally underestimated would be correctly recorded. This means that all the costs associated with a project will be known and included in the company's costing system.

Any direct savings which may have been quantified would be included in the costing system but these would normally have been based on using the largest value which would be accepted, while estimates of costs would have been based on the lowest value. In consequence, even the quantified estimates would often not be achieved.

Costing systems are based on the use of forecasts, and because intangible benefits could not be quantified in the initial investment appraisal, they could not be included in the costing system. Because the nature of intangible benefits was not understood, there was a belief that if the investment was made, the benefits would quickly appear and somehow would render the project viable.

One of the main reasons why the concepts of intangible benefits developed is that, while managers can normally quantify benefits which occur in their own department, the intangible benefits will normally appear in a different part of the company to that in which the investment is made. For example, investment in FMS can improve delivery performances, resulting in an increase in sales, or the use of CAD to produce quotations can increase sales and reduce the number of unprofitable orders.

As AMT has become more complex, the time to install, commission and get it fully operational has tended to increase. For example, while it would have taken only a few weeks to get a conventional machine tool installed and fully operational, it may take one or two years to do the same with FMS. Even when the equipment is fully operational, it may still take a long time for the project to reach its level of full savings.

With CAD, for example, the productivity of draughtsmen, compared with the use of a drawing board, is much greater when modifying existing drawings than when creating new detail drawings, but it is not until after the drawings have been put onto the CAD database that they will require modifiction. With MRP systems, many of the benefits will not occur until the full system is operational.

The result is that intangible benefits cannot be included in the costing system because they have not been forecast in quantified terms. When they do eventually occur, they will not be attributed to the project and will appear as an unplanned operating variance. Because of this, any investment which is made as an act of faith, where savings greater than costs were not quantified, will invariably appear to have increased the cost of manufacture according to the costing system. The situation can then be made worse if this apparent increase in cost is reflected in an increase in selling price which may, in turn, result in a loss of sales, thereby turning the perceived failure of AMT into a self-fulfilling prophesy.

Companies trying to establish whether a project is successful can only compare actual performance against the original expectations. While it will be quite easy to see if a project is achieving the technical objectives which would have been defined in the project specification, and is performing to this specification, it will not be possible to decide if it is financially successful if there were no financial estimates against which to make a comparison.

No matter how profitable a project may actually be, if it has not been correctly evaluated and the benefits forecast and quantified, the costing system will still show that it is a financial liability. This means that because of the large number of AMT investments that have been made without an evaluation, much of the reported financial failure of AMT may be wrong and is only a result of the way that AMT has been recorded in costing systems.

When an investment appraisal is carried out using a single set of estimated values, which will normally be the most optimistic, these will be the figures which will be included in the costing system. However, when the evaluation is done correctly, and a range of estimates produced (e.g. optimistic, pessimistic and most likely), the question arises as to which set of values to include in the costing system because only one set can be used. Most companies would tend to use the 'most likely' set of values, but the conservative approach would be to use the set of values which would give a net present value of £0.

Much of the perceived failure of AMT may only be apparent and not real, but the cause of this is not that there is something wrong either with AMT or costing systems. The reason for the perceived failure is rather that managers have not realized that intangible benefits would not be attributed to a project in the costing system. Because it has now been shown that there is no such thing as an intangible benefit, and that all benefits can be forecast and quantified, the underlying cause of the problem can be eliminated.

MACHINE UTILIZATION

When a company buys a new machine tool, there can be pressure from senior management who want to see it operating full time as soon as possible. As well as such physiological pressure to achieve full utilization, there can also be financial pressure.

Depreciation is now becoming a major element in the rate/hour for a machine in the costing system, especially for expensive machines such as CNC and FMS, and this can lead to pressure to increase the planned utilization. By doubling the forecast number of hours per week which a machine will be operating, the depreciation element in the cost rate can be halved.

It has often been assumed that FMS can only be justified if it can be kept running for 24 hours a day, seven days a week. Doing this would not only reduce the depreciation rate per hour, but also help to increase the savings in labour and operating expenses by increasing the workload transferred from other machines. However, one of the main financial benefits of FMS can be its ability to improve delivery performance to customers, but to be able to do so, the output of the FMS has to be varied to suit the way in which order intake varies, both in terms of sales volume and product mix.

Figure 6.1 shows the fluctuations in workload on a group of machining centres in an engineering company, while Fig. 6.2 shows how the load on the lathes varied at the same time. The fluctuations were caused by changes in product mix rather than sales volume as the company had a full order book at the time. Although companies installing technology such as FMS should do so on the basis of using planned maintenance, there will always be unplanned breakdowns for various reasons and these will add to the problems of utilization.

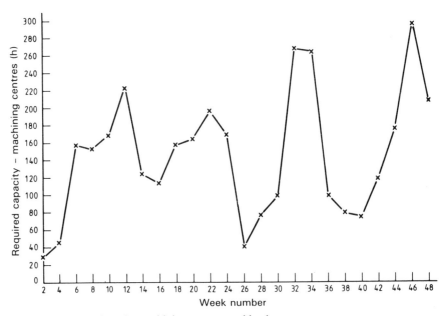

Fig. 6.1 Fluctuations in machining centre workload.

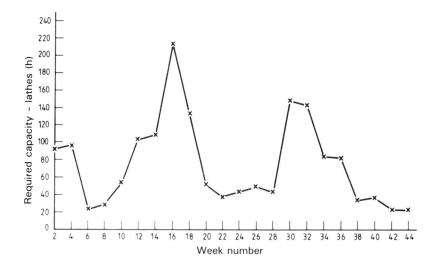

Fig. 6.2 Fluctuations in lathe workload.

Dealing with fluctuations in sales and machine availability when using conventional batch manufacture in a traditional layout factory means having long lead times, high levels of work-in-progress and inflexibility of delivery. Because these exist, they may conceal the magnitude of the short-term fluctuations in demand and, as a result, production engineers may be unaware of the size of the problem they have to deal with in trying to reduce lead times and stock levels.

The objective with FMS is to be able to respond to customers' needs without the penalties imposed by conventional manufacture. Although it may be possible to plan some standard components, which are produced for stock, to help level out the fluctuations in FMS load, the closer the load comes to full utilization, the greater will be the loss of flexibility. Planning work to provide maximum utilization is likely to be counterproductive because the flexibility needed to deal with short-term fluctuations in customers' orders, which was the main financial objective for investing in FMS, will be lost.

One of the objectives in carrying out an investment appraisal for any project is to provide the information needed to record the project in the costing system. Part of this information are the estimates for costs and savings and the forecast timing of all cash flows. In addition, in order to calculate the value for depreciation which is included in the cost rate for a machine, it is necessary to forecast the level of utilization. Machine utilization can be between 1 and 168 hours per week. For example, with special purpose plant, such as deep-hole drilling or broaching machines, which may have been bought for a specific task, the planned utilization may be extremely low, possibly only 1 h/week. Because the alternative may have been an inability to do the work at all, or having it done on conventional machines in a highly expensive manner, investment in special machines may be quite viable, even if they are going to have a very low level of utilization and correspondingly high level of depreciation.

If the level of utilization has not been forecast correctly, the depreciation rate per hour will be incorrect. For example, if depreciation is calculated on the basis of 80 h/week utilization, but the actual utilization is only 8 h, the depreciation value included in the rate per hour for the machine will be only 10% of its correct value.

If the forecast utilization is wrong, the allocation of overheads other than depreciation will be only slightly inaccurate because the machine involved will be one of many to which the overhead costs are allocated. If in the above example the other machines represent 1000 h/week, the error in estimating the utilization of one machine means that the overheads will be spread over 1080 h/week instead of 1008, thus the percentage error will not be great unless the forecast for all machines is extremely inaccurate. In the past, when the capital value of machine tools was relatively low, errors in forecasts of utilization were not too important, but as capital values increase and depreciation becomes a larger proportion of machine rates, the need for accurate forecasts of utilization also increases.

The effect of machine utilization on costing systems can be seen in companies that have tried to introduce **group technology (GT)**. In the 1960s, when much of the early work on GT was being done, few companies had NC machine tools and the capital cost of the machines being put into cells was low. As a result, the low machine utilization rates associated with GT cells was not seen as a problem affecting standard costs. With the widespread introduction of CNC, the difficulty of creating GT cells has increased considerably not only because of the need to justify the cost of buying additional machines, but also because the low utilization of expensive machines may appear to increase standard costs.

It is important that the decision to set up GT cells is evaluated, so that as with any other investment the financial benefits are identified and quantified. It is only by doing this that the potential increase in standard costs caused by reduced utilization will be offset by the savings. If this is not done, the introduction of GT cells, however viable, will appear to show an increase in costs and be reported as a financial failure. As with AMT, much of the perceived failure of GT in the past may be caused by failing to quantify the benefits and include them in the company's costing system. Another problem area associated with the allocation of depreciation occurs when a machine is bought to provide additional capacity, or to replace an old machine, in a situation where there are still going to be other machines of the old type in use.

When CNC is bought to replace manual machines, then the new machine is going to be more productive than the existing ones. The fact that the rate per hour for the new machine may be higher than the old ones should be compensated for by the shorter operation times. Provided the new value of operation time × rate per hour is less than the old value, it will be cheaper to produce on the new machine.

A problem arises if the output rate of the new machine is similar to the older existing ones, and the new machine is given a different, and higher, cost rate than the old one because of its capital value. It will then appear to be cheaper to produce work on the old machine.

If the justification is based on increasing, or replacing, existing capacity without an additional cost reduction, the new machine would need to have the same rate as the existing ones, even though this may require the rate of all machines to reflect the new higher capital value of the group of machines. In some cases, however, the new rate per hour may be lower, as would happen if the old machines has a high operating cost such as caused by excessive scrap and rework or long set-up times.

If the justification for investment included a significant cost reduction, then it would be preferable for as much work as possible to be planned for the new machine, and the cost rate should reflect this. For example, investing in CNC where the higher rate per hour would be offset by shorter operation times. The objective must be to set a cost rate which results in work being planned for the most efficient machine.

The establishment of cost rates for new machines must reflect the reasons for investment given in the financial evaluation. Provided the potential problems are understood at the time when an investment appraisal is carried out, the required data can be provided.

PRODUCT LIFE CYCLES

Manufacturing plant is bought in most companies for general use, and it is used to produce a variety of different components, possibly for several different products. The plant will normally have the flexibility to cope with any changes which result from the introduction of new product designs. In such cases, the plant would be kept until it had reached the end of its working life, and this life has no connection with the life of any products.

Some companies, however, especially those in high-volume manufacture, have traditionally installed new plant, such as transfer lines, when introducing a new product range. Such companies treat the investment in new plant as an integral part of the decision to invest in making the new product; the cost of the plant being included in the development cost of the product. The assumption being that the physical life of the plant (plant life) would be the same as the production life of a product (product life) and that the plant would be scrapped when production finished.

While product life cycles were long, it was possible to use this approach; but there is now increasing pressure on companies to introduce products with shorter and shorter life cycles. At the same time, there may be increasing needs to be able to customise products rather than just offering a standard specification. Not only does this mean that product life can be much shorter than potential plant life, but companies can no longer afford a long changeover period for installing and commissioning new plant for each product change. To lose six months between products every ten years may have been acceptable, but to lose six months every two years is not.

To meet this change in product requirements, companies are increasingly having to invest in plant, such as flexible transfer lines, which not only can be used for successive products, but for producing parts for several different products at the same time. The result is that for such companies the traditional link between product life and plant life no longer exists. This means that the investment decisions for products and plant must be dealt with separately, as is done in most batch manufacturing companies.

For many companies the transition from dedicated plant to flexible plant will have been gradual, in the same way that other companies have changed from being labour intensive to being capital intensive. As a result, their financial systems may not have been changed to reflect the way the company has changed.

In such companies it is not just the procedures for investment appraisal that have to be changed, the costing system has to be changed as well, for there is no longer a direct relationship between product cost and plant cost. Plant costs now have to be allocated between several products, each of which have a different product life, and the utilization of the plant may not be the same for each product.

PRODUCT COSTS AND INVESTMENT APPRAISAL

Although investment appraisal and costing must be treated as two separate techniques, there are some aspects which are interconnected. In conventional investment appraisal the values of costs and savings are estimated and a DCF return is calculated from these values. This return becomes the criterion for assessing profitability and comparing alternative investment projects. Once an investment decision has been made, the estimated values are included in the costing system.

A different approach to this is sometimes taken by companies that have a choice between different methods of manufacture for a product. The investment decision is made by calculating the expected cost of the product when using each of the alternative manufacturing processes; this cost includes the cost of the plant. Investment is then made in the process which appears to give the lowest product cost.

In single-product industries, such as the generation and supply of electricity, there may be only one major criterion – e.g. the unit cost of supplied electricity. When trying to select the method of generation in which to invest (e.g. coal, oil, nuclear, wind), the projects being considered are all mutually exclusive. The method used is to calculate the unit cost of electricity as produced by each alternative generating method; investment is then made in the method which will produce the lowest unit cost.

With utilities, such as electricity generation, projects can be mutually exclusive because there is only one objective – e.g. to identify the method which produces electricity at the lowest cost. Investment in generating capacity does not have to be compared with investment in any other project. Nor does the utility need to know the profitability of the investment, only that the return will be greater than their cost of capital.

However, if a manufacturing company wanted to consider investment in plant to generate its own electricity it would not only have to ensure that the investment would be profitable; but it would also have to be able to compare its profitability with that of all the other types of capital projects being considered within the company. Investing in plant to generate electricity would prevent the available financial resources from being spent on other projects which may be more profitable.

Usually companies have many more potentially profitable projects than they have capital available. Presenting projects for approval on the basis of 'we can either spend £250 000 to reduce the cost of all our electricity from £0.042/unit to £0.038/unit or we can spend £375 000 to reduce the cost of product A from £123.75 to £112.00' is not very meaningful.

In utilities, such as electricity generation, there is only one major investment decision to be made, so considerable management effort is devoted to getting a correct answer. With manufacturing companies, even if the method used overcomes the problems of the incorrect use of depreciation described in an earlier chapter, there are other fundamental problems inherent in the use of such a methodology.

Potentially the largest financial benefit, and the most important reason for investing in AMT, is the effect it can have on sales. This means that any comparison of unit product costs, with and without AMT, must include the effect which increasing the sales volume will have on the allocation of overheads. However, the allocation of overheads can be highly inexact and often quite arbitrary, especially in a company making more than one standard product.

Investing in AMT may not only affect the sales volume of products, but an increased ability to customize and update the design may also change the product life. It is not just that product life and plant life will be increasingly different, the ability of AMT to speed up the introduction of new products means that product lives will be changed by investment in AMT and this must be reflected in the investment decision.

Making investment decisions on the basis of product costs means investing in whichever product provides the lowest product cost, but the differences between the costs may be very small; for example the costs may be:

Product cost with AMT   £999
Product cost without AMT   £1000

In this case, because the cost of using AMT is the lower, investment would be made in AMT. However, a difference of only 0.2% in one of the costs could have reversed the decision. Unfortunately, inaccuracies of 10% or more are quite possible, especially if some of the plant can be used for more than one product.

The process of calculating product costs can be highly complex and laborious, and because a complete cost structure has to be calculated for each potential sales volume and product life, it is difficult to make allowance for variations in factors such as product and plant life. The result is that it becomes impractical to use **sensitivity analysis** to check on the sensitivity of the decision to variations in the original assumptions. The problem of calculating an accurate product cost for each alternative becomes even worse if investment in AMT will allow the product to be redesigned, but in many cases AMT only becomes viable if the product has been redesigned to make use of the technology.

The fact that costing is inexact is not critical when the information is used for its intended purpose of ensuring that all costs are absorbed in selling prices because allowance can be made for the inaccuracies of the information. If necessary, a more sophisticated version of the costing system can be introduced to increase the accuracy.

The danger lies in the use of costing information to make decisions for which the costing system was never intended, such as giving a 'yes'/'no' verdict on an investment where the verdict depends on the differential between two inexact values. Trying to use cost accounting information directly in an investment appraisal will almost always produce an incorrect result, leading to the wrong investment decision being taken. However, there are cases where costing information has to be used indirectly.

For example, an investment in automated assembly may enable a product to be redesigned, thereby reducing the product cost and resulting in an increase in sales. To evaluate such an investment the cost of the redesigned product has to be estimated, so that the Marketing Department can be asked to predict what effect this will have on sales volume.

In such cases, the fact that the estimated product cost will be inexact is not critical because Marketing do not need an exact value. Even if they had the exact cost, it would be unrealistic to expect them to provide an exact forecast of sales volume. Investment decisions should be based on a range of values (e.g. optimistic, pessimistic and most likely), so that the assumptions made about the effect on sales volume of reducing product cost can be related to the range of potential DCF returns.

Chapter

7 Risk and uncertainty

Any investment must be based on assumptions about what is going to happen in the future and therefore subject to uncertainty. Some of the assumptions made may be obvious but others may be implicit in the decision to invest, for example, that the company is assumed to have a long-term viable future and will remain in existence for at least as long as the expected project life.

Although such assumptions may not always be apparent to engineers evaluating specific projects, they will be reflected in factors such as the cost of capital. Thus new small companies in high-risk industries will have to pay more to borrow money from shareholders, banks, etc. than do long-established, large companies with a proven track record. In addition to the assumptions made about the company, there are others which are relevant to a specific project. The uncertainty in these is reflected in the technical and commercial risks that the project will not achieve the objectives planned in the evaluation.

The element of risk inherent in a project is not just the probability that various events will occur, but it is also concerned with the magnitude of the rewards and penalties which can result from those events happening. This means that the allowances which are made for uncertainty must not concentrate solely on the probability of various events occurring; they must also relate the probability of occurrence to the changes in the DCF return which will be caused by the occurrence.

The reason why any potential risks associated with a project must be identified is not just to make allowance in the final evaluation. By identifying areas of uncertainty, and the financial consequences of the planned objectives not being achieved, it may be possible to reduce the element of uncertainty by modification to the technical specification, or to the plans for implementation.

TECHNICAL RISK

This is the risk that the machine or system will not be able to perform to the required technical specification. Here the need is not only to be able to perform to specification when brand new, but over the whole of the planned working life of the project. For example, a CNC machine must be able to produce components within the estimated cycle times and to the required quality standards not just during its acceptance trials, but right up to the end of its life, which may be in eight or ten years time. Production engineers try to eliminate risk by detailed specification, by observing similar machines or systems in use in other companies which have a similar type of production and, if applicable, having their components produced on the machines being considered for purchase.

With computer systems, such as CAD or MRP, it is important to examine any proposed system in use in a company having not only compatible types of product being produced in similar quantities, but where the company organization and control systems are similar. Any such system which is examined should have been in use for some time so that the practical operating problems will have been discovered.

When a project which is being considered is going to use technology which has not yet been developed or is unproven, the assessment needs not only to include any possibility that the technology may turn out to be more impractical, or that development may take far longer and be much more expensive than planned. It needs also to take into consideration the financial consequences to the company if the project is not practically viable. In such cases, the allowance for risk is not just a financial allowance, but may include plans for a fall-back project if the required technology cannot be developed.

COMMERCIAL RISK

The specification of a project, such as planned capacity and equipment utilization, will be based on assumptions about factors such as the future level of product sales. The commercial risk is that while the project may perform correctly to specification, the projected level of sales will not be achieved. Therefore the value of the savings will not reach the levels planned in the evaluation. It is important to be aware of any allowances which are made for risk, such as overspecifying the equipment or reducing the planned working life, because this can result in 'double counting' if there is also an allowance for risk built into the required discount rate.

ALLOWING FOR RISK

When using established technology, it is possible to minimize the element of technical risk in a project by using techniques such as detailed attention to the specification, selection of suppliers of proven ability, inclusion of penalty clauses in the contract, etc. However, there is still the possibility that the project may achieve all its technical objectives, but not its financial ones.

Unfortunately, the commercial assumptions made in a project do not lend themselves to treatment in the same way as the technical specification. Much of the uncertainty involved is due to factors, such as the national economic climate or actions by competitors, which are not directly within the company's control.

A number of mathematical techniques have been developed to deal with risk in investment appraisal such as *probability analysis, Monte Carlo simulation, decision trees* and a *capital asset pricing model.* Unfortunately, most of these are complex to use and it is not easy for managers to decide from the results of using some of the techniques whether or not a project will be viable.

An additional problem is that the use of probability techniques can encourage a false belief that it is possible to calculate accurately the future outcome of a project. However, investment appraisal is not an exact science, it is only an aid to decision-making, with the results being only as good as the assumptions and estimates which are used. By their very nature, any forecast of future events must be subject to uncertainty and inaccuracy.

One of the techniques used by companies in trying to allow for risk is to use a single discount rate, which is set sufficiently high to compensate for any element of risk. Unfortunately, doing this is dangerous because it can bias the selection of investments towards the high-risk projects.

For example, if the cost of capital to a company is 15%, it may use a rate of 20% as the minimum discount rate at which projects are accepted in order to allow for risk. Such a company may be faced with a choice between two projects, one being a very low-risk project which could provide a 19% return and the other a high-risk project which might possibly provide a 20% return, with a much higher probability that the forecast savings would not be obtained. Setting the discount rate at 20% would reject the first project in favour of the second.

The use of a high discount rate in such a way has done nothing to eliminate the selection of the high-risk project, and in no way differentiates between the perceived level of risk in projects. It does nothing to penalize projects which have the potential to provide a high rate of return, but equally can have a high probability of failure. In fact, by reducing the possibility of selecting low risk–low return projects the probabilty is increased that more high-risk projects will be selected.

An alternative approach is to use a risk classification system where the company specifies the cost of risk-free capital and then, as shown in Fig.

7.1, defines a table of risk categories, each with its appropriate minimum hurdle rate. While this overcomes the problem associated with using a single discount rate, the difficulty in practice is deciding the appropriate category for any particular project.

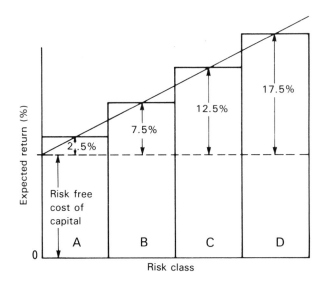

Fig. 7.1 Risk classification

The most meaningful practical technique is **sensitivity analysis**. Here a range of possible outcomes of a project are quantified and an evaluation is carried out for each one. It is then possible to submit the project for approval, giving details of the assumptions made and the effect which each of these will have on the DCF return. The advantage is that the project can be presented in terms which are understandable to the managers who have to approve the investment decision.

Before the development of computerized appraisal techniques, the work involved in evaluating a single set of estimates for a complex project was very time-consuming and prone to error. The difficulty of evaluting more than one set of values not only encouraged a pass/fail attitude, but also implied the use of sensitivity analysis was highly restricted.

In complex AMT projects a large number of cost and saving factors may initially be identified as being relevant, twenty to thirty being quite common. Although it will be possible to obtain a single value for most of the costs, where suppliers can provide a specific quotation, most of the savings will be subject to uncertainty. In theory, an initial evaluation should be carried out using the most likely values for all factors. A series of evaluations would then be done using the optimistic and pessimistic value for each factor, in turn, to determine how sensitive the DCF return would be to variations in each. If an evaluation was to be carried out for every one of the possible permutations, there would be an enormous number of evaluations and the process would be completely impractical – not just in terms of the time taken to do the evaluations, but more important, the difficulty of using the results to make a meaningful decision.

Fortunately, experience now shows that while a large number of factors may be identified as relevant in a project only variations in a very small number, in practice, will have a significant effect on the result. If conservative estimates (maximum cost–minimum savings) are used in an initial evaluation at the start of an investigation, it will be obvious from looking at the magnitude of the values which ones are important.

The objective is to identify the small number of savings factors which will have a major effect on the result, and then concentrate resources on improving the accuracy of estimates. It is also important to ensure that the specification which is selected is designed to achieve the benefits. Also that their achievement is included in the objectives and timetable set for implementation.

Where projects involve the use of technology which is proven, but whose use is unfamiliar to the company, there can be a danger of some areas of cost not being foreseen and therefore excluded from an evaluation. Allowance for this involves detailed investigation to try to identify all the potential cost implications. Although projects which use technology that is unproven, or still has to be developed, will have costs that are subject to uncertainty, the costs can be forecast with reasonable accuracy in the majority of projects. It is mainly in the area of savings that uncertainty exists.

The objective in using sensitivity analysis is to present the project in such a way that managers, possibly from different disciplines, can understand the key assumptions which have been made and which are critical for the success or failure of the project, and the effect these assumptions will have on the return on investment.

The final objective in using sensitivity analysis, then, is not to identify a single set of values which will provide the minimum required return, as happens with the pass/fail approach, but to help managers assess the validity of the assumptions they are making about the project; and to understand how important these are both to the technical and financial success of the project.

NEW TECHNOLOGY

When investing in proven technology, the main areas of uncertainty are the commercial risks involved because the technical risks can be minimized. When the technology is new, and possibly still having to be developed, or where it is to be used for a new and unproven application, there are a number of potential outcomes of the project which have to be allowed for, namely:

1. It may work but not perform fully to specification.
2. It may take much longer than forecast to develop.
3. It may cost much more than forecast to develop.
4. The technology may prove to be impractical and not work at all.

One of the reasons for carrying out an evaluation is to try to identify the nature of these risks and assess the consequences of project failure. By evaluating the penalties of project failure it is possible to assess whether the magnitude of the potential benefits – if the project succeeds – will compensate for the risk of failure. By identifying the main areas of uncertainty at the outset, it will be possible to establish criteria which can be used to monitor progress, so that early warning of failure can be given and possible corrective action taken.

Part of the process of allowing for risk is to investigate the consequences of project failure. A question which should always be asked is: 'what will be the effect on the company if the technology does not work?' This should consider contingency plans for the provision of fall-back options. If failure is likely to have serious consequences for the company, it may be necessary to reduce the scope of the project to avoid the use of 'state of the art' technology, while at the same time having to accept a reduction in potential benefits.

If the potential benefits are so large that it is worth attempting to develop new technology, it may be possible to reduce the element of risk and penalty of failure by identifying at the outset the key factors in the technology which have to be developed in order to make the project viable. Concentrating resources on solving these key factors at the outset may not be the cheapest, or fastest, way to develop the project, but it would reduce the period during which the company was exposed to uncertainty about success or failure.

Where uncertainty exists, the initial evaluation should consider the following:

1. Identify the nature of the risk.
2. Define both the penalty of failure and rewards of success.
3. Try to minimize the consequences of failure, for instance, by the provision of fallback options.
4. Establish measurable targets against which progress can be monitored, so that corrective action can be taken as soon as possible.

If problems arise once a project has been started, and a significant amount of money has already been spent, there can be a reluctance to abandon the project and waste money already spent. Alternatively, the feeling may be that continuation is only going to throw good money after bad. As soon as it is discovered that a project is seriously overspent, or behind programme, an evaluation needs to be carried out to decide whether it should be continued or abandoned. The first requirement is to determine whether the problems which have caused the time and money overrun have been cured, or if further haemorrhage is likely. Having decided that, an evaluation is then carried out to compare the future costs and the benefits of continuing with those of abandonment.

As with any other evaluation, the comparison is between two different sets of future cash flows. In most cases, the money already spent cannot be recovered by abandoning the project, except for any resale or scrap value of assets already purchased. Although the unrecoverable investment to date should not be included in the evaluation, any future payments already committed, or penalty payments for cancellation which will be incurred if the project is abandoned, must be included as a cost element in the set of cash flows representing the abandonment alternative.

8 Cost of capital

Because the cost that a company has to pay for capital is the basis for both the discount rate used to calculate the NPV of a project and the hurdle rate against which to compare the IRR, the cost of capital has been regarded as a critical factor in the traditional approach to investment appraisal. Considerable debate has taken place about the correct value to use. For example, whether it should be the current rate of interest that a company pays to borrow money from its bank by increasing its overdraft or the cost of raising additional long-term capital from the shareholders or some complex combination of these and other factors.

There are so many potential variations in the way that capital is obtained that each company has its own ideas about the value to use and there is no generally agreed best way of deciding the correct cost of capital. Because investment appraisal has always been treated as a technique which gives a final pass/fail verdict on projects, the cost of capital has been seen as critical since this is the criteria used to make 'yes'/'no' decisions. Even the name *hurdle rate* helps emphasize the concept of a final hurdle that has to be overcome.

Where projects are accepted on the basis of a single set of figures, as is done in the pass/fail approach, managers will always tend to submit their most optimistic set of estimates. The result is that if these are only just good enough to get the project over the hurdle rate, the probability is that the required return will not be achieved in practice. Since accountants know that managers are normally over-optimistic in their estimates of savings, companies try to compensate by using a rate which is higher than the cost of capital.

Any financial evaluation is based on assumptions about what will happen in the future and any such predictions must be liable to error. Because an evaluation should calculate a range of likely outcomes for a project, the decision whether or not to invest is no longer critically dependant on the hurdle rate which now becomes more of a guideline. Consequently, much less emphasis needs to be placed on calculating an exact rate. However, because an evaluation must take into account the effects of taxation, the hurdle rate used must be 'after tax'. Provided that any interest which has to be paid on the money borrowed for a project can be deducted from the company's tax liability, the hurdle rate will be lower than the 'before tax' rate.

For example, if a company borrows £1000 at 10%, the interest will be £100 a year. If this interest can be offset against taxation at 35%, the cost of the interest will be reduced to £65. As a result, the cost of borrowing will be equivalent to a 6.5% interest rate.

Manufacturing industry is constantly being exhorted to invest in AMT, the message being that technology is essential if industry is to become competitive in international markets. Despite this, surveys of the rate of introduction of AMT show that many companies have still made little or no investment in AMT. People who try to find reasons for the low rate of AMT investment often put the blame on high interest rates, or the reluctance of financial institutions to lend money to industry. This is convenient because it means that the fault lies not with industry's management, but with the financiers. Unfortunately, for such apologists, a closer examination of the problem shows that while they may have a limited effect, neither the level of interest rates nor the availability of finance should be a major constraint on AMT investment.

The significance of interest rates can be illustrated by using the example of a robot which will cost a total of £30 000 to buy and install. The cost of capital will vary between companies, depending on how they have raised the finance, and interest rates will also vary depending on the economic climate, but it is assumed that the cost of capital for one company is 12% while a competitor pays only 6%. For simplicity the effect of taxation is ignored as are running costs.

A company raising finance for an investment must have selected a project which will generate sufficient savings to do four things, namely:

1. Repay the capital borrowed.
2. Pay the running costs.
3. Pay interest on the outstanding sum each year.
4. Make a profit to compensate for any element of risk.

Table 8.1 shows the required cash flows if the working life is assumed to be three years and the cost of capital is 6%. It is assumed that some of the capital is repaid at the end of each year and interest is calculated for the whole year. Although the costs would be slightly lower if repayments and interest are calculated on a monthly or quarterly basis, this is compensated for by excluding the additional savings required to compensate for risk and to make a profit.

If three different physical working lives are assumed for the robot (3, 5 and 10 years), Table 8.2 shows the annual savings which would have to be

Table 8.1 Cash flows for three-year life

	Year 0 £	Year 1 £	Year 2 £	Year 3 £	Total £
Initial capital	30 000				30 000
Interest @ 6%		−1 800	−1 235	−634	3 669
Capital repayment		−9 423	−9 988	−10 589	30 000
Minimum savings		+11 223	+11 223	+11 223	33 669

Table 8.2 Savings required for £30 000 investment

Working life (years)	Interest rate %	Required annual savings £	Extra annual saving £	Percentage of initial capital cost %
3	6	11 223	–	–
3	12	12 490	1 267	4.2
5	6	7 122	–	–
5	12	8 322	1 200	4.0
10	6	4 076	–	–
10	12	5 310	1 234	4.1

made to repay the capital cost and pay interest, calculated on the same basis as in Table 8.1. Again, running costs are ignored. For each of the three project lives the additional annual savings needed to pay for the higher interest rates remains reasonably consistent. Although the additional savings required becomes a larger percentage of annual savings as the required annual savings reduces, the proportion of initial capital cost does not change significantly.

When investment in AMT is aimed at making a company more competitive, rather than just improving manufacturing efficiency, it has the potential to provide an extremely high return. As a result, when companies concentrate on identifying such projects, the cost of raising the required finance is not a critical factor because the expected return will be far larger than the cost of capital.

The effect of high interest rates on restricting AMT investment is of much less significance than other factors. For example, the ability to identify the company-wide benefits which can be obtained from AMT is more prevalent in some companies. This, in turn, leads them to invest in more projects, thus increasing their rate of introducing AMT.

One of the main factors affecting the rate of AMT investment is that the majority of companies still use payback rather than DCF, with companies using payback normally looking for short-term returns. If one considers the example of the £30 000 robot in Table 8.2, to provide a two-year payback would need annual savings of at least £15 000, ignoring running costs. Table 8.3 shows the implications of this.

Table 8.3 Effect of using two-year payback

Working life (years)	Annual savings £	Total savings £	Return on investment %
3	15 000	45 000	23.3
5	15 000	75 000	41
10	15 000	150 000	49

As each aspect of AMT becomes established, the rate of innovation decreases and reliability increases. As a result, the expected physical working life increases, so that for much of AMT five years has become conservative and ten years is not unrealistic. This can be seen in cases such as CNC machine tools, where the technology is well established and most companies now keep machines until they are worn out, rather than replace them because more advanced designs are available.

In the example in Table 8.3 the project would need to generate savings of £15 000 a year to give a two-year payback. However, many AMT projects take a considerable time to install and commission. If it was assumed in the example that only 50% of annual savings were achieved in the first year, to get a two-year payback would need savings of £10 000 in the first year and £20 000 a year thereafter, as shown in Table 8.4.

Table 8.4 Savings required for a two-year payback

	Year 0 £	Year 1 £	Year 2 £	Year 3 onwards £
Initial capital	−30 000			
Minimum savings		+10 000	+20 000	+20 000

Arguments about whether interest rates should be 6% or 12% seem irrelevant when the methods used by companies to select projects can result in them rejecting investments, as shown in Table 8.3, which will have a life of five years or more and which could provide a DCF return of over 40%, because they do not provide a two-year payback. Another reason put forward to excuse the low rate of investment is the reluctance of financial institutions to lend money to manufacturing industry and examples are quoted of enormous sums of money being invested abroad, or in service industries, rather than in manufacturing. In fact there seems to be little evidence to support this idea, and it is quite common at AMT conferences for there to be a speaker from a bank or venture capital company saying there is no shortage of capital available.

The real problem seems to be the inability of managers to evaluate projects in such a way that they can convince their own company's accountants that the project is sufficiently attractive to make it worth while raising the finance. Asking for money to finance an act of faith is not likely to appeal to a banker. Financial institutions are often accused of taking a short-term view of investments but examples, such as the Channel Tunnel, show that this is not the case. However, because of the high costs and long start-up times of major AMT projects, it is important to calculate the realistic cash flows expected over the whole life of the project, so that the company's bankers, and if necessary shareholders, understand the full implications.

INFLATION

High rates of inflation is also offered as a reason why companies find it more difficult to invest in long-term projects. However, the cost of money borrowed from a bank or other source comprises three main elements:

Interest rate = interest charge + risk factor + inflation factor

The risk factor can be seen in the higher interest rates that small companies in high-risk industries have to pay to borrow money, compared with large, well-established companies.

When a company borrows money, it has to repay the same amount plus interest. Because this repayment may be made several years after the money has been borrowed, its value in real terms will be reduced by inflation. This means that to prevent the money they are lending losing its real value, banks increase their interest rate to compensate for inflation. The fact that the rate of inflation may be high is part of the reason why interest rates are high, it is not an additional constraint on AMT investment.

There are two main techniques used in investment appraisal to allow for inflation. The first is to increase all the estimated annual cash flows by a suitable percentage to represent the expected future rate of inflation. This is technically the correct way of allowing for inflation, but in practice it makes the evaluation more difficult and requires estimates for the expected rate of inflation in each year through the project's life. The second method is to use cash flow values based on today's prices and make the allowance for inflation by reducing the hurdle rate. This approach is much easier and less prone to error in the calculations, and it is the one normally used in practice.

In using this second method, however, there will always be a slight margin of error. Although inflation will affect annual costs and savings equally, this does not apply to capital allowances offset against taxation. While the figure for costs and savings will increase each year in line with inflation, the amount of tax relief from capital allowances will not increase as it is based on the original capital value.

To illustrate the effect of inflation, the following shows the net cash flows of a project without any allowance for inflation:

Year 0	Year 1	Year 2	Year 3	Year 4	Year 5
−10 000	+3 000	+3 000	+3 000	+3 000	+3 000

Assuming an inflation-free rate of interest of 1%, plus a risk premium of 7%, giving an 8% discount rate, the project will provide an NPV of £1978.

Increasing the annual cash flows at a compound rate of 10% to allow for inflation gives the following:

Year 0	Year 1	Year 2	Year 3	Year 4	Year 5
−10 000	+3 300	+3 630	+3 993	+4 392	+4 832

The discount rate also has to be increased by 10% compound rate to allow for inflation, thus:

$$1 + R = (1 + 0.08) \times (1 + 0.10)$$
$$R = 18.8\%$$

using this rate with the revised annual cash flows, again, gives an NPV of £1978. If the evaluation is done without increasing annual values, the discount rate would be 8%, but if the annual values are increased to allow for inflation, the rate would be 18.8%. If £10 000 was borrowed at 18.8% interest, the annual repayments over five years would have to be £3256 (giving an NPV of £0).

In carrying out a financial evaluation it is important to ensure that the hurdle rate contains the correct allowance for inflation. There is a danger that if annual cash flows have been not increased to include expected inflation, this may not have been offset by reducing the hurdle rate to eliminate the inflation allowance.

9 Monitoring performance

When investment appraisal is treated as a final hurdle that has to be over-come, the values used in a justification are normally the most optimistic ones which will be accepted. As a result, there is a high level of probability that costs will overrun and forecast savings will not be achieved. In such circumstances, the use of **post-audits** to monitor projects only leads to a state of conflict, with the manager responsible for the project trying to invent excuses for what has gone wrong or attempting to put the blame for failure on someone else.

The normal approach to performance monitoring is to have a formal review of the original financial estimates, possibly one or two years after the initial investment, the objective being to confirm whether or not the estimates were right in the first place. In theory, this approach improves the forecasting ability of managers in the long term.

In practice, however, the involvement which many departmental managers have in the selection and justification of major projects will be a one-off event. A more practical advantage is that if managers know that their estimates will be subject to a formal post-audit, they may tend to be more realistic in their estimates.

One of the reasons for using investment appraisal is to quantify all the costs and benefits, so that a project can be correctly reflected in the costing system. As long as all the benefits have been quantified, and none excluded as intangible, the costing system will provide an automatic system for performance monitoring.

Any variations from the forecast cash flows, both for costs and savings, should be identified by the costing system and reported as an operating variance. This means that any major deviation from the planned implementa-tion, in terms both of the magnitude and the timing of cash flows, should be detected as soon as problems start to arise such that corrective action can be taken. Performance monitoring therefore changes from being a one-off audit and becomes an ongoing control.

One of the aims of investment appraisal is to relate the projected cash flow changes to the technical objectives and the timetable set for their implementation. Part of the process of performance monitoring therefore is to compare the progress of implementation with the planned timetable, so that appropriate action can be taken if problems arise which will delay the achievement of the technical objectives. The overall aim is to establish both the financial and technical objectives and then ensure that they are being achieved.

Because of the problems encountered in evaluating complex projects in the past and the belief being that the benefits would somehow become apparent once the investment had been made, many existing AMT applications were installed without a realistic financial evaluation. This means that a formal post-audit would be impractical because there are no quantified estimates to compare with actual vlaues.

The inability to include all the benefits of projects in costing systems has often meant that they are wrongly reported as being a financial failure. By carrying out a new financial evaluation in such cases, and quantifying all the identified benefits, it can be seen whether any changes are necessary in the objectives and the timetable for any further implementation. Doing this will show whether projects are white elephants to be abandoned or that their poor reputation is undeserved.

When companies are investing in projects such as CAD and MRPII, managers may have little prior experience of the systems and, as a result, the original objectives and timetable which are set may be limited or unrealistic. Carrying out regular re-evaluations as implementation progresses, and as operating experience is gained, will help to identify any potential areas of saving which were not considered in the original evaluation.

The aim of using post-audit in this way is not to check whether the original estimates were correct, which should be done through the costing system, but to re-examine the assumptions on which the original evaluation was based in order to identify any changes that are needed in the planned implementation.

10 Product quality

The historical development of **quality control**, which grew out of traditional inspection departments, has conditioned people's perception of quality, so that it is often regarded as a necessary evil. Fortunately, it has now been found that the basic philosophy underlying this development has been wrong and a completely different approach is now required, which helps to show that investing in *quality improvement* can be most profitable.

Until the late 1960s or early 1970s, quality was seen as a function of manufacturing, with the results of poor quality being scrapped or rejected components. Putting these right was seen as the 'cost of quality'; this cost included not only correction of faults discovered in manufacture but also the warranty and service costs of faults discovered by customers. Because of the way quality was perceived, efforts to improve it concentrated on having large numbers of inspectors, whose job was to try to check as many components as possible in order to detect faulty components, often at the end of the manufacturing process. The underlying philosophy of this concept of quality was that operators created the faults, and an inspector's job was to try to find them.

Some companies used quite sophisticated statistical techniques to calculate the optimum number of components that had to be checked to ensure that a minimum percentage of faulty components got through to the customer. For critical components the policy was often to carry out a 100% inspection of critical dimensions.

The fact that most companies had some form of bonus payment scheme, such as rate-fixing or time study, meant that operators could suffer a financial penalty if their work was faulty and this was found out. It was in the operators' interest therefore to try to hide any faults in the hope that, if they were found out at a later date, it would not be possible to identify the person responsible. A common practice was that an operator, finding that he had scrapped a component, would record that he had produced the total qualtity for the bonus system and then 'lose' the faulty one.

Works Managers work always under considerable pressure to achieve delivery dates and output targets and, as a result, they may conceivably try to coerce inspectors into letting products be shipped with known faults. Doing this would help them achieve their targets while passing on the problem to the Service Department, often reporting to a different director. Because of the potential conflict of interests it was normally considered to be essential that the Inspection Department should be responsible to a director, such as Engineering, who was not also responsible for Manufacturing.

In the 1960s people began to realize that this philosophy of inspection was expensive and inefficient and that it made more sense to attempt to concentrate efforts on preventing the faults being made in the first place, rather than trying to find them afterwards. To help emphasize that this was a new approach, the name *quality control* was applied to this philospohy in order to differentiate it from Inspection.

One of the main principles was to make operators responsible for the quality of their work and, as such, they were expected to do their own inspection, but without financial penalty if they reported any faults.

That concept was seized upon by managers who saw it as a way of eliminating much of the disruption of production caused by finding out at the end of the manufacturing process that components had to be replaced. For many managers an even bigger bonus was that by making operators inspect their own work, often without extra payment, it was possible to get rid of most of the inspection labour force, which was regarded always as expensive and unproductive.

The concept that it was better to try to prevent faults occurring, rather that just trying to find them after the fault had been made, led to the understanding that the original cause of many defects was not in the manufacturing process, but originated from the initial design and planning; for example, incorrect or ambiguous drawings and documentation, or designs which were unnecessarily complicated and which required the achievement of unrealistically close tolerances.

The importance of identifying the cause of defects before they happen is shown in surveys which suggest that about 70% of the faults found in manufacturing are caused by pre-manufacturing activities, such as:

1. Incorrect specification.
2. Poor planning.
3. Incorrect or poor design.
4. Errors and omissions in documentation.

While the realization was growing that it was necessary to start at the initial design stage to improve quality, a fundamental change was taking place in industry. Because of increasing competition, it was no longer good enough to have products which were technically excellent; they had also to be able to compete on price and delivery. The fact that improving quality was equated to reducing costs helped the introduction of quality control. At the same time as the concepts of quality control were being developed, the increasing pressure on companies to reduce costs led to the development of **value analysis (VA)**. The basis of VA was the realization that traditional cost reduction was inadequate because it was based on each department trying to improve its own performance with there being little communication between departments. The idea of VA was to set up multi-disciplinary teams (e.g. Production, Design, Finance and Sales) to examine each component of a product, in turn, to attempt to reduce its cost, starting with the most expensive.

As happened with quality control, it soon became obvious that most of the cost of a product had been built into the design before manufacture started, thus the level of savings which could be achieved by looking at current products was very limited. However, major savings were possible if the analysis was carried out at the initial design stage. To emphasize that this was a different approach it was called **value engineering (VE)**.

As traditional industries continued to decline, while Japanese industries were expanding, considerable efforts were made to identify any factors which could explain the difference. One of the most obvious differences was the quality and reliability of products, and looking for the cause of this, it was found that many Japanese companies operated *Quality Circles*, a concept which seemed to be completely unknown outside Japan.

All the advocates of 'flavour of the month' technology jumped on the band-wagon with the message that if companies introduced Quality Circles, all their problems would be over, which of course they never were. In fact the concept of Quality Circles is very similar to VA, that is where a group of people hold regular meetings to discuss ways of improving a product and reduce its cost.

In one case, the emphasis is on starting with the most expensive components in a product; in the other case it is starting with the most significant manufacturing problems, which are normally quality ones. The main difference being that VA is treated as a management function, while Quality Circles are based on using shopfloor workers. The Japanese having realized that the people working on the shopfloor have a much better understanding than management of the detailed problem of manufacture and that, if correctly organized and motivated, they can make a significant contribution to improved efficiency.

Despite this change in the understanding of the cause of defects, companies still measure quality in terms of cost – e.g. scrap, rework, etc. Even if this extended to include factors such as design change costs, reprinting and re-issuing drawings, and so on, the measurement of quality is treated still as being the cost of failing to do the correct thing. Attempts to improve quality tend to start by trying to measure the 'cost of quality' with consider-able debate taking place about the magnitude of this 'cost' and efforts being made to identify all the factors in a company which contribute to quality cost.

Quality-related investments tend to be defensive by nature, such as having to reduce scrap and rework, or the company being forced to install plant, such as X-ray facilities or test equipment, in order to adhere to the external standards set by customers. Alternatively, quality is regarded as an overhead which includes such costs as inspectors' and quality control staff wages, gauging equipment, maintenance of standards room, etc. As a result, investment in equipment, such as coordinate measuring machines, is seen as a way of reducing the overhead cost.

The traditional concept of quality improvement, whether Inspection, Quality Control or Quality Circles, is based on reducing the cost implications of poor quality. In quality control, as with inspection, efforts to improve quality are designed to reduce the level of defects in a company's products and the techniques used, such as **statistical process control (SPC)**, have been developed to help improve product reliability.

Unfortunately, when quality is treated as a cost, the only way of improving it is to reduce the cost. This can result in a law of diminishing returns where companies have to spend more and more to achieve less and less improvement. Equally important is that it reinforces the attitude that the aim of improving quality is the improvement of reliability.

Although 'better-quality products' is often quoted as being a benefit of AMT investment, this is treated as a rather abstract concept or as an interesting phenomenon which cannot be quantified, except in the traditional terms of scrap, rework, etc. It is only now that it has been shown that there should be no such thing as an intangible benefit that the full economic implications of 'better-quality products' can be evaluated.

As described in the earlier chapter on intangible benefits, the need is to redefine the generalized statement into quantifiable terms, and then identify which ones may be relevant, thus 'better-quality products' may mean some or all of the following:

1. Reduced scrap.
2. Reduced rework.
3. Reduced disruption caused by scrap and rework.
4. Reduced warranty and service costs.
5. Reduced cost of inspection and quality assurance.
6. Reduced cost of concessions and design changes.
7. Reduced cost of documentation and change control.
8. Reduced need for safety stocks.
9. Increased sales of better quality products.

The benefits of quality attainment may be far-reaching, yet they may not always be obvious. For example, the uncertainty caused by possible scrap and rework normally causes Material Control departments to adopt a range of expensive strategies, such as extended lead times, increased order quantities, carrying buffer safety stocks, etc. By eliminating, or reducing, the possibility of scrap and rework, a company can rethink its material ordering policy.

Although there may be a lot of different benefits from improving product quality, the one which is potentially by far the largest is increased sales of better-quality products. This is not only because the magnitude of the benefits from increasing sales can be very large, but previous efforts to improve quality have concentrated on reducing the 'cost of quality'. As a result, considerable work will already have been done to reduce the levels of scrap, rework, etc. and the scope for further significant improvement will be very limited. When increasing sales, rather than reducing cost, is seen as the main objective for quality improvement, a fundamental change in approach is needed because product quality can now be seen as a potential asset, the difference being that an asset can be increased in value without restriction.

As soon as product quality is viewed as a potential asset, with the objective being to maximize its value, the way it must be dealt with has to change completely. The starting-point must be to identify the perception which potential (as well as existing) customers have, not just of the products, but of the company as well. The customer's perception of the company and its products is much wider than reliability. It will be formed by factors such as advertising image, company reputation, product appearance, user friendliness, packaging, product specification, instruction manuals, delivery performance, customer support and service facilities.

In changing the emphasis from cost reduction to increasing customer satisfaction, it is important to find out whether the existing product specification and quality standards are correct. Some aspects of a product, such as appearance, may not be defective, but the standard can be insufficiently good to match the customer's perceived requirements. Even if the product is completely correct to specification, then if the specification does not meet the customers' real needs, there is a danger that products are providing an elegant and expensive solution to the wrong problem.

With many products, the first-time customers find out whether or not they are reliable will only be after they have bought them. Although customers may be upset when they open attractive packaging to find that the product is unreliable, at least they have already bought the product. If the packaging is unattractive, the customer may not even buy the product, however reliable it may be.

Reliability is only one element of quality and there is no point spending a lot of time and money in further improving the reliability of products which are already to a higher standard than customers require. The need is to get the correct balance of all the elements and concentrate management and financial resources on the most cost-effective aspects.

When improving quality is treated in terms of reducing cost penalties, it is relatively easy to identify the most expensive problems on which to concentrate resources. However, when quality is viewed as an asset which encompasses a wide range of factors relating to increased customer satisfaction, it is much more difficult to identify the areas of a company, which may not be in manufacturing, where resources must be concentrated.

The approach to quality improvement must start by defining the needs of potential customers, both short term and long term, and then to identify the changes which need to be made to improve the customers' overall perception of the company and its products. Once the required changes have been defined, it will be possible to relate the costs of making the various changes to the financial benefits which can result. Because the required changes can affect several different areas of the company, such as advertising, product redesign, appearance and packaging, it may be possible at the same time to introduce several improvements. However, the need is to develop an overall plan for improvement.

The traditional view of quality as a necessary evil means that resources are allocated grudgingly, the attitude being, 'how little do we have to spend to keep customers happy?' When quality is seen as an asset, and when investment in quality improvement can be shown to be very profitable, management will be more willing to allocate all the necessary resources.

Chapter 11 Just in Time (JIT)

Normally the decision to introduce **Just in Time (JIT)** is not seen as an investment decision which has to be evaluated in financial terms. However, introducing JIT can involve considerable expenditure, as well as providing financial advantages. In addition, as happened with GT, attempts to reduce lead times and stock levels can have an adverse effect on machine utilization, so that if the financial benefits of JIT are not quantified, the result may be an apparent increase in standard costs.

An enormous amount has been written about JIT, but most of this is based on the level of such platitudes as 'Just In Time not Just In Case'. In practice, most companies find that their real problem is not just that they manufacture 'Just in Case', but they manufacture 'Just Too Late'.

Unfortunately, JIT is portrayed as a philosophy rather than a practical production technique. As a result, it is all too easy to say that all components should be produced just in time, and it is difficult to argue against the suggestion that this is what companies should be aiming to do, even if few companies in practice can actually do so. Because of the way that JIT is presented, saying that the objective is unrealistic means that one is thought to be negative and reactionary.

Introducing JIT is seen as a way of overcoming the problems of *batch manufacture*. It is very easy to be critical of batch manufacture because it appears to be a highly inefficient way of producing components in comparison with *mass production*. Thus numerous authors have identified the fact that components produced in batches spend a very small part of the total lead time actually having work done on them.

For example, batches may spend over 90% of the lead time in a queue waiting for a machine, and an individual component may then spend over 90% of the batch machining time waiting for its turn to go onto the machine. Even when a component is on the machine, the actual cutting time may represent less than 50% of the operation time. The result is that it is easy to show that, although lead times may be long, components spend less that 1% of that lead time actually having work done on them.

The fact that this is uneconomical seems self-evident and, as a result, it is assumed always that batch manufacture must be replaced by some other technique for producing components. Since the days of F. W. Taylor at the beginning of this century, people have been trying to overcome the apparent inefficiency by developing new ways to control batch manufacture.

Controlling batch manufacture is a highly complex balancing act which has to trade-off a number of conflicting interests, including:

1. The need to keep expensive manufacturing facilities operating at maximum utilization, which means keeping a uniform flow of work.
2. The need to keep direct labour fully utilized.
3. The need to produce components in the largest batch sizes possible, in order to reduce the number of set-ups which are regarded as a non-productive cost.
4. The need to keep lead times to a minimum, in order to improve the ability to respond to changes in customer demand.
5. The need to operate with the minimum levels of work-in-progress and finished components.
6. The need to cope with variable factors such as machine breakdowns, labour absenteeism, scrap and rework.

Unfortunately, the success or failure of the various techniques developed, such as GT, have been measured on the basis of technical criteria, or by using very limited financial criteria which were not able to encompass all of the factors listed above. In some cases, even this limited assessment has not been done and the justification for the proposed technique has been purely subjective, with the use of emotive arguments based on the assumption that batch manufacture is 'a bad thing' which must be replaced.

Advocates of JIT start with the assumption that the ultimate objective is to make components and products *just in time*, and that companies should concentrate all their resources on trying to achieve this objective. However, manufacturing in most companies is highly complex, with there being few aspects that cannot be improved if sufficient resources are employed in so doing. The concentration of resources on trying to make parts just in time may be the wrong priority because other changes may be needed which are more important. Because of this, it is necessary to evaluate the introduction of JIT not only to ensure that the expenditure is justified, but to compare JIT with other potential changes in the company.

Production engineers spend much of their time trying to reduce set-up times and improve component quality, in the same way that purchasing departments keep trying to improve the delivery, quality and price of bought-in components and materials. Provided that they have been doing their job properly, scope for further improvement will be limited.

By concentrating sufficient management resources on any aspect of a company's operation there will be some improvement; in fact many of the benefits claimed in the past for other 'new' management techniques came from the concentration of attention, rather than the technique itself. Because of this, managers who are considering new ideas, such as JIT, must seek to identify the real potential benefits which the technique can provide, so that they can compare them with the alternative of concentrating attention on other aspects of the company's operation.

Much of what has been written about JIT starts with the assumption that the most important improvement that a company can make is *inventory reduction*; this perceived need to reduce inventory is the justification for concentrating resources on JIT. Usually the reasoning that is given is that because direct labour is no longer a major cost element, attention now must be directed elsewhere and inventory is seen as the next largest cost factor. However, the importance of inventory reduction is rarely, if ever, questioned in an objective way because carrying inventory is assumed always to be 'a bad thing', and anything which reduces it must be 'a good thing'. Consequently, the justification for JIT is normally emotive rather than analytical.

The first question that has to be asked is: 'what are the costs and the benefits of JIT?' The potential benefits have not only to be identified, but they must be assessed in such a way that they can be compared in financial terms with the benefits which could be achieved by other changes in the company.

Although there are large variations between companies, all companies are faced with the same basic problems – e.g. delivery, price, product quality, obsolete designs, excess inventory, matching customers' specification, etc. What is unique within a company is the relative importance of each of these problems. It is now possible for a company to analyse the problems that it is faced with, and calculate the magnitude of the benefits which can be obtained by solving them. Any comparison between the magnitude of these benefits has to be related to the cost and feasibility of achieving them.

Although the need to reduce inventory is normally portrayed as the reason for concentrating on JIT, the changes required to produce components and products just in time not only reduces inventory, but also improves delivery performance which, in turn, can result in increased sales. As discussed in an earlier chapter, the benefits of inventory reduction, although large in themselves, may be quite small in relation to other potential benefits such as increasing sales through improved delivery performance. If the basic objective changes from inventory reduction to improved delivery performance, the question is whether concentrating on JIT is still the correct thing to do.

Increasing sales volume (or just as important, preventing sales being lost), and increasing profit margins, for instance, by the ability to charge a premium on selling price, can depend on a lot of different factors, of which delivery performance is only one. The need is to consider whether using JIT to improving delivery is the correct approach when the objective is to increase sales. In other words, will the application of JIT as opposed to other methods result in an increased ability to satisfy the needs of customers? Unfortunately, in many cases, the answer is 'no'.

In theory, if a company could produce all components and products just in time to suit the needs of customers, it would also be able to win all the orders where delivery performance was the critical factor. Of course, if it were practical, companies would have started making everything just in time a long time ago! The difficulty is that there are two major variables which have to be allowed for: one is the uncertainty of the supply process; and the other is the fluctuation in order intake. Dealing with these two variables has major cost implications in trying to improve delivery. Figure 11.1 shows how order input can vary in a company. To be able to supply a demand which fluctuates like this, by producing products *just in time*, both the manufacturing and purchasing facilities have to be capable of responding to rapid and major changes in demand. Traditional manufacturing relies on long lead times and high stock levels to cope with short-term fluctuations in sales volume and product mix. As a result, many production engineers may be unaware of the magnitude of these short-term fluctuations because they only have to allow for long-term changes in average demand levels.

When lead times are long, the company shown in Fig. 11.1 may be able to supply customer demand by having capacity for approx. 800 units. However, as lead times are reduced it will be necessary to increase capacity to over 1000 units; but there will be time when the factory output will drop well

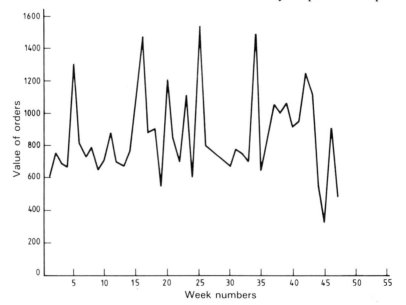

Fig. 11.1 Fluctuations in order input.

below the 800 unit level. If the original utilization was 100%, and there was no increase in sales volume, the increase in capacity would mean that average utilization would drop to 80%, resulting in an increase in standard costs. Providing the additional capacity to give the company the increased flexibility of production to respond to sales fluctuations would involve considerable expenditure. Increasing flexibility represents a cost, not a benefit.

Advocates of JIT suggest that what has to be done is to reduce set-up times to zero and eliminate scrap and rework by improving the quality of the manufacturing process, the ultimate aim being the ability to make all components in batches of one. But, as discussed earlier, the control of batch manufacture involves a trade-off between a number of conflicting interests. In every case, the constraint is the requirement to keep costs to a minimum; if cost were not a constraint, batch manufacture would present no problem.

Unfortunately, improving only a few machines, often by investing in new and expensive ones, may not be much help overall. The components produced on these machines probably have to go through several other processes, which would also need to be improved. Merely speeding up the throughput of some components may not change product delivery; it may result only in components arriving in the stores earlier, thereby increasing the value of inventory.

A technique that production engineers have always adopted (which used to be called *family planning*) is to select the small number of components that have the greatest effect on product delivery and price, and concentrate on improving delivery of these by setting up groups of machines where each group is dedicated to the production of one family of critical components. Setting up such dedicated groups of machines is expensive because their utilization is low. As a result, it is only viable for a small number of components where 'family planning' is more economical than the alternative of achieving delivery performance by carrying expensive inventory. In selecting such families there is a marked Pareto-effect, whereby as the value of the components being considered reduces, it quickly becomes more economical to increase stock levels rather than set up machine groups, in order to provide the flexibility needed to respond to sales fluctuations.

With bought-in components, the choice is either between buying at the most economical price, with delivery and order quantity being determined by the manufacturing process used by the supplier, or alternatively, buying components to be delivered just in time as required by the user. When the company buying components is the supplier's main customer, it may be possible to insist on parts being delivered as required without a major cost penalty. However, most companies buy a large number of different parts from a large number of suppliers where the relatively low value of orders means that the suppliers are not highly dependent on the purchaser.

The reality is that most suppliers would probably be prepared to deliver components just in time, if asked, but would increase their prices to cover the increased delivery and paperwork costs, as well as the cost of having to keep the parts in their own stores until required. The supplier would not normally change the way the parts are made, all that would happen would be that the supplier, rather than the purchaser, would carry the inventory. This would be reflected in an increase in purchase price, which would be greater than the saving in inventory value.

The primary objective is to increase the company's ability to supply customers with what they want, when they want it. This goal can be achieved in two ways, either by carrying high levels of inventory or producing everything just in time. As a result, the financial benefit of JIT is not the effect on sales volume, but the avoidance of carrying stock.

By correctly defining the principal objective (i.e. increasing sales volumes and profit margins) it is possible to identify the action needed to achieve this (e.g. improved product delivery performance). Only by so doing is it possible to define the correct way in which this can be done. In some cases, it may be necessary to increase stock levels 'just in case' a customer may want to place an order with a very short delivery time.

With any management philosophy, it is important to start by defining the real objectives, the cost of achieving them and the nature and magnitude of the benefits. Evaluating these may show that concentrating on other priorities may be more important. However, in order to remain competitive, companies must keep trying to improve all aspects of their operation, whether it is design, manufacture or marketing. The advantage of new concepts, such as JIT, is that they make managers stop and rethink their priorities, and by so doing may help identify unseen areas of inefficiency.

12 Investment strategy

In order to remain competitive, companies must continuously improve their plant and machinery, as well as their management control systems. In trying to do this, companies have a wide choice both of machinery and computer systems, but unfortunately most of the literature concerning this is based on the assumption that a company has already decided to invest in a specific area of technology, such as FMS; and what they need is help to identify the optimum specification.

When the objective for investing in AMT is improved departmental efficiency, the approach will have limited validity because the largest financial benefits come from the effect that AMT can have on the total company. For example, although investing in FMS can result in savings in labour, WIP, etc., the major benefits come from the effect it can have on sales. Unfortunately, in many companies the decision to invest in a specific aspect of AMT happens because there is a manager with a strong personality who wants to improve his own department, or because the company has been persuaded to invest in the latest management fashion. Even if the company-wide benefits of such an investment can be achieved and it is profitable, making the investment may have prevented the company from spending resources on other projects which are more important.

Because of this, any company considering investment must start by identifying the areas where resources have to be concentrated. The objective when considering AMT should not be to improve individual departments on a random basis, or to keep installing the most up-to-date technology, rather the aim must be to optimize the company's profitability and its long-term competitive ability.

One of the problems encountered in trying to decide where to concentrate resources is that, in most companies, the manufacturing facilities and control systems are a result of the historical development of the company and may no longer be suitable for meeting the needs of the market-place. The existing manufacturing facilities in a company can strongly influence the way that new products are designed, but these facilities may not be appropriate for the types of product needed in the future. Unfortunately, the rate of change within most companies tends to be gradual, so that the need for a radical change may not be obvious until it is too late and the company can no longer afford the cost, or have sufficient management resources, to make the required changes.

It is wrong to concentrate resources merely on improving the existing organization, rather the starting-point must be to define the type of manufacturing organization needed for the future. To do this, the company must identify the needs of the market-place in which in the future it hopes to compete. One of the main reasons why Japanese companies are so successful is that they are very good at doing just this.

It has often been suggested that a company should develop a manufacturing strategy. Unfortunately, the inability to measure the effect of the proposed changes in financial terms has meant that any such strategic plan is of a purely subjective nature, thus little more than an act of faith.

All companies are subject to many conflicting priorities and, as a result, changes in one department may be in conflict with the aims and interests of other departments. Thus quality may be improved at the expense of having to increase selling price, thereby reducing sales, while inventory may be reduced at the expense of restricting the flexibility of sales response.

In trying to develop a strategy, the costs which have to be considered are not just the direct costs associated with each investment, but the potential indirect costs which result from the effect the investment can have on the rest of the company. Starting with an overall strategy for change allows the company wide costs of each option to be identified, so that they can be compared with the potential financial benefits. Only in this way will the strategy be objective and not subject to personality bias.

One of the traditional approaches in developing company strategies has been to survey a number of companies in order to identify a 'best management practice' and then trying to adapt this to all other companies. This approach is incorrect because, although it may identify some areas for improvement, it does not identify those areas where resources must be concentrated to optimize results. A further problem with this approach is that it tends to result in the development of management fashions. The effect of this can be seen in study groups that have gone to Japan, seeking to identify the secret of their success, and returned with Quality Circles, FMS, JIT, etc. All companies are different, so that the needed changes even by companies competing in the same market will be unique to each one. Every company must be able to develop its own specific strategy. Even if a particular management technique works in some companies, this does not mean that it should be adopted by all companies because other techniques may exist which could be more appropriate.

While it is possible to predict the ideal types of product that a company needs (including price, delivery, quality, quantity, stock levels, etc.), it would normally require such major changes to the whole organization to produce products to this optimum specification. Because of this, few companies could afford to make all the changes required and there has to be a compromise between the current situation and the ideal.

Using a common evaluation technique, investment in manufacturing plant and machinery can now be compared with concentrating resources in techniques such as JIT and GT, or with investing in other areas of the company such as product innovation, marketing and distribution. This means that companies can be treated as a total economic entity, of which manufacturing is only one element. As a result, the development of any strategy should start by considering the needs of the total company and then go on to re-examine the role of manufacturing in order to define the type of machinery and systems which the company will need in the future. The rate of implementing the required changes identified in the strategy will be subject to conflicting pressures between the cost and disruption involved on the one hand, and the financial consequences on the other to the total company if the changes take too long.

When considering investment in the past, the aim of managers has been to use technology to improve manufacturing efficiency and consequently the development of manufacturing technology and management control systems has been aimed at meeting this perceived need. The ability to produce quantified company strategies will, for the first time, allow the role of manufacturing within companies to be re-examined from basic principles. Not only will this allow maufacturing to change from being a self-contained department within a company and become an integral part of the whole organization, but it also means that as the objectives for investment change, the way that technology is being developed will also change.

13 Industrial relations

There is a widespread belief that the introduction of automation will destroy jobs. Often the future is depicted as relying on completely automated factories which will produce all our needs without any human operators. It is widely believed, especially when unemployment figures are rising, that within a few years automation will have created mass unemployment (or mass leisure). However, the same view of technology has been held for a long time, not just in the days of Henry Ford and the Model-T, but by the original Luddites. Not only have all the past predictions proved false, but there is now evidence that automation can create jobs, not destroy them.

In trying to examine the impact of AMT on employment, one of the problems encountered is that automation has often been used in the past as an excuse for changing working practices, and thereby reducing manning levels. In many cases, if working practices had been changed by negotiation, any subsequent reduction due to the introduction of automation may have been negligible. In fact the use of automation in such cases might not have been needed.

Although many industries have experienced large reductions in the size of their labourforce, surveys suggest that these have tended to coincide with changes in national economies such as the effect of the 1973–4 oil crisis. Investment has tended to take place during periods of economic expansion, so that the effect of introducing robots, CNC machine tools, etc. on the size of labourforces may have been negligible. The emphasis on labour-saving in the introduction of AMT is largely a result of financial distortions caused by the way that managers attempt to introduce automation, rather than the ability of automation to replace humans.

Production engineers spend much of their time trying to reduce costs and improve production efficiency; but they are mainly trying to reduce the costs that they can measure and influence. While these are primarily the costs of manufacture, their efforts are restricted by the difficulty of making significant changes in some areas of manufacturing cost. Thus they are forced to place undue emphasis on those factors which they could change.

In the past, direct labour was often the largest cost element in manufacturing companies and commonly represented 40%–50% of total manufacturing cost. This has gradually been reducing, so that for many companies direct labour may now represent only 10% of total cost. The reduction in direct labour means that the cost of the material content in products can now be a high percentage of total product cost. Although efforts may be made to reduce this, the scope for reduction can be limited if the product design cannot be radically altered.

The experience of **value analysis** and **value engineering** has shown that in order to make major savings in material costs a complete re-examination of product design is needed. The changes therefore may be restricted to such examples as altering a sand casting to a die casting, or a fabrication to a forging.

Manufacturing overheads are another major element in total cost, but many of the factors that compromise this, such as depreciation, are difficult to change. In fact investing in AMT to improve operating efficiency will increase capital values and thereby increase depreciation. Although indirect labour costs may represent a relatively small percentage of total overheads, they can represent a large percentage of the costs which production engineers are able to change and therefore considerable resources may be concentrated on making reductions. Not only is much of manufacturing overhead fixed in the cost accounting concept that it does not vary as sales volume varies, but it is also physically fixed by the nature of the factory and is not easily susceptible to change for cost reduction. The result is that direct and indirect labour receive more attention than other factors.

The emphasis on labour-saving is further increased by costing systems. Although companies have normally changed from being labour intensive to capital intensive, labour/hour rate is still the most common allocation basis in standard costs. In allocating costs on the basis of a rate per labour hour it appears – wrongly – that a reduction in the number of direct workers will also reduce the allocated overheads.

For example, if the actual cost of labour is £5/h (representing wages and employment costs) and the costing rate is £25/h, reducing labour appears to save £25/h. In reality, the saving in cash terms may be only £5/h, the remaining £20 being unaffected by the change and existing still after the change is made.

Because of the complexity of costing systems, labour/hour rates will be recalculated only occasionally, possibly once a year, not every time there is a small change in the size of the labour force. This means that although the unaffected overhead costs will exist still, they will not be allocated to other cost rates until the rates are recalculated.

Although many managers realize that cost information is suspect, the information is often used to measure departmental efficiency, sometimes reinforced by a **Management by Objectives scheme**. As a result, they are often happy to go along with a system which makes it much easier to justify investments and appears to show that they are doing a good job in running their departments.

Managers select technology which will optimize the savings which they can quantify, especially labour. As a result, robots are portrayed as 'machines that replace people'; CAD is seen as a way of reducing drawing office labour; and the objective of FMS is portrayed as unmanned manufacture, which is the ultimate labour-saving. Not only does this attitude make little economic sense, it can lead to major industrial relations problems. Using CAD as an example, it is possible to see how unrealistic this emphasis on labour-saving can be.

A number of surveys have been carried out that show that when companies have tried to justify investment in CAD, they have done so almost exclusively on the basis of reducing drawing office labour. These surveys show that productivity improvement ratios of 3 : 1 are often used, but higher ratios such as 4 : 1 are not uncommon. The implication of such ratios is that once CAD is fully implemented, two-thirds (or three-quarters in the case of 4 : 1) of the original staff will not be needed.

Calculating the productivity improvement of CAD would seem to be something which managers could do exactly, but in an experiment carried out by a company using CAD, a range of existing components were redrawn on both drawing-boards and CAD with the times being measured; the overall difference was 1.7 : 1 in favour of CAD. This improvement was based on the time taken to reproduce a drawing, not to produce an original design. Although there will be some tasks, such as using parametrics, where much higher productivity improvements can be achieved, this will be offset by the fact that draughtsmen may only spend about a third of their time working on a drawing board.

Although ratios of 3 : 1 or higher are always used, there is no factual evidence to suggest that the introduction of CAD results in redundancies. There is not an increasing number of unemployed draughtsmen, if anything there is a growing shortage of experienced draughtsmen. The conclusion is that the claims of improved productivity are highly subjective and of doubtful validity, with there being virtually no factual evidence that quantifies the effect in a scientific manner.

Needless to say, the chances of an enthusiatic and effective implementation of CAD are low when the primary objective is to reduce the number of draughtsmen. When as inevitably happens, the labour-savings are not achieved, the temptation for management must be to blame an uncooperative workforce, rather than accept that the original estimates were unrealistic. The high capital cost of CAD and the emphasis on labour-savings has led to pressure for two-shift working which, as well as being seen as anti-social and resulting in industrial relations problems, may also be very inefficient for control purposes.

Because the introduction of CAD has been aimed at reducing jobs, companies have often been forced to pay substantial premiums to get it accepted. Not only can this lead to future problems with other groups of workers seeking parity, but if the labour reductions do not materialize, in practice, then the payments were unnecessary. There is evidence to suggest that some companies have avoided investment in CAD because of the industrial relations problems they foresaw.

A further problem is that if CAD is purchased on the basis of an unrealistically high estimate of productivity gain, the size of the purchased system will be much too small not just in terms of the number of terminals, but also the central processor. When this happens, it will create the impression – probably incorrectly – that the CAD system is a failure.

When the expected productivity gains are not achieved, it is easy to find excuses; one of the reasons frequently quoted is the failure of companies to spend enough money on training. However, the lack of training is not always caused by the small amount that companies are prepared to spend. Pressure of work means that companies feel they cannot spare the time for their staff to be trained.

The emphasis on using labour-savings to justify investment in automation has resulted in manufacturers trying to optimize the ability of technology to replace humans, but with only limited success. With robots, for example, although their development has concentrated on features such as positioning speed, vision and touch, they are still very inefficient at replacing humans for anything but the most simple and repetitive tasks.

The aim with FMS has been to achieve unmanned operation. Despite the compexity of the control systems which have been developed, the response to any unplanned failure during periods of unmanned operation is normally for the system to shut down until the start of the next shift. With relative costs which may be £5/h for an operator and over £50/h capital cost of an FMS, unmanned operation does not make much economic sense if it is going to result in lost machine time.

To achieve the full potential of FMS the need is for the activity of the system to be independent of the activity of the operators, so that the FMS will keep running if the operators leave it for short periods such as to go to the stores or have a tea-break. The FMS is not unmanned and the operators are still available if anything goes wrong to take corrective action quickly in order to keep the system running. Running FMS in this way may not require additional labour, but a more flexible allocation of the hours being worked.

As discussed in an earlier chapter, the main potential benefits which can be obtained from AMT, in declining order of importance, are:

1. Increasing sales (or preventing sales being lost).
2. Increasing the profitability of orders.

3. Reducing cost of material content in products.
4. Reduced operating costs.
5. Reduced labour costs.
6. Reduced inventory levels.

Overcoming the problems of evaluating AMT has shown the need for a major change in the objectives of investment. Not only are the potential benefits much greater than had been thought previously but it has been found that the earlier emphasis on labour-saving was wrong.

Changing the emphasis to increasing the sales of more cost-effective products is not only more profitable, but it can result in an overall increase in the labour-force. By changing investment objectives away from saving labour, AMT will no longer be seen as a threat to jobs and, as a result, the implementation of projects is likely to be much more enthusiastic and effective.

14 Selecting technology

When managers start to investigate the possibility of investing in AMT, they have normally already decided the area of technology in which they want to invest. Typically the attitude is: 'I think we ought to invest in CAD [or FMS, CNC, robots, etc.], let's try to find an application which we can justify.'

Having found a potential application, they then go on to attempt to identify the benefits, but when they cannot identify enough direct savings to justify the investment, they will start to think up intangibles. This not only presents them with a problem in quantifying the benefits, it is also difficult to relate the benefits to the technical specification required to achieve them. When benefits identified in this way are quantified, it is found that although they may have a value, the value of many of them is negligible. In some cases, the value may even be negative because the additional cost required to achieve the benefit will be greater than the value of the benefit.

The danger is that by selecting technology in this manner, the selected specification is unlikely to be optimum and, in addition, the chosen area of AMT may not even be the one on which the company should be concentrating its financial and managerial resources. Starting to select technology by first defining the problems which have to be overcome means that it is possible to identify changes in the company that are needed, and from this, it is possible to establish the objective used to select the required technical specification.

When one looks at AMT in terms of its financial advantages, it can be seen that different aspects of AMT can be used to help solve the same problems. For example, CAD, MRP/MRPII and FMS can all be used to improve delivery performance and help to reduce stock levels, while CNC, robots, FMS and MRPII can all help to reduce direct production costs such as labour, WIP and operating expenses.

In selecting and evaluating AMT the major benefits should have been defined by identifying the major problems that need to be solved. However, there will normally be several other benefits which can be significant, in addition to the large number which are probably insignificant. When a company is investing in an area of technology with which it is unfamiliar, it may be unaware of some of the potential benefits and, as a result, may not include the ability to achieve these benefits in the technical specification.

When evaluating any project, the identification of costs is just as important as identifying benefits; this is especially the case with computer systems, such as CAD and MRPII, where the start-up and running costs can be considerably greater than the initial purchase and installation cost. For example, the typical annual cost of maintenance and insurance for a computer system may be between 10% and 15% of the purchase price. As a result, for a system with a working life of ten years the total cost of maintenance and insurance will be greater than the initial cost.

In order to help identify all potential costs and benefits, the following chapters include lists of both. It must be remembered, however, that the problems faced by any particular company will always be somewhat different to those faced by other companies. Therefore the lists must not be treated as being fully comprehensive.

Always technology is developing, with extra features becoming available which may increase the range of potential benefits and may also increase costs. An example of the way that costs change is that as computer technology has developed it is increasingly possible to operate quite large computers in a normal office environment, without the need for a special air conditioned computer room, thus helping to reduce the installation costs. At the same time, the complexity and size of systems is increasing, so that their start-up may involve a considerable cost for data entry.

Early computer applications were designed to automate existing procedures such that their introduction often had little effect on the rest of the company, but as AMT has become more complex its introduction can affect several other departments. For most applications, AMT must no longer be used simply to automate the existing procedures, and to obtain the major potential benefits means that the company's organization will need to be changed which, in turn, may involve considerable costs.

As discussed in earlier chapters, a number of factors have to be considered in evaluating any project, namely:

1. Physical working life.
2. Residual value at end of life.
3. Cost of capital.
4. Company tax situation.
5. Availability of grants.
6. Capital expenditure avoided by a purchase.
7. Capital assets made available for sale.
8. Planned utilization (for costing system).

In producing the lists of costs and savings in the following chapters all the intangible benefits which could be identified have been redefined into quantifiable terms. The lists have been refined on the basis of considerable experience of evaluating projects in industry.

While a single factor, such as improved product quality, can produce benefits in several areas such as reducing production costs and increase sales, several factors could result in savings in the same area, for example, both improved delivery and reduced selling price can increase sales. To try to avoid such duplication, the lists have been divided up into type of saving, rather than the cause of the saving. There is of course some duplication between the separate lists because different aspects of technology can provide the same type of saving and each list can be considered in isolation.

15 CNC machines

Although lathes and machining centres are the best-known types of **computer numerical control (CNC)** machines, the application of computer control to machines now covers almost every manufacturing process – e.g. grinding, pipe bending, sheet metal work and PCB manufacture. Although much of the discussion also applies to all the other types of CNC machine, for simplicity this chapter deals with investment in CNC lathes and machining centres. Despite the fact that CNC machine tools are probably the most widely used and understood aspect of AMT, with NC and CNC machines having been available for over twenty years, many companies have still not invested in them and even quite large companies may only have one or two CNC machines.

A major restriction on the rate of introduction of CNC has been the methods used by companies to attempt to justify investments which, as shown in an earlier chapter, have consistently understated the benefits of CNC. However, it is not only within companies that an incorrect methodology has been used, most authors who have tried to illustrate the advantages of CNC have understated the benefits in the examples they have used. In some cases, the return calculated has been less than half the value if a correct methodology had been used.

An examination of the literature advocating investment in CNC identified twenty numerical examples, of these nineteen used the same basic method to calculate the return on investment. This was to calculate the existing and proposed cost of manufacture for a representative component, or group of components; the difference between the two costs being used as the basis for calculating the return on investment. Taking the figures in the examples, and avoiding the incorrect use of depreciation and overheads, calculating the return showed that only one example gave the correct result; nineteen out of twenty had understated the return on investment.

When CNC machines are bought as individual machines, it is normally assumed that the only factors which will alter are those directly related to the machines being replaced and the rest of the factory will be unaffected.

This attitude is reflected in the list of costs and savings given later. However, if a number of machines are being bought, or if an investment in CNC is part of a wider project, then this assumption would no longer hold good and a much wider range of factors would have to be considered.

An investigation into the possible use of CNC is likely to identify several problems in the way that existing machines are being operated. In order that the savings which will result from solving these problems can be included in the evaluation, there can be considerable temptation to assume that these problems will be solved by installing CNC. It is important to consider these problems realistically and accept that, despite a resolve to make sure that the same problems do not occur with the new machine, the reality will be that once management interest has been transferred elsewhere, the original problems will probably return. If it were easy to eliminate the existing inefficiencies, the problems would no longer exist. Therefore, where problems are identified, their solution should only be included as a saving in the evaluation if detailed planning has been carried out into ways to eliminate them, and these plans are likely to be implemented.

It is often suggested in articles about CNC that set-up times will be reduced. However, many of the factors affecting set-up times are not machine dependent, for example, booking on/off, going to tool stores, waiting for inspection, reading drawings, gauging, etc. Even the time savings that can be achieved in factors such as tool setting may well be offset by extra time being taken in activities such as tape proving. A detailed investigation of existing practices may show that set-up are already minimized by foremen, who often load work in sequence to reduce tool changing. Any planned saving in set-up time which is included in an appraisal must be measured in relation to the actual current practice and the proposed change clearly identified.

BATCH QUANTITIES

Many authors suggest that the introduction of CNC will enable batch sizes to be reduced, thereby reducing the level of WIP and producing a saving which helps justify the investment. On the other hand, some suggest increasing batch sizes to improve the ratio of run time to set-up time, with the reduction in set-up costs being used as a saving. There are several different methods which can be used by companies to decide on batch quantity sizes, for example:

1. Net requirements for a period (e.g. monthly).
2. Net requirements for an order period (i.e. lead time).
3. Fixed quantity.
4. Multiples of fixed quantities.
5. As order intake.

6. Economic batch quantity (EBQ) assuming fixed demand.
7. EBQ with variable demand.
8. EBQ with price breaks.

Of these, the concept of an *economic batch quantity* appears to offer a way of balancing the conflicting aims of reducing the costs of set-ups and inventory. Unfortunately, most of the literature about EBQs is simplistic and based on components that have one operation where the costs of only one machine have to be considered. Even so, the formula to calculate an EBQ with reasonable accuracy may contain over twenty factors.

One of the main problems, in practice, of applying any EBQ formula, is that most components will require more than one operation, and involve several different manufacturing processes, but they will have only one batch quantity. The EBQ cannot change from one operation to the next and the batch quantity which may be optimum for one operation will be wrong for all the others.

Batch sizes are normally fixed by the *material control* ordering system, so that apart from a few special batches to try out the machine and tooling, the purchase of a single machine is unlikely to result in a change in ordering policy, especially if the change involves altering the rules within an MRP computer system. Much of the literature describing the advantages of CNC

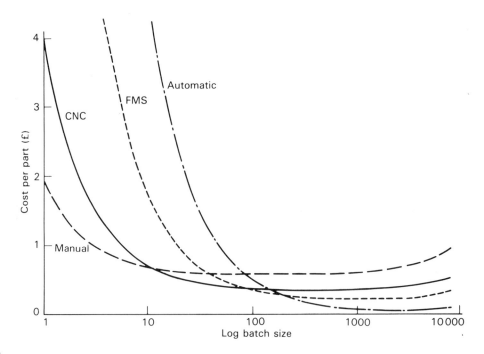

Fig. 15.1 Traditional view of batch size/machine type relationship

suggests that it is only viable for medium batch size production (with 15–50 off being a typical range). In practice, there are a large number of factors which can affect the profitability of investment in CNC, with batch size being only one of these.

Many articles about CNC include a diagram, such as in Fig. 15.1, suggesting that for any specific batch size there will be an appropriate level of technical sophistication required; however, there are a number of factors which determine the type of machine chosen, the main ones being:

1. Batch quantity and number of such batches a year.
2. The ratio between set-up time and per piece time.
3. Component complexity.

It can now be seen that, for the correct application, CNC can be viable from one-off production up to large volume manufacture. Unfortunately the widespread belief that CNC was only suitable for medium batch production has meant that many companies may not have considered investment.

To illustrate the relationship between batch size and machine viability, an example is taken of the replacement of manual machines by CNC. Three representative components are selected, each of which has a per piece time of 1.8 min on the manual machines and a set-up time of 30 min on both types of machine. One component is regarded as simple, another is average while

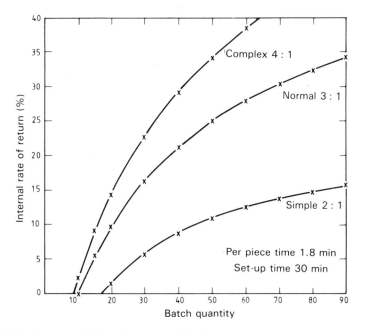

Fig. 15.2 Change of IRR as batch quantities increase.

the third is complex. It is calculated that the ratios of old : new per piece times will be 2 : 1, 3 : 1 and 4 : 1 respectively. Figure 15.2 shows how the internal rate of return (IRR) increases as the batch quantities increase for each of the three components.

If the old per piece time is 18 min, rather than 1.8 min, the set-up time is still 30 min, and the old : new ratios stay the same, the new times will be 9.0, 6.0 and 4.5 min respectively. Figure 15.3 shows the new relationship between IRR and batch quantities. In Fig. 15.2, CNC becomes viable only above batch sizes of 20, whereas in Fig. 15.3 it can be viable for batches of 2-off. In most companies there will be a range of components which comprise the projected workload, thus making the simplistic assumptions behind Fig. 15.1 even more unrealistic. In fact there is no range of batch quantities for which CNC is automatically viable.

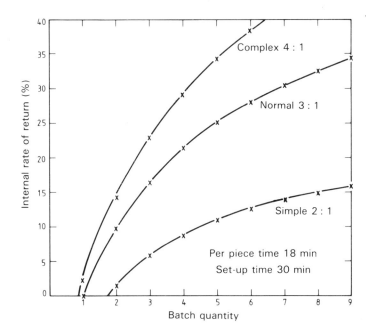

Fig. 15.3 New relationship between IRR and batch quantity.

In a company, always regarded as a 'one-off'-type company by its managers, CNC had never been seriously considered. The load on their manual lathes ranged from simple parts taking 6 min to complex ones taking 2.5 h each. When walking round the shopfloor, the large number of very small batches gave the impression that everything was made in ones and twos, and an analysis of the batch sizes gave the following results:

Batch quantity	Percentage of total batches
1 off	42
2 off	21
3–9 off	25
10–30 off	7
Over 30 off	5

However, when the analysis was done on the basis of load, rather than the number of batches, the figures became:

Batch quantity	Percentage of total load
1 off	20.5
2 off	17.2
3–9 off	23.0
10–30 off	10.3
Over 30 off	29.0

Although over 60% of all batches were less than 3-off, this represented less than 40% of the load, and detailed analysis showed that there were sufficient components suitable for CNC to make investment viable.

MACHINE UTILIZATION

As with set ups, there is a temptation to assume that the utilization of the new machine will be better than the old ones, especially when surveys of existing machines are likely to show that more than 50% of the total available time is non-productive. Although, as shown in Fig. 15.4, a large number of factors can affect utilization, only a few of these may alter as a result of buying a new machine. Any planned improvements which are included in an evaluation must therefore relate to specific factors where the proposed changes in operating procedures have been clearly defined. Because the motivation in an evaluation is normally to try to justify an investment, the emphasis will be on trying to identify areas where utilization can be improved; however, it is equally important to identify any areas where utilization will be adversely affected. For example, although CNC machines are becoming increasingly reliable, the lost time due to both planned and unplanned maintenance is likely to be higher than for manual machines.

Unlike manual machines, time is needed on CNC to prove out new programs, not only when the machine is new, but throughout its life as new components are planned for the machine, or existing designs and programs are altered. If any improvements in set-up times and machine utilization, which will result from changes in factory organization, are

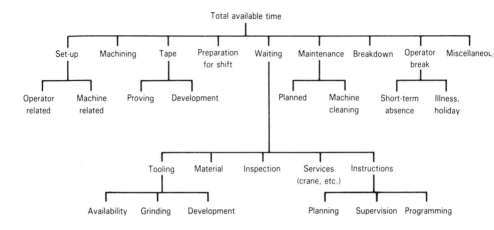

Fig. 15.4 Factors affecting utilization.

going to be significant factors in the financial justification, consideration should be given to whether the changes can be introduced without expenditure on the new machine. If this were possible, questions should be asked about why the changes have not been made already and how realistic are the new plans.

CNC machines do not need much operator involvement when they are running, as compared with manual machines, and as a result it is often suggested that they can be run with one operator looking after two or more machines, the aim being to increase the savings by reducing labour costs. If multiple machine/man operation is considered, any potential loss of utilization has to be taken into account. If an operator is working two machines, while setting either of the machines the other machine is also likely to be stopped waiting for a component change. This can also happen when the operator is resetting tooling. Unless the machines are being use for large-batch quantities of components with long cycle times, or they have automatic component change, the increased loss of utilization for both machines can easily offset the increased savings in operator wages.

For example, if the set-up time on a single CNC machine is 30% of the total batch time – and when two machines are being run by one operator – one machine will be stopped while the other machine is being set-up; to produce 70 machining hours on each machine would require:

	Machine A	Machine B
Machining hours	70	70
Set-up hours	30	30
Lost time	30	30

It would therefore take 260 h to produce 140 machining hours, compared with 200 h if the machines were run by one operator per machine. In such cases, the reduction in utilization must be compared with savings in operator wages.

In an evaluation it is important to avoid any double counting and to correctly identify whether factors have to be dealt with as costs or savings. For example, with some CNC machines that are producing very accurate components it may be necessary to run the machine for a considerable time at the start of the morning shift to ensure that it is fully warmed up before starting production. In such cases, the result is a loss of potential output, but this reduction in utilization is not a cost; instead it represents a reduction in the potential savings.

Another problem with CNC is that, unlike manual machines, it may not be practical to start machining a complex component with a long cycle time if the program will not be finished before the end of the shift when the operators will have to leave. This, again, reduces potential savings.

SCRAP AND REWORK

One of the major benefits of CNC compared with manual machines is their ability to produce complex components with a high degree of accuracy and repeatability. Not only does this provide the ability to design more complex components, but it can give considerable savings in scrap and rework. When this represents a major element in the evaluation, care is needed in the way that savings are quantified. Considering machine-related factors only, reducing scrap provides three direct benefits:

1. Saving in material costs.
2. Improvement in utilization of the new machine compared with the old.
3. Saving in previous operations which have to be performed on replacement components.

Allowances should also be made for the fact that batches of replacement components are likely to be small and therefore will have a higher ratio of set-up time to run-time.

If the level of scrap concerned is relatively low, it may be sufficient to value the scrap using the simple formula which is often used for WIP, namely:

Component value = raw material cost + 50% (labour + variable overhead)

If the reduction in scrap is a major factor in the evaluation, a more detailed analysis will be needed. Care must be taken to avoid the double counting which can result from including both the saving in the operators' wages from improved utilization resulting from reduced scrap, and the element in the value which represents the same operator's wages.

Reducing rework avoids the cost of carrying out the rework, and this will improve machine utilization if the rework is being carried out on the machine where the fault was created. However, with any rework caused by a CNC machine, consideration must be given as to how the rework will be carried out because, unlike manual machines, CNC may not have the ability to deviate from program, so that any rework may have to be done on another facility.

In addition to the direct savings from reducing scrap and rework, there are likely to be secondary benefits such as avoiding the disruption caused by interrupting production and changing set-ups which results from having to split batches. There may also be reductions in quality-control costs because the repeatability of CNC may enable the inspection of critical dimensions to be reduced.

In estimating the savings which will result from improved quality it is important to do this on the basis of expected quality standards over the whole of the machine's life, not just when it is new. As machines start to wear, the accuracy of their repeatability will reduce and component quality may deteriorate. Because of friction and inertia, the tolerances to which many CNC machines can be programmed will (even when new) be better than those to which the machine can produce components, especially if only small distances are being moved between coordinates.

START-UP TIME

Manual machines are normally bought to replace existing machines or to provide additional capacity. This means, then, that all the jigs, fixtures and tooling which are needed will normally be available and as soon as the machine has been commissioned it can be fully loaded.

Unlike manual machines, a full workload cannot be transferred to a new CNC machine as soon as it is operational because programs have to be written for each component and more than one program is often required for some components (e.g. machining the second end of a component on a lathe). Even if the CNC machine is replacing an earlier NC machine, new programs will be needed because the new control system will be completely different. Most articles advocating investment in CNC disregard the time taken from the initial commissioning of the machine to the stage where it is fully loaded and the maximum level of savings is being achieved. Because of the considerable improvement in productivity achieved by CNC, where one CNC machine is normally able to replace several manual machines, a large number of components may have to be programmed, and in a company making small-/ medium-size batches several hundred programs may be needed.

In order to estimate how long it will take for the new machine to become fully loaded, it is necessary to calculate the total number of programmes needed. In doing this an allowance has to be made for the fact that considerably more than 100% load will have to be programmed to achieve full utilization. This is so because it will be necessary to compensate for fluctuations in product mix and sales volume, which is a normal feature of batch manufacture; allowance has also to be made for re-programming to cope with design changes.

The rate at which programs can be reproduced is dependent on variable factors such as machine type, component complexity, programmer expertise and availability of computer assistance. In trying to estimate the average rate of programming, allowance has to be made for the time taken to prove programs on the CNC machine, as well as the time take to write the program.

There is little published information available about programming time, but it is likely that over an extended time period a programmer may be able to program components only at an average rate of between two and four per week.

COMPONENT SELECTION

An assessment of start-up time may show that full utilization will not be achieved until a long time after commissioning, possibly one or two years. It is important therefore that the first components to be programmed are selected in a way which will optimize the initial savings and utilization. The main advantages of CNC compared with manual machines are largely the result of the following factors:

1. Machine design allows higher metal removal rates.
2. Faster tool positioning.
3. Operations can be combined.
4. Complex shapes can be produced with single-point tools (e.g. eliminates need for radius, form and chamfer tools).
5. Programmer can plan optimum tooling, number of cuts, etc.

This means that the potential saving in machining time becomes greater as components become more complex. With most CNC machines, not all the components in the potential workload will be selected for programming, therefore it is possible to improve the financial viability of CNC by selecting those components which will provide the greatest improvements in productivity.

In the following example it is assumed that the set-up time for CNC is the same as for the old manual machine:

Batch quantity	Set-up time	Old piece time	Old batch time	CNC piece time	CNC batch time	Saving
100	30	5	530	2	230	300
12	45	35	465	10	165	300

If the criteria used to select components from the old machine was the largest batch size, or to maximize load, the first component would be selected. If, however, the choice was made on the basis of trying to maximize savings the second one would be selected. If the ratio of savings is calculated where:

Savings ratio = Set-up plus run time on old machine
───────────────────────────────────
Set-up plus run time on new machine

The ratio for the first component would be 2.30 : 1, and 2.82 : 1 for the second. If this were to be applied to all the components selected for a CNC machine, the profitability of the investment would be considerably increased. Ideally the first parts selected are those which will give both the greatest savings and the greatest initial load to improve utilization.

Where a small number of different components are going to be produced in large quantities, considerable effort can be devoted to optimizing the selection of components. However, in companies producing small/medium batch quantities, where a large number of components will be programmed for CNC, it can be difficult to identify the components which should be transferred to the new machine.

Traditional techniques for component selection, such as looking round the stores, are not very effective. However, MRPII systems can be used to produce lists of all the components which are planned for selected groups of existing machines, giving their annual usage and per piece times. These lists can then be used to help identify the components which are likely to provide the greatest *savings ratio*.

Table 15.1 shows a typical sample of the turret lathe load in a company listed in batch-quantity order. The new per piece times were estimated

Table 15.1 Components from turret load

No	Description	Batch quantity	Set-up	Per piece	Load
A	Collar	8	30	12	126
B	Rod	6	42	12	114
C	Spindle	4	30	6	54
D	Pinion	3	30	105	345
E	Washer	2	30	6	42
F	Sprocket	2	60	180	420
G	Shaft	1	30	120	150
H	Sleeve	1	42	90	132
I	Chainwheel	1	48	120	168

Table 15.2 Load arranged in saving ratio order

No	Batch quantity	Set-up	Old P/P	New P/P	Savings ratio
D	3	30	105	30	2.88
F	2	60	180	51	2.59
G	1	30	120	34	2.34
I	1	48	120	34	2.05
A	8	30	12	4	2.03
H	1	42	90	26	1.94
B	6	42	12	4	1.73
C	4	30	6	2.5	1.35
E	2	30	6	2.5	1.20

for CNC and the savings ratios calculated, on the assumption that set-up times were unchanged. Table 15.2 shows the load rearranged on the basis of saving ratio. When the total load was analyzed in this way, the larger batches tended to be at the top of the list, but this was not always so, and one consecutive sequence of batch sizes was: 3, 1, 1, 8, 24, 4, 2 and 6. Although it was easy to select the first few components to program when the load was not printed in saving ratio order, the subsequent selection was significantly different from the list in Table 15.2 which would optimize the potential savings.

VIABILITY OF CNC

Considerable improvements in productivity can be achieved by investing in CNC with figures ranging from 2.5 : 1 to 4.5 : 1 being quoted by various authors. This means that provided double-shift working is used, it is possible to justify many CNC machines purely on the basis of labour savings.

However, this improvement in productivity means that the new machine will have a considerable appetite for work and it may be difficult to find sufficient components to keep the machine fully loaded, unless some components are planned which provide a much smaller productivity improvement. In calculating the savings it is important to examine the whole of the potential workload, not just calculate savings on the basis of the small sample of components which will be the first to be programmed and which will provide the greatest savings. When evaluating more expensive CNC machines, the benefits from labour saving may be inadequate to justify the investment. Although improving labour productivity is important, there can be no other benefits which can be financially more attractive.

Although there is a wide range of types of machine and potential applications, it is possible to give advice on some of the factors which should be considered:

1. If the existing machines have got to the stage where they have to be replaced, investing in CNC will avoid investment in conventional machines, thus reducing the capital cost which has to be justified. However, to avoid double counting, if allowance is made for avoiding capital expenditure involved in replacing old machines on a 'like with like' basis, the savings in operating costs must relate to the replacement machines, not the existing ones.

2. The condition of the existing machines may be such that potential sales are being lost because of poor quality, delivery or lack of capacity. Many companies can reach the stage where the only way to stay in a particular market, or to enter a market, is to invest in new machines. In such cases, the contribution to overhead recovery from the extra sales is used in the appraisal.

3. Reducing the amount of work sent out for subcontract, or being able to take on subcontract work, can help to make an investment profitable, but as described in an earlier chapter, many companies understate the value of this by their incorrect use of standard cost data.

4. Investment in CNC may mean that subcontract work can be taken on, which will also provide work for other processes where spare capacity is available.

5. Because one CNC machine can replace several manual ones, especially if the CNC machine is double-shifted and the manual ones single-shifted, there can be a considerable saving in required floorspace. This benefit can be included in the evaluation, provided that it represents a cash flow saving.

6. Companies that are buying their first CNC machine may not have the maintenance expertise needed and will rely on having a service contract with the manufacturer, or with a specialist maintenance company. Not only does such a contract have to be included in the running costs, but allowance has to be made for the potential loss of utilization because even quite minor faults may stop the machine for several hours, or even days, until a service engineer can make a visit.

7. Where a company is only operating a single shift, but wants to run a CNC machine on two shifts to justify the investment, the additional costs involved are not just a shift premium for the operator, but the cost of heating and lighting the factory through the second shift. Safety considerations may make it unacceptable for an operator to be working a machine alone in the factory on a long-term basis; as a result, other shift workers may be needed, thus adding to the cost of shift premiums.

8. Unless a radical change occurs, such as starting a night shift, it is unlikely that there will be a change in the number of indirect personnel, such as supervision, as a result of a single machine purchase.

9. Costs for heat, light, power, etc. are unlikely to change by much as,

although the new machine may replace several existing ones, the total amount of metal removed will still be the same.

10. Because of the high cost of CNC machines, companies will normally have trained more than one operator per shift, in order to provide cover for holidays, sickness etc., thus adding to such costs as training and operator upgrading.

11. Where the investment in CNC is part of a wider project, the potential benefits can be much wider in scope. It may be that if individual machines are evaluated in isolation, they are not viable; but if the total project, including CNC, is evaluated, it may be viable.

COSTS AND SAVINGS OF CNC

The following list of costs and savings include only machine-related factors:

INITIAL COSTS

- Initial capital cost.
- Installation (foundations, power supply, crane, etc.).
- Training (operators, programmers, maintenance).
- Tape preparation equipment.
- Tool pre-setting equipment.
- Special tooling and toolholders.
- Subcontract, overtime and other costs of lost time during start-up.

RUNNING COSTS

- Programmers' wages and employment costs.
- Programming costs (e.g. tape purchase).
- Maintenance (including any maintenance contract).
- Extra expenditure on heat, light, power, etc.
- Operator upgrading.
- Additional shift premium or regular overtime payments.
- Location and workholding fixtures.
- Tooling costs increased by faster cutting conditions.

SAVINGS

- Operators' wages and employment costs for replaced machines.

- Wages and employment costs for secondary operations (e.g. marking out).
- Reduced scrap.
- Reduced rework.
- Reduced quality-control costs.
- Reduced disruption of production from lower scrap and rework.
- Reduced work sent out to subcontract.
- Subcontract work taken on.
- Reduced tooling costs (less form tooling, specialized tooling, etc.).
- Reduced jig and fixture costs (e.g. eliminate drill jigs).
- Reduced WIP from combining operations.
- Reduced component cost from redesign.
- Effect on sales of having better-quality products.
- Effect on sales of being able to design more complex products.

16 Flexible manufacturing

Some aspects of AMT, such as CNC, CAD and MRP, are well established and understood and the rate of technical innovation is relatively slow. Although this is still not the case with **flexible manufacturing (FM)**, the technology is becoming established and FM is no longer something which only very large companies can afford to experiment with. The stage has now been reached where companies of any size can consider investment.

The first problem is what is meant by FM. There is still no generally accepted definition, but FM, as discussed in this chapter, is taken to mean the following:

Manufacturing stations that are under computer control, so that they are capable of processing a number of different components, without the need of any significant human intervention to adapt the workstations to the different operations required, and which allow a variable quantity of different parts to be processed in sequence rather than in batches.

As with any definition, this one should be used as providing guidance rather than being a rigid rule. Using this definition, the concept of FM cannot only be applied to metal cutting machine tools, but to a wide range of processes such as PCB manufature, sheet metal production and product assembly.

The common theme is the introduction of flexibility into a manufacturing process to enable a company to increase its competitive ability. Although most of the principles can be applied to any manufacturing process, for the sake of simplicity, this chapter deals with the machining of prismatic and rotational components.

When FM is looked at from a financial rather than a technical viewpoint, it can be seen that there are four different concepts in terms of the type of benefit which can be achieved, namely:

1. Single machine flexible manufacturing modules (FMM).
2. Multi-machine flexible manufacturing systems (FMS).
3. Flexible transfer lines (FTL).
4. Fully integrated flexible manufacturing factories (FMF).

Most of the early development of FM was into FMS using machine centres or lathes, but the manufacturers of other types of machine, such as grinding, gear cutting and coordinate measuring, have been developing the technology which allows their machines to be used as either stand-alone FMM or integrated into FMS, FTL or FMF.

The first attempts to build FMSs were in the 1960s with Molins System 24 and the Variable Mission systems built by Cincinnati and Herbert Ingersoll. Unfortunately, the Molins System 24 was abandoned before completion and Herbert Ingersoll went into liquidation, thus it was only the Cincinnati system, in the USA, which continued in operation. The result of this was that when interest in FMS revived in the late 1970s there was virtually no operating experience available for companies planning to design FMS, and there was a high level of perceived risk and uncertainty. The designers of systems in the 1970s were unable to evaluate them in financial terms, because no one knew how to do so. As a result, the decision to build an FMS was a pure act of faith, with the designs being based on technical rather than business objectives. Although it is easy to be critical of these early systems, much of what seems obvious now only appears so with the benefit of hindsight.

One of the reasons why people were unable to evaluate FM is that they perceived 'increased flexibility of production' as a major benefit, but could not see how to include it in either the technical specification or a financial evaluation. Reports about early FMS suggest that they have suffered from a lack of flexibility and this is probably because the required flexibility was not defined and specified at the design stage.

Early attempts to define flexibility concentrated on trying to do so in such as way that the flexibility itself could be quantified such as the degree or percentage of flexibility. In fact, although the required flexibility has to be defined, flexibility itself does not have to be quantified because it is part of the technical specification. What has to be quantified are the financial benefits which the technical specification, including flexibility, provides.

The need to define flexibility is twofold, not only do the benefits which can be obtained from flexibility have to be included in the investment appraisal, but the technical specification must reflect the required level of flexibility. A company needs to be able to define the nature of the flexibility required in such a way that any proposed specification can be examined to see if it will be adequate.

As the complexity of FM is increased from FMM to FMF, so the nature of the financial benefits change and, as a result, so does the nature of the required flexibility. This means that each level of FM has to be considered separately. By identifying the benefits of FM it is possible to define the flexibility required to achieve those benefits and from this define the required technology.

The high cost of FM means that the technical specification must not be selected just to suit existing components and products. Consideration must be given to the way that products are likely to change in the future throughout the life of the plant. Even with the existing components, it is necessary to consider whether they can be redesigned to make maximum use of the potential benefits of FM.

The aim must not be simply to change the existing designs, so that components can be produced by FM, the requirement is to adopt a multi-disciplinary *value engineering* approach which starts by considering why the components are needed and what their function is. In doing this, it is necessary from the outset to have an understanding of the potential scope of FM, so that final components design can optimize the benefits of using FM.

By using this approach, products are likely to be redesigned and, as a result, the required technology may well change. The situation may then be similar to that experienced in some companies which redesigned their products in order to use automated assembly only to find that the design had been simplified to the extent that automated assembly was no longer required.

There is a need for considerable *production engineering* effort in finalizing product designs. It is only when all the detailed planning and programming is complete that operation times, tooling and fixture requirements can be established. In addition, it is not until the operation times have been established that the machine tool load and the required number of machines can be calculated. It is only then that it is possible to establish the detailed specification for machines and equipment.

Value engineering can be a lengthy and iterative process of producing revised designs, estimating production times, establishing capital costs and evaluating the investment. The product costs then have to be compared with that of alternative designs, possibly using different manufacturing processes. Fortunately, the required techniques are no different to those traditionally used by engineers.

MACHINE UTILIZATION

Investment in stand-alone FMM, as with CNC, is normally aimed at improving machine shop efficiency, whether by replacing existing machines or providing additional capacity. As such it would be considered as an alternative to investing in 'conventional' CNC machines. The design of FMM is normally based on that of CNC machines, so that the cutting speeds, feeds and depth of cut would be similar. The difference between FMM and CNC is not metal removal rates, but the potential to increase the percentage of available time that is spent cutting metal.

In order to achieve the maximum advantage from FMM, compared with CNC, the machine must be able to function independently of the operator. The aim being that, unlike CNC, when the operator leaves the machine, such as to go to the stores or for a meal break, the FMM will continue to run without any loss of output and, if required, be able to produce components in batches of one-off.

Two features are required in order to obtain the maximum improvement in utilization:

1. The FMM must have the ability to monitor its own performance and take any corrective action when necessary.
2. The concept of a batch set-up has to be eliminated, so that the FMM can change between different components with no more time penalty than the change between identical components.

In trying to establish what the improvement in utilization will be when compared with an equivalent CNC machine, the difficulty is that the conditions within any company will be unique, even different machines within the same company will have different levels of utilization. An additional problem is that studies of utilization always have somewhat different definitions for the categories used.

A number of studies of machine-tool utilization have been published and the correlation between them is sufficiently close that they can be used to illustrate the way that FMM utilization may compare with CNC. The result of the studies was as shown in Table 16.1.

Table 16.1 Summary of utilization studies

	%
Machining	54.5
Reset tools	3.7
Breakdown	6.25
Tape proving	6.6
Setting	9.0
Inspection	3.4
Wait work/tools, etc.	5.65
Miscellaneous (includes operator absence)	10.9

In trying to compare utilization a number of assumptions have to be made, namely:

1. The rate of production and utilization of CNC and FMM will be the same when the machines are running.
2. If the CNC machine uses shuttle pallets, there will be no difference in load/unload times.
3. The time to reset tools will be proportional to machining time, and is the same percentage for both machines.

4. Breakdown time is proportional to machining time, and is the same percentage.
5. The same type of work is considered for both machines.
6. Relatively few components are considered for both machines, so that tape proving can be ignored after the intitial start-up period.
7. The FMM will run independently of the operator, so that the setting, inspection and wait work/tooling applicable to CNC will not apply.
8. The FMM will run during most of the miscellaneous CNC idle time such as tea-breaks and operator absence; an arbitrary value of 75% is assumed.

Based on these assumptions, the categories in Table 16.1 are divided into two groups, the first being those factors which will apply to both FMM and CNC, the second being those which only apply to CNC. Eliminating tape proving, and dividing the miscellaneous time as discussed above, gives results as shown in Table 16.2. Although this gives the percentage of the available time spent on different activities, the comparison must also take into account any differences in available hours. Assuming that the CNC machine is worked on double-shifts (five day and four night shifts a week), each of which represents 39 hours a week, the FMM will be able to work for more hours

Table 16.2 Allocation of available hours

	%	
Machining	58.3	
Reset tools	4.0	
Breakdown	6.7	
25% of miscellaneous	2.9	
Sub-total	71.9	(applies to both FMM and CNC)
Setting	9.6	
Inspection	3.6	
Wait work/tools, etc.	6.1	
75% of miscellaneous	8.8	
Sub-total	28.1	(applies to CNC only)

Table 16.3 Comparison of working hours

	CNC	FMM
Standard shift hours	78	78
Meal-breaks	0	4.5
Shift-end	0	2.5
Available hours	78	85.0

because it can work during meal-breaks and carry on beyond the end of a shift. If the FMM runs during a 30 min meal-break each shift, and for 30 min beyond the end of each day shift, the available hours per week will be as shown in Table 16.3.

For CNC 58.3% of the available 78 h is spent machining, thus:

$$\text{CNC machining hours per week} = \frac{58.3 \times 78.0}{100} = 45.5 \text{ h}$$

With FMM there are two areas of improvement: first, a greater percentage of available time is spent machining; and secondly, an increase in available hours. Considering the first, only 71.9% of total CNC time is applicable to FMM, thus the percentage of available FMM hours spent machining is:

$$\frac{58.3 \times 100}{71.9} = 81.1\%$$

The increase in available hours then gives:

$$\text{FMM machining hours per week} = 85.0 \times 81.1 = 68.9 \text{ h}$$

Thus one FMM will do the work of:

$$\frac{68.9}{45.4} = 1.5 \text{ CNC machines.}$$

As discussed in the earlier chapter on CNC, there can be a considerable reduction in machine utilization if one operator is looking after more than one machine. The ability of FMM to continue working independently from the activity of the operator means that a multiple machine/man operation may be achieved without loss of output.

The technology required to enable FMMs to run independently of an operator is now well established for some types of machine, such as machining centres, and the additional cost penalty of an FMM compared to an equivalent CNC is considerably less than 50%. For many companies therefore an investigation into the utilization of their own machines may show that investment in FMM will be more attractive than investment in CNC.

SINGLE-MACHINE FMM

Here, in comparison with CNC, the main areas of financial advantage are:

1. *Capital avoidance.* Investment in FMM will avoid expenditure on alternative machines such as CNC.
2. *Labour-saving.* By increasing machine utilization, and by operating in

multi-machine/man configurations, the total labour requirement can be reduced.

3. *Quality improvements.* By eliminating the concept of a set-up the quality problems associated with set-ups are also eliminated.

The increased complexity of the machine and programs may mean that it will be longer before full utilization is achieved, and there will be some areas where FMM costs may be considerably greater than CNC, thus the start-up costs which may be greater are:

1. Programming and tape proving.
2. Work-holding, where multiple fixtures may be needed.
3. Tooling, toolholding and pre-setting equipment.
4. Additional training.

Although most of the running costs will be similar, there are some areas where there may be an increase, namely:

1. Maintenance: due to the increased complexity of the technology.
2. Upgrading of operators and programmers.

The programming and provision of work-holding fixtures for any component will be very expensive, so that relatively few components will be planned for an FMM. Although the objective is to be capable of producing components in batches of one, this is not because components with a low annual usage will be produced, but rather that the aim is to be able to respond to fluctuations in demand – if necessary, on a daily basis.

An additional reason for being able to produce components in batches of one, without any time penalty, is to reduce the number of work-holding fixtures that are needed. If the FMM is to be kept running while the operator is absent, such as during meal-breaks, sufficient fixtures will have to be pre-loaded with components to ensure that the machine will not run out of work before the operator returns. If the FMM is unable to change its set-up automatically, it may be necessary to make several very expensive work-holding fixtures for every component planned for the FMM. The financial benefits of FMM determine the flexibility needed to achieve these, namely:

1. The flexibility to enable the machine to produce the required range of component geometry, thus the FMM must have:
    (a) sufficient number of axis;
    (b) sufficient length of these axis;
    (c) sufficient number and variety of tools;
    (d) sufficient range of speed, feed and power to deal with variations in materials.
2. The flexibility to deal with any future design changes, or the introduction

of new products; this may extend the specification beyond that which is required for current component designs.

3. The flexibility to change set-up between any planned component without direct intervention of the operator, thus the FMM must have:-
   (a) sufficient program memory;
   (b) sufficient tool store capacity for at least two different components;
   (c) the ability to recognize and change between different components;
   (d) sufficient computer logic to deal with different component characteristics.
4. The flexibility to deal with changes in product mix; this can be achieved by the FMM imposing no penalty of time or reduced quality when changing between different components.
5. The flexibility to deal with changes in product volume. By having the capability to function independently of the human operator, such as being able to run during meal-breaks or between shifts, the capacity of the FMM is not curtailed by having to run for discrete shifts, as is the case with CNC, thus the number of hours per week which the FMM can run can be flexible.
6. The flexibility to be able to deal with variations in component raw material, for example, out of shape or hard castings.
7. The flexibility to respond to tool wear or failure without creating unnecessary scrap or rework, and by taking corrective action, avoiding the loss of utilization which would result from the machine stopping as soon as wear was detected.

In addition to the flexibility required to operate as stand-alone machines, some companies may invest in FMMs with the intention of linking a number of FMMs into an integrated FMS at a later date.

To achieve the required flexibility, a number of features are required, namely:

1. Automatic component load/unload on the machine.
2. Automatic change between different components with no time or quality penalty.
3. Continuous monitoring of tool wear and breakage, with the ability to take corrective action automatically, so that machining can continue.
4. Automatic swarf removal.
5. Automatic correction of out of tolerance machining.
6. Ability to check component raw material and respond to variations.
7. Computer and machine interfaces, so that workpieces, tooling, status information and command instructions can be transferred to and from the machine.

The technical specification must reflect these requirements, but the extent to which they can be achieved is different for prismatic and rotational components.

PRISMATIC COMPONENTS

Machines are normally based on machining centre configuration which provides automatic component changing; however, sufficient pre-loaded pallets are needed to enable the machine to keep running for the longest expected period of operator absence. A potential constraint is the capacity of the tool magazine because not only is there a need to provide back-up for all the tools subject to rapid wear or breakage, but to eliminate the constraints of set-ups the magazine needs to contain tools for all the components to be produced.

As part of the ability to monitor tool wear, control systems record the cutting life of each tool, so that they can be replaced after a predetermined time. They also record the tool size, including any allowance for wear, in order to apply the correct spindle offsets.

Removing tools from the magazine might cause problems if this data is not recorded in such a way that it can be attributed to each individual tool when the tools are replaced. This situation can arise if the magazine is too small and tools have to be taken out and replaced later – so doing means that an element of unpredictability is introduced.

When all tools that are needed can be retained in the system, under computer control, the operators have the confidence to allow the machine to keep changing components without intervention. Taking tools out of the system and replacing them later, probably into different positions in the magazine, removes this confidence, so that operators want to monitor the changes in components, thus reintroducing the constraints associated with set-ups.

An increasing number of FMS manufacturers can supply a central tool store with automatic transfer to and from machines, such that once a tool has been put into the system, it is continually under computer control and all the information about tool size, cutting life and location are known by the FMS control system. Because these stores may be of any size, they can contain all the tools required for all the components planned for the FMS, thereby removing the constraints encountered when a range of different components have to be produced. As the cost of such systems reduces, they will become available for FMM, as has already happened with sheet metal manufacture.

Once all the required tools are stored under computer control, the changing of tools in the machine magazine can be planned for each change of component in order to minimize down-time. As the order in which components are scheduled through the system will keep changing, so will the number of tools which have to be changed. Ideally the change of tooling should be scheduled, so that the first tools required for the next component are inserted in the magazine while the machine is still operating.

As computer-controlled tooling systems become more sophisticated, the problems of scheduling tooling associated with machining centres will be eliminated. In defining the required technical specification the criterion to be borne in mind is:

If a complete change of tooling is required when components are changed, the machine will start to operate on the new component as soon as the first tool is changed. The objective being the ability to change between different components in under a minute, even if a complete change of tooling is required.

Although this may seem a difficult objective to achieve, some manufacturers claim that they can already achieve this.

Control systems increasingly have the ability to monitor tool wear and breakage and automatically replace worn tools. However, the ability to respond to tool breakage is often limited to stopping the machine to await an operator. Based on experience of manual and CNC machines, this appeared to be a major constraint; however, operating experience of FM now suggests that the incidence of tool breakage is very low, except for a few tools such as very small-diameter drills.

Tool breakage is expected in some cases, and then the computer program needs to include tool checking routines with conditional instructions if breakage is detected, otherwise tool breakage may be symptomatic of other problems; thus checking by an operator is essential. Unplanned tool breakage in normal operation is sufficiently unusual that stopping the machine should not have a significant effect on utilization.

When using FMMs for large volume manufacture, the component raw material, such as pressure die castings, is normally very accurate, but as quantities reduce, so material accuracy will decrease. When FMMs are used for medium/small-volume production, such as for a large range of similar components, they will need the capability not only to measure material variations, but take corrective action such as extra cuts or adjusting machine off-sets.

ROTATIONAL COMPONENTS

Automatic change between different components can produce work-holding problems if there is significant variation in size, the problem being in changing chuckjaws, component load grippers and automatic tailstock movement. Some manufacturers now claim to have overcome these problems, but it is essential to identify the full range of component sizes to ensure that the machine selected has got sufficient flexibility.

Component changing is normally done with either an overhead gantry running along the axis of the machine or a robot mounted in front of the machine. Although the latter may be the cheaper method, it can impose operational constraints because robots (being potentially dangerous machines) should be fully guarded, for safety reasons; thus having a robot on the front of a machine may restrict the operator from approaching the machine to monitor performance while it is running. Unlike machining centres, tool storage capacity should not represent a constraint because the variety of tools is normally small in comparison with the tools magazine size.

HYBRID COMPONENTS

Machining centres have the ability to combine opertions, such as milling and drilling, on one machine, and now there is a trend towards developing machines which combine machining centre operations with turning. Initially, this has been done by adding the facilities for drilling and milling to vertical boring lathes and horizontal lathes; and although power and rigidity was originally limited, the trend is towards machines which combine the full machining centre and lathe capabilities.

Such machines offer the possibility of designing highly complex components which could not be produced in separate operations. In addition, the quality advantages of producing complex components complete in one operation are considerable – reducing the number of set-ups and eliminating problems of concentricity. Although hybrid machines are still very expensive, their costs are likely to reduce considerably as designs become established, such as happened in the past with the early NC machining centres.

MULTI-MACHINE SYSTEMS

Many companies will find that while FMS may be viable, it is possible to obtain all the benefits by investing in an equivalent number of FMMs at a much lower cost. When evaluating FMS therefore it is necessary to identify what additional benefits can be obtained from an integrated system to justify the additional costs.

While an FMM can provide considerable improvement in output compared with an equivalent CNC machine, a FMS may produce less work than the equivalent number of FMMs because of the problem of balancing the load on all the machines in the system. In comparing the output of FMS with FMM there are three factors that have to be taken into consideration, namely:

1. Productivity.
2. Machine Availability.
3. Utilization.

Productivity is the efficiency with which the machine produces components while it is running, and because FM is normally based in CNC technology, there is unlikely to be much difference between the productivity of CNC, FMM and FMS.

FMS is normally based on FMM technology and both can operate during meal-breaks and between shifts. As a result, the hours when they are available, although considerably greater than for CNC, will be similar. The difference between FMM and FMS is in utilization, with different percentages of the hours available being used for producing components.

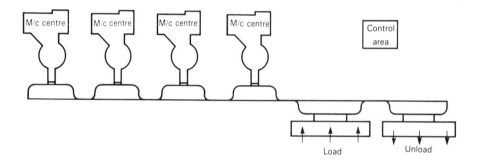

Fig. 16.1 Interchangeable-type FMS

The loss of utilization of FMS compared with FMMs is highly dependent on the design of the FMS, thus an interchangeable-type system, such as shown in Fig. 16.1, where all the machines are of the same type, will tend to have a much higher machine utilization than a complementary-type system, such as presented in Fig. 16.2, which comprises a number of different types of machine. Although it may be possible to keep one type of machine in a complementary FMS fully utilized, it is likely that the work content of the planned components will provide an equal balance of load between the different types of machine. Most of the financial benefits of FMS, which are additional to those obtainable from FMM, come from the ability to achieve shorter, more predictable and more reliable delivery of the components planned for the system, which should be the components that affect product delivery.

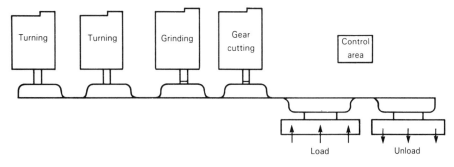

Fig. 16.2 Complementary-type FMS

Most companies suffer from fluctuations in sales volume and product mix, such as is shown in Fig. 16.3, and, because the financial benefits of FMS come from the ability to rapidly respond to market needs, it is unlikely that the load on the FMS, and therefore its utilization, will be constant. While it may be possible to improve utilization by planning additional components, which can be dual-sourced, there is a danger that in so doing the problem of utilization is merely transferred somewhere else in the company.

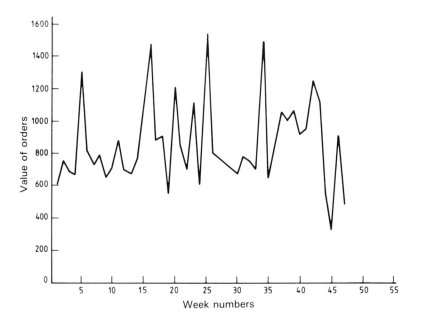

Fig. 16.3 Fluctuations in order intake.

One of the implications of FMS investment is that it can involve a major change in the balance between fixed and variable costs. When companies are labour intensive, a large proportion of the standard cost can be varied as output varies, such as by hiring and firing labour, thus making costs relatively insensitive to changes in sales volume. On the other hand, much of the standard cost with FMS represents depreciation of the capital cost. Unlike labour, the total value of depreciation cannot be changed as sales change, therefore the standard cost is highly dependent on forecast sales volume.

The result is that if sales reduce, utilization decreases and standard costs will increase. If selling prices are then increased because of this, a further reduction in sales can result, starting a vicious downward spiral. By realizing that the danger exists, it is possible to avoid the problem by not automatically changing selling price to reflect changes in standard cost.

To illustrate the magnitude of the problem faced by companies trying to achieve full utilization, a duration of 1 h on a four-machine FMS may correspond to 6 h on a CNC machine and 15 h on manual machines. If the four-machine FMS has a maximum of 110 h a week available (440 machine hours), and the product mix and volume fluctuates by ± 10%, the planned load could be 100 hours ± 10 h. Thus to ensure full utilization it may be necessary to transfer up to 20 h a week of FMS load from elsewhere. This would represent up to 300 h a week fluctuation in the load on the rest of the machine shop.

Considerable emphasis was placed on trying to achieve unmanned manufacture in the design of early FMS because this was seen as the ultimate saving. In some cases, in order to avoid tooling problems, unmanned operation was achieved by reducing the output of the FMS.

However, most of the potential labour-savings can be achieved by investing in FMMs, and the difference in manning levels between FMS and the equivalent number of FMMs will be very small. As with FMM, the need is not so much unmanned manufacture, but the ability to run independently of the operator.

Trying to run unmanned for long periods may be counterproductive because it can result in a loss of utilization and output. It may not result in any overall reduction in the number of operators, but may just mean having all the operators on one shift, the only saving being in shift premium costs.

In comparison with FMM, the main financial benefits of FMS are:

1. The effect on sales volume of being able to quote shorter delivery times, while at the same time improving the company's reputation by increasing the reliability of delivery promises.
2. The ability to quote a premium or higher selling price for improved delivery.
3. Reduced level of work-in-progress because of shorter manufacturing lead times.

4. Reduced need to carry finished component and finished product stock to meet customer needs.
5. Reduced lead times and lower stock levels allows for faster introduction of new products.
6. The effect on sales volume of being able to quote for more orders due to the increased ability to match product specification to customer's requirements.
7. Reduced manufacturing cost of making a product which only has those features needed by each customer, rather than a standard product containing surplus features.
8. The effect on sales volume of being able to offer a cheaper customised product.
9. Predictability of delivery reduces the need for the traditional methods of achieving delivery such as subcontract and overtime.

The flexibility required to achieve these benefits is:

1. The flexibility needed to produce the required range of component geometry has the additional requirement that multiple manufacturing processes may now be involved.
2. The flexibility to schedule components through a system where the number and sequence of workstations visited by components can vary.
3. The flexibility to move components between workstations in a situation where not only the operation times may be different for each of the processes involved, but the times for any workstation's load will change relative to the other workstations as the product mix changes. These changes will be additional to the overall changes in load caused by fluctuations in sales volume.
4. The flexibility to cope with future design changes and the introduction of new products, not just in terms of machine size and configuration but the capability of dealing with changes in the balance of load between the various workstations. This not only requires sufficient workload capacity, but also control systems are needed which can deal with the changes.
5. The flexibility to deal with the failure at any work station, whether this is associated with faulty components, tooling problems, mechanical or electrical breakdown, etc., in such a way that disruption and loss of output from the whole system is minimized.

Many manufacturers now offer standard modular FMS and the concept of these is becoming well established. Although most of such FMS are based on machining centres, possibly with the addition of inspection, deburring and washing-machines, some of the larger manufacturers now offer multi-process FMS – e.g. machining centres and lathes.

The advantage of standard modular FMS is not just that customers can buy proven technology, but that the very high development costs of FMS do not have to be paid for by each customer; thus the development of very sophisticated systems is rendered economical. In order to provide the flexibility needed to achieve the financial benefits, a hierarchy of control systems is required, namely:

1. *Machine tool controllers*, which operate the machine functions.
2. *System controllers*, which operate inter-machine functions such as pallet transporters.
3. *Management control*, which schedules the flow of work within the FMS.
4. *Outside control*, which directs work to and from the FMS.

While FMS can operate without having the level 4 control directly connected to the others, it is essential that the first three levels are fully integrated.

Most FMS have been developed by manufacturers using their own machines, but as the scope of FMS expands, the need will be to combine multiple processes using FMMs from several manufacturers. Some control system manufacturers are developing systems whereby customers can buy different makes of machine tool and combine them into an FMS. At present, this only works if all the machines selected have the same make of control system, and although this can overcome the problems of control systems associated with multi-process FMS, the potential user may still have major problems in the physical transfer of workpieces and tooling due to lack of standards.

As FMS becomes a practical production facility a major requirement is that operators must be able to control the system in such a way that they can consistently achieve production output targets. The advantage of standard FMS is that although the control systems are highly complex, they are becoming easier to use because the complexity of the system is not seen by the operator. The result is that FMS can now be run by experienced machine operators rather than by computer experts.

FLEXIBLE TRANSFER LINES

When product life cycles were long, companies in high-volume manufacture invested in dedicated transfer lines because the advantage of very low unit costs outweighed the disadvantages of high capital cost and the long changeover times between products. The fact that production may have to be stopped for several months to install new transfer lines acted as a constraint on new product development. Because of the increasing pressure on companies to keep updating product designs, or to introduce new products, plus the need to be able to customize products, traditional dedicated transfer lines are becoming uneconomical.

With FMS, the objective is to extend to batch production the benefits of short lead times and control of output associated with transfer lines, while retaining the flexibility of batch manufacture. With FTL, the objective is the converse, namely to retain the advatages of line control while adding the benefits of the flexibility associated with batch production.

In large-volume manufacture there are two types of application for FTL: one is for FTL as an alternative to a dedicated line for full-scale production, while the other is to use an FTL for the introduction of new components. The advantage of this second application is that dedicated high-volume lines can be designed to suit components which are already in production, and the initial teething problems associated with new products overcome.

Because the second type of application would have to be able to produce a wide range of components, the need would be for a considerable amount of flexibility, such as is needed in an FMS. Consequently, the design of such a line would tend to be similar to FMS. It is therefore the first type of application which needs further consideration because the requirements are very different from those of FMS.

One of the advantages of FTL, as an alternative to a dedicated line for full-scale production, is that it may be possible to produce more than one component on a line, thus reducing the capital and operating costs. Another advantage of an FTL is that it can cope with component variations such that, unlike a dedicated line where all components have to be the same or require a long changeover time, it becomes easier to produce products which can be customized to suit various market needs.

The benefits of an FTL to a dedicated line, are:

1. The effect on sales volume and selling price of being able to introduce new products more frequently.
2. The effect on sales volume and price of being able to produce product variants because components no longer have to be identical.
3. Reduced loss of output (i.e. sales) during product changeover.
4. Reduced cost of capital and installation and cost of product changeover in the future.
5. The benefits of improved quality (e.g. extra sales and reduced warranty payments) resulting from the ability to introduce design improvements during a product's life.
6. Increased ability to expand the line's capacity to deal with future increased sales.

In addition to the above, considerable improvements in operating performance are possible such as increased utilization and faster cutting conditions. However, the financial benefits of this come not so much from reduced operating expenses, but from the ability to achieve the planned output with less machines in the FTL, thus reducing initial capital costs.

The requirement for flexibility in an FTL, which is considered as an alternative to a dedicated transfer line, is therefore:

1. The flexibility to enable future new products to be produced without the major rebuilding or replacement which is a feature of dedicated lines.
2. The flexibility to enable design changes to be introduced, such as for improved quality or reduced cost, throughout the life of a product.
3. The flexibility to monitor tool wear and breakage on all tools, so that individual tools can be changed as required, thereby allowing the line to run at optimum cutting conditions and avoiding the loss of utilization which is a feature of conventional lines.
4. The flexibility to enable component variations to be produced, so that products can be customized.
5. The flexibiliy to produce more than one component on one line.
6. The flexibility needed to enable the line to run independently of the operators, so that it is not constrained by shift times and therefore can be operated to suit sales requirements by responding quickly to changes in sales volume.
7. The flexibility to modify the amount of work done at each workstation in order to improve line balance.
8. The flexibility to perform more than one function at any workstation, thus reducing the number of workstations required.
9. The flexibility to increase the capacity of the line to suit future sales increases by inserting additional standard design workstations and then balancing the line.

While FMS is bridging the gap between batch and mass production, for large-volume manufacture with very short cycle times the use of FMS based on CNC configuration may be too expensive because it would be uneconomical to have a matching centre at each stage in the line. However, manufacturers are now developing the required technology such that it is possible to buy modular units for building into an FTL which have the required flexibility, without many of the features of CNC machining centres.

In selecting such units a number of features are required. One of these is the ability to monitor tool condition, and corresponding component quality. The aim is that all the tools can be run at optimum cutting condition, and automatically changed within cycle time, before component dimensions go out of tolerance. Here the objective is the ability to operate the line with zero downtime. The ability to introduce design improvements and new products, plus the potential of producing variants, means that the spindle positions relative to the workpiece must be variable, and that the spindles must be capable of holding alternative types and sizes of tool.

One of the constraints of conventional lines is that each workstation can normally only perform one type of function, whereas by incorporating toolchanging in an FTL, it has the potential ability of carrying out more than one type of function per workstation. Here the advantage is that of greater scope for the line balancing and the possibility of reducing the number of workstations.

At present, transfer lines are designed for a specific component for which future sales volume has to be predicted. This means that lines either have to be designed for over-capacity at extra cost, or the company has to accept the potential limitation on sales volume. The development of standard modular systems, such as with FMS, will help overcome these constraints by providing the ability to extend the line as sales increase by adding additional modules and rebalancing the line.

FLEXIBLE FACTORIES

Companies are increasingly operating in volatile markets which have rapid changes in sales volume and product mix, and where there is a constant need to introduce new products and enhance existing designs. Where large batch or mass production would be appropriate, some gains can be made from investing in FMS or FTL, but these benefits may be insufficient to remain competitive and the company may have to invest in a completely integrated factory. In such a factory the total process from goods inward, through component production and assembly to despatch, including all material movement, is under direct computer control.

While the initial capital costs of an FMF can be very high, so too can the financial benefits. This means that a company setting up a new manufacturing unit (e.g. in an overseas market) may find that the additional capital cost of an FMF was more than compensated for by the additional sales and reduced operating expenses. For a company already established in a market, and faced by a competitor who has invested in FMF, the investment in a similar facility may represent the only way to remain in that market. In extreme cases, the penalty of not investing is for the company to cease to exist.

An FMF will probably comprise a number of FMM, FMS or FTL which are integrated, so that when trying to define the requirements of flexibility in an FMF, the need is to identify the additional requirements, namely:

1. The flexibility which the individual elements need to enable them to operate as part of the total system.
2. The flexibility which enables the company to supply any potential customer with the specification they want at the time they want it.
3. The flexibility to change the products produced to suit future changes in market requirements.

4. The flexibility to operate with minimum stock levels and without the cost penalties normally associated with operating in fluctuating markets.

A distinction has to be made between an FMF and a factory where the co-ordination is done by computer systems, such as MRP/MRPII, which rely on human interfaces for data and output. One of the features of conventional factories is the lack of data accuracy which results in a considerable element of uncertainty. Thus uncertainty in conventional factories is compensated for by introducing safety factors such as buffer stocks or extended deliveries.

The inaccuracies are such that the advocates of performance measures for control of MRP systems suggest setting target levels of 95% accuracy of inventory records, but even if companies are able to achieve such a target they will still have a 5% error rate. The objective with FMF is to integrate the whole factory operation under direct computer control, so that by eliminating data errors it is possible to achieve 100% predictability. It is only when this becomes possible that all the safety factors in stock and lead times can be eliminated.

In building an FMF the requirement is not for computer integration (e.g. via MAP, etc.), which needs interaction between systems, but the ability to transfer management control information in predetermined format. Because this can be achieved by linking currently available non-compatible computers to transfer alpha numeric data in ASCII code, it is possible to build an FMF and obtain the financial benefits using existing technology.

SELECTING INVESTMENT IN FMS

Because the nature of the financial benefits obtainable from FMS are different to those from CNC, this will be reflected in the criteria used for component selection, and this in turn affects the selected design of FMS. In a previous chapter, it was shown that it is possible to maximize the savings from CNC, by selecting components which maximized productivity. In the early days of FMS, it was assumed that a similar process of component selection was needed, with simulation being used to help the trade-off between component savings and system cost.

The technical complexity and lack of operating experience meant that the designers of FMS in the late 1970s saw the use of simulation as being essential to help overcome the uncertainty and high level of perceived risk. The subsequent publicity given to the use of simulation then led to the widespread belief that any company considering investment in FMS had to start by using simulation to model their requirement.

Manual techniques for building a model which could be manipulated in order to stimulate how the real world would behave have been used for a long time in a wide variety of applications; in fact the builders of Stonehenge probably built a model to try to simulate tipping up the stones. It was the advent of computers which meant that by the late 1970s the technology was available not only to build FMS, but to use computer simulation to predict its operation.

Because computer simulation was being developed at the same time as the concepts of FMS, a lot of early research was not aimed at developing FMS, but at developing simulation techniques, using FMS as a model. As a result, by the mid-1980s there were probably more simulation packages available than there were actual FMS. Fortunately, the stage has now been reached where both FMS and simulation have progressed from the experimental stage to practical production technology, so that the way simulation is used has now changed.

There are four main uses for simulation in FMS:

1. Specification and selection by customers.
2. System design by manufacturers.
3. Control of FMS operation.
4. Teaching and research in universities, colleges, etc., where it is impractical to buy an FMS.

Once it is realized that the nature of FMS benefits are different to those of CNC, it can be seen that the criteria for component selection must also be different. As the major benefits of FMS come from having shorter, more reliable and predictable product delivery, as opposed to component delivery, the components selected must be those key components which directly affect product delivery.

Many years before coding and classification systems were developed, production engineers were selecting major components for special attention and grouping together the machines needed to produce them. This system of machine grouping was called 'family planning' (FP) and was based on commonsense analysis and experience and few factories operated without a number of these families of machines.

Group technology (GT) attempted to formalize this process and apply it to the general machine shop by using a classification system to group components and machines. Although the problems of low machine utilization in GT cells can normally be offset by using low-cost manual machines, the high capital costs of FMS means that it would prove to be grossly uneconomic for general machine shop components. It is only when FMS is used for FP groups of high-value 'A'-class items that it can be economic.

The first stage of component selection should be to define existing product delivery performance and compare this with the performance that the Marketing Department specify as being necessary if the company is to compete in its selected market.

In trying to improve delivery performance it is important to examine the total delivery lead time because it has been found that in many companies the pre-manufacturing time for producing documentation represent almost 50% of quoted delivery time. Concentrating efforts on improving pre-manufacturing activities may be more cost-effective than investing in FMS. In order to identify the changes needed to improve delivery performance **critical path analysis (CPA)** techniques should be used because it is only those components which lie on the critical path that need to be considered for FMS.

The use of CPA will also help to identify any improvements needed in bought-out components or materials, or any changes needed in pre-manufacturing procedures. Using CPA will result in a Pareto-effect, such that reducing the lead time of a very small number of components will have a significant effect on delivery. But as the number of components considered increases, the effect on delivery decreases, a point is soon reached where a rapidly increasing number of components have to be changed to produce an increasingly small improvement in delivery.

Relating the cost of FMS investment to the benefits of improved delivery performance will show a cut-off point where the rapidly increasing size and cost of FMS cannot be justified by the small additional improvement in delivery. For most companies, this cut-off point will be easy to identify without detailed analysis because FMS capacity can only be increased in step form by having additional machine tools. At the same time, delivery performance is improved in steps (e.g. daily, weekly or monthly as appropriate), with each improvement rapidly increasing the number of components which would have to be planned for the FMS.

As the benefits of FMS come from improved delivery performance, it is important that FMS output can respond to fluctuations in order output, both for sales volume and product mix. In a traditional batch manufacturing factory the high level of WIP and long lead times means that the workload is insensitive to short-term fluctuations in sales input. As a result, production engineers may be unaware of the magnitude of the problem they will be faced with in having to respond directly to short-term fluctuations. Figure 16.3 showed the way that order input can vary, and in Fig. 16.4 it is shown how, even if the company has a full order book, the load on a group of machine tools can vary as product mix varies.

The main benefits of FMS result from its effect on sales, but as a result of achieving these benefits, the level of sales will increase which, in turn, requires an increased capacity in the FMS. In order to estimate this increase, it is necessary to try to predict future events, but however good the analytical techniques, the result can never be exact. Fortunately, the modular design concept of FMS helps to eliminate the need to estimate an exact figure.

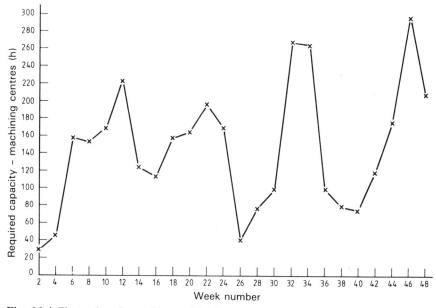

Fig. 16.4 Fluctuations in machine-tool load.

With interchangeable types of FMS, a company needs to estimate the minimum capacity required in the short term and the maximum potential long-term capacity, in order that they can buy a system which initially contains the minimum number of modules, but which too has the capability of having additional modules installed as the required output increases.

With a complementary-type FMS, there will normally be one type of machine which determines the capacity of the system; and with modular designs, it will be possible to add an extra machine of this type to increase capacity in the future. However, this may mean that a different machine type now controls capacity, so that further increases in the capacity of the whole system needs a different type of machine to be installed each time capacity is increased.

Fortunately, the planning techniques involved are the same as those which always have been used to design and balance transfer lines. Although many factors need to be considered in calculating required FMS capacity, the result does not have to be exact because the installed system can only comprise discrete numbers of machines – i.e. 2, 3, 4, etc.

Provided that allowance is made for future expansion, the required size of system can be established using conventional **industrial engineering** techniques. There is no point using simulation to calculate that a system needs 3.56 machines because the decision will be either to install three machines and leave space for a fourth, or to install four machines at the start. In addition to the number of modules to be built into an FMS, there are a number of other variable factors which need to be specified:

1. Size of machine tools.
2. Number of machine tools.
3. Size of component buffer store.
4. Size of auxiliary tool store.

As with calculating the number of machine tools, the sizes of component buffer and tool stores need only to be calculated on the basis of initial requirement and maximum future requirement. Any underestimation of initial capacity can be corrected later by installing extra modules – as long, of course, as the system selected and the floor space allocated allow for this. Other variables which may not affect the FMS manufacturer's specification, such as the number of fixtures or special tools required or the number of load/unload stations, are not critical because they can be increased as required on the basis of operating experience.

In considering the need for simulation, one has to start by identifying which are the factors that can be varied as a result of using simulation. In so doing, it will usually be found that with standard modular designs all the factors which can be varied are those where it is not critical to obtain exact estimates of future requirements. Not only is it unnecessary to calculate an exact figure, but it is unrealistic to expect that such a figure could be calculated.

In the past, many potential users of FMS were put off by the perceived risk involved, thus an essential objective for manufacturers is to portray FMS as proven technology. The ability to select standard FMS from a catalogue and to be able to visit companies to see similar FMS in operation not only makes it easier for engineers to relate FMS technology to their own requirements, but also helps to eliminate the perceived risk associated with early FMS. Unfortunately, the use of simulation as well as suggesting that each FMS has to be designed to suit each individual, also encourages the belief, because many engineers do not understand simulation, that FMS operation must needs be taken on trust, or that FMS investment is suitable only for those large companies which have the required technical expertise.

The attitude, in the past, has been that simulation was essential, but the stage has now been reached where many manufacturers no longer use it for their standard systems. The attitude which should now be adopted is that simulation should only be used where the need is proven and where the required data cannot be obtained using conventional techniques. By concentrating on the use of traditional techniques, such as value analysis and CPA, not only are companies able to use their own staff to do the selection but they will have a much greater understanding of the objectives and function of the FMS than if they have used simulation, which probably required the use of outside experts.

For most FMS, the only variable factor which might require simulation is the loading of automatic guided vehicles (AGV) or rail guided vehicles (RGV). Because RGV loading is highly dependent on the sequencing logic (such as 'push' or 'pull' loading) built into each FMS – and this logic will be different for each manufacturer – it is extremely difficult to reflect this logic in a simulation program. The use of simulation will not alter the way the RGV is going to operate because this is determined by the logic in the FMS computer system (which has to exist before the simulation is carried out), so that the only factor determined from using simulation is the number of RGVs.

Where the machine cycle time is very short such that even on a small FMS (e.g. two or three machines), the RGV utilization will be high; the components are likely to be sufficiently small that a conveyor system, rather than an RGV, can be used for transport. For most FMS the number of RGVs (normally either one or two) will be self-evident. Where the number is not obvious, experience has shown that conventional method study will provide just as reliable a result as simulation. Fortunately, the decision is not a critical one because, where there is any doubt, manufacturers will design the FMS such that it can operate with two RGVs, but initially will install only one.

FMS for special applications would normally be of the complementary type, comprising machines from more than one manufacturer, the FMS being designed and built by the company which is going to use it or by a company that specializes in such work. The experience of companies that have designed and built such one-off FMS has shown that there are major design problems, but the problems do not relate to the factors which can be determined by the use of simulation.

The problems encountered relate to the integration of the control systems of individual machine tools, RGVs and so on, into the required hierarchy of control needed for FMS, or such physical problems as the ability to transfer components on pallets between work stations which may be at different heights and use different methods of work-holding. For special-purpose FMS designed by the user company, an extra factor discouraging them from using simulation is that while manufacturers, consultants and academics may have an ongoing use for simulation, companies designing their own FMS normally have a one-off requirement. The high cost and long learning curve of simulation, combined with a probable lack of confidence in the result, will dissuade companies from buying a package.

Not only may the use of an experienced outside consultant be very expensive, but the person doing the simulation has to make a large number of assumptions – many of which may be implicit. The danger is that the consultant may not appreciate the implications of these assumptions in the operation of the company while, at the same time, the company may be unaware that these assumptions have been made. The result, which has already been seen in practice, can be the failure of the FMS to achieve its objectives.

If simulation has been used to design an FMS, it seems logical also to use simulation to optimize its running. This belief was encouraged by the experience of some of the early FMS, where there were major problems in trying to optimize machine utilization. Simulation was used to try to resolve these conflicts. However, most of the problems that arose were the result of design limitations in the FMS, for example, the set-up constraints imposed by the lack of a central computerized tool store and automatic tool replenishment system. As designs have improved so the problems disappeared, and with them the need to use simulation.

In the control of FMS the need is to be able to calculate the optimum loading sequence for components based on constant updates on the availability of machine tools, fixtures, pallets, tooling, workpieces, etc. Fortunately, the work flow will tend to be unidirectional, and the number of components and machines to be scheduled will be relatively small, so that the number of permutations that have to be considered will also be relatively small. As a result, real-time computer scheduling can be used to achieve optimum throughput.

FMS CASE STUDY

The case study here is based on actual company figures, although for clarity some of these figures have been simplified and several minor benefits omitted as they did not have a significant effect on the result. The company in this case study has an annual turnover of £9 million and makes hydraulic pumps and valves. The variety of options they can offer customers is large, so that although some standard items are made for stock on the basis of sales forecast, most components are manufactured in batches to suit orders received, the batch sizes representing a month's requirements.

The main castings were machined in a self-contained section which comprised a mixture of conventional milling and drilling machines and some early 'first generation' NC machines. There were fourteen machines in total, of which some were single- and others double-shifted; however, this tended to vary as load changed. Because of the age and condition of the machines, reliability was an increasing problem, as was declining quality standards. The company therefore had four main alternatives to consider:

1. Do nothing: this was rejected because the consequence would be declining quality and delivery, with resultant long-term loss of market share.
2. Subcontract: this was rejected because it would have resulted in loss of control of the components which were critical for product delivery.
3. Replace with CNC machines.
4. Replace with an FMS.

It was decided that the last two alternatives should be investigated in detail, and as CNC investment was the cheapest and easiest option, it was considered first.

The workload on the casting machining section was studied in detail and considerable effort put into replanning the components; in some cases, this involved design changes. On the basis of the new planned times and sales forecast, it was calculated that five CNC machining centres, double-shifted, would be required. The expenditure would be £700,000, and this would be spread over three years.

The next stage was to investigate FMS, and because investment in FMS was perceived to have a considerable element of risk, the evaluation was carried out using conservative estimates. Here the assumption was that if the project appeared viable using these figures, it would be an attractive investment in practice. Costs therefore tended to be over estimated and benefits were underestimated.

An examination of the planned workload, including an allowance for the increase in sales expected to result from the improved delivery provided by FMS, showed that by using the FMS for a 24-hour, five-day week, a three-machine system would have adequate capacity, leaving the weekends for maintenance, or to cope with any peaks in the workload. In calculating the required capacity it was assumed that the machining times would be the same as for CNC, but there would be a considerable increase both in machine utilization and operating hours.

One of the main objectives in using FMS was to reduce component lead times, and to do this required improvement in the total process time which included inspection and washing. As a consequence, a co-ordinate measuring machine was incorporated into the FMS. A washing machine was also considered, but the extra cost was not thought to be justified because the existing washing facility had spare capacity and did not represent a bottleneck. Including an additional washing machine into the FMS would not significantly reduce lead times.

The total cost of the FMS was £1 100 000, of which the machine tools and measuring machine represented 75%. One of the features of the FMS, compared with CNC, was the high cost of fixtures and tooling. The CNC machines would have been run by setter/operators using relatively simple fixtures and setting tools as required; but with the FMS, all tools would require pre-setting and special pre-setting equipment was needed. While the tooling itself was mainly standard, a large number of special toolholders were needed.

Fixtures proved to be a major item of expenditure because more than one fixture had to be made for many components, in order that enough work could be loaded to run the system between shifts, and also to give the flexibility that was needed to cope with fluctuations in workload. The aim was to plan the workload on a daily basis; and to keep down the number of fixtures many were designed such that multiple components could be loaded. In some cases, two operations were executed on one fixture, so that components could be produced complete. The total cost of fixtures and tooling equipment was £150 000.

One potential problem with the FMS was floorspace because, unlike CNC where the machines could be fitted into existing spaces, a large area was needed in one location for the system and peripherals (computer room and tool pre-setting area). Although this area was not much different in total to that occupied by the old machines, the FMS had to be installed and running before the old machines could be removed. Provision had also to be made in the layout for the possibility of future expansion of FMS capacity. Fortunately, it was possible to find enough space elsewhere in the factory, although some cost was involved in re-layout.

Because the company had reached the stage where their minimum invest-ment was £700 000 for five machining centres, the evaluation was to compare the additional cost of FMS with the additional benefits. While the additional costs were relatively easy to identify, great care was needed to avoid any double counting of benefits because many of the benefits of the FMS would also have to be obtained with CNC. For example, there were considerable savings in scrap and rework costs, but most of these could be achieved with CNC; similarly, the savings in labour had to be based on five operators per shift for CNC, rather than the much higher original level.

Because of manufacturing lead time and the consequent inflexibility of the ordering system, Marketing had been unable in the past to quote for short delivery orders except the limited range of stock models. The very short lead times of FMS would not only allow more enquiries to be quoted for, but as delivery would be better than their major competitors, a high proportion of these extra quotes should result in orders.

The company assumed an eight-year working life, with zero resale value at the end of that time; the figures used in the evaluation are as follows:

1. Capital cost of £1 100 000, phased over three years; the three machine tools would be delivered and paid for at the end of year zero and commissioning would be completed by the end of year 1. Because programming and fixture design would not be completed until year 2, £50 000 was budgeted for that year.
2. Capital cost of five CNC machines at £140 000 each would be avoided, this was spread over three years.
3. The FMS would operate with three people on days and two on nights, thus saving two day-shift and three night-shift operators. The basic wage of £165 a week is increased for labour on-costs (National Insurance, welfare costs, etc.) and shift premium to give an annual cost per operator of £11 412 for days and £15 177 for nights. Savings are assumed to be:

year 1 – one night-shift; year 2 – one day and two night; and year 3 and onwards – two day and three night.
4. Using CNC, the components would still be produced in monthly batches, but with FMS the total lead time would be under one week. Not only would this reduce shopfloor work-in-progress, but the change in ordering would also reduce finished component stocks. The book value of the stock reduction would be £125 000 and, of this, the cash flow value would be £75 000 in year 2, the tax advantage of the stock reduction being £17 500 in year 3.
5. Marketing estimated that sales should increase by at least 5%, giving a contribution to overhead recovery of £157 500 a year from year 2. Although competitors would eventually improve their delivery performance, the annual saving will still be valid because, without FMS, the company would then have started to loose market share.

One of the problems in an evaluation is estimating the timing of cash flow changes, especially with complex projects such as FMS where there are likely to be a lot of unforeseen problems. Because the FMS chosen was of an established design, with other similar systems already in operation the main risk perceived was not that the system would be unable to produce the components, rather that it would take a long time to become fully operational.

In the evaluation it was assumed that by concentrating on critical components to start with, many of the savings would be obtained by the end of the first year, but it would be two years before the level of full savings was being achieved.

Tax is calculated on the basis of a 35% rate and capital allowances on the basis of a first-year allowance of 25%, with the allowance in subsequent years being 25% of the remaining reducing balance.

The table shows the annual cash flows used in the evaluation. For interest, the first evaluation was carried out using only the figures which related to improved manufacturing efficiency, namely labour and stock reduction. This showed the return to be 7.6% internal rate of return (IRR) and −£84 738

	Year 0	Year 1	Year 2	Year 3	Years 4–8	Year 9
Capital cost	−670 000	−380 000	−50 000	–	–	–
Capital avoided	280 000	280 000	140 000	–	–	–
Capital tax	–	34 125	34 344	17 883	Reducing	3 183
Labour-saving	–	15 177	41 766	68 355	68 355	–
Stock reduction	–	–	75 000	–	–	–
Extra sales	–	–	157 500	157 500	157 500	–
Revenue tax	–	–	−5 312	−52 243	−79 049	−79 049
Net cash flow	−390 000	−50 698	393 298	191 495	Reducing	−75 866

net present value (NPV) which, when compared with the 15% after tax of capital, showed the project was not viable.

However, when the effect on sales was included, the return increased to 35.2% IRR and +£311 642 NPV. Because the estimates allowed for the perceived risks involved, and were generally considered to be conservative, the evaluation showed that the investment was attractive.

Chapter

17 MRP and MRPII

The use of computers for material control and production control has led to the development of material requirements planning (MRP) and manufacturing resources planning (MRPII) systems. Because MRPII is often considered to be an extension of MRP, and the management techniques used for selection and evaluation are similar for both systems, for convenience of discussion MRP and MRPII will be referred to as MRPII.

Surveys of companies show that MRPII is one of the most common AMT investments, but although MRPII involves considerable initial expenditure and high ongoing running costs, most companies have regarded its introduction as 'inevitable', rather than as an investment which has to be evaluated. This attitude has been encouraged by a belief that computer systems, such as MRPII, are somehow different and cannot be evaluated in the same way as machine tools. This attitude to MRPII can have serious consequences, such as the following:

1. Withdrawal of management support if the benefits which result from the use of MRPII cannot be identified.
2. MRPII can require major expenditure before any returns are forthcoming, but the lack of quantified objectives prevents progress being monitored in terms which are understandable to top management (e.g. costs, benefits and return on investment).
3. Without financial objectives, the type of system selected and the time scale for implementation is decided by subjective means. The problem is normally compounded by a lack of MRPII experience in the company.
4. Introducing MRPII represents a long-term commitment, with the implementation normally extending over several years; without detailed financial objectives, any disruption caused by failures elsewhere in the company may be blamed on MRPII.
5. In the absence of a financial justification, with the decision to invest

often being made by a 'project champion' who is convinced it is essential, MRPII becomes vulnerable to management changes or priority reappraisals.

6. Introducing MRPII may be championed because it is the 'fashionable' thing to do; as a result, there is a danger that if the financial advantages have not been estimated, it will be abandoned if fashion changes, as has occurred with techniques such as group technology.

7. Companies which could achieve substantial benefits from MRPII may fail to introduce it because of the high costs involved and the inability to show that it will be profitable.

Any company considering MRPII is faced with a number of decisions; the first is whether to invest in MRPII or to concentrate financial and management resources on improving other aspects of the company's operation. Assuming that MRPII is identified as the required area of investment, the next decision is to define the level of sophistication needed.

Managers trying to select the most appropriate system may be very knowledgeable about material and production control, but have little or no experience of computers and computerized MRPII. At the same time, they may be faced with a choice of over a hundred systems, with the suppliers of each producing arguments as to why their own system is the most suitable.

When installing a new CNC machine tool, it is often possible to influence the initial cash flows by selecting those components which will provide the greatest savings as the first to be programmed. With MRPII, the scope for influencing the initial profitability can be much greater, partly because of the much longer implementation period and partly because of the ability to change the sequence in which the various elements of many MRPII packages can be installed.

COSTS AND BENEFITS OF MRPII

The main ways that a company is affected by MRPII are:

1. Reduced paperwork and lower clerical costs.
2. Reduced disruption of production.
3. Controlled stock levels.
4. Shorter and more reliable product delivery times.
5. Increased ability to supply customers with the required product specification.

The first three areas are those considered when MRPII is viewed as a way of improving manufacturing productivity, and contain the direct savings which managers normally are able to quantify. However, it is the last two areas which contain the major financial benefits and these represent the effect which manufacturing can have on the total company.

Just as important as quantifying benefits is the need to quantify both initial and running costs. Companies which have no previous experience of MRPII may be unaware of the major long-term costs commitment being made with an investment whose running costs over the system life are likely to be considerably greater in total than the initial cost.

The following checklists have been compiled to help managers identify potential areas of costs and savings; it is not claimed that they are comprehensive, but they are designed to help identify the main areas to be included in an evaluation.

COSTS

Installation and start-up costs

- Computer hardware.
- Computer installation, including building alterations.
- Software purchase.
- Internal costs for customizing purchased software.
- External costs for customizing purchased software.
- Writing software in-house.
- Consultancy costs to assist with both system selection and implementation.
- Project team costs for selection of system.
- Company-wide education of personnel, such as senior managers, who need to understand the system.
- Education and training of people who will directly operate the system.
- Cost of temporary staff to input data or to run duplicate system.
- Overtime or shift premium for existing staff to input data or run duplicate system.
- Cost of temporary staff for checking and reconciling stock levels.
- Overtime or shift premium for existing staff to check and reconcile stock levels.
- Cost of disrupted production during implementation, including lost sales.
- Cost of subcontract or overtime to avoid lost production during implementation.
- Redundancy costs.

The costs of a feasibility study should not include any expenditure which would still be incurred if the decision can be made not to proceed. Thus the only costs included are those which will arise after a decision has been made to invest. Two categories of education are included to emphasize that it is not just the people who will directly operate the system that need training, managers in other disciplines (e.g. sales and design) need to understand what MRPII does and how it can help their departments.

There is not a rigid division between initial costs and running costs, for example, a company may introduce MRPII in a number of discrete stages or modules, with the installation costs being spread over several years and the annual running costs increasing in line with the expansion of the system.

Running costs

- Hire or lease of hardware and/or software.
- Maintenance contract for hardware and software.
- Insurance.
- Operating costs (e.g. electricity).
- Consumables (e.g. special stationary).
- Hardware expansion.
- Software updates.
- System management.
- Computer support staff.
- Ongoing education and training for new personnel.
- Additional clerical personnel for data entry.
- Additional works personnel for perpetual inventory checking.
- Staff upgrading.
- System back-up facilities.
- Premiums for regular overtime or shift working by computer staff.
- Concentrating on implementing MRPII may prevent other planned improvements being undertaken.

Most authors emphasize the labour-saving which can be achieved with MRPII, but MRPII involves high levels of data entry; controls are needed such as perpetual inventory checking; and computer support staff may be needed. Therefore, as well as identifying savings, it is equally important to identify departments where extra staff may be needed to operate the system.

BENEFITS

Labour-savings

- Clerical labour (from reducing paperwork systems).

- Indirect production labour (from reduced progress-chasing, work-moving, etc.).
- Stores labour (reduced kiting).
- Inventory control labour (reduced need to reconcile stock levels).
- Direct production labour (fewer set-ups of split batches and improved productivity).
- Direct support labour (e.g. inspectors and supervision).
- Reduced overtime payments.
- Lower recruitment and training costs (from lower personnel numbers).

Some improvements will not directly reduce labour; for example, while supervisors should spend less time progress-chasing, the number of supervisors may not be reduced, rather they will spend more time improving the efficiency of their departments. The saving therefore is not reduced labour, but improved productivity.

Stock reduction

Various factors within a company can contribute to an overall reduction in stock levels:

- Manufacturing WIP (as a result of shorter lead times).
- Assembly WIP (reduced delays from avoiding unplanned shortages).
- Raw materials (improved ordering policy and supplier progressing).
- Finished components (resulting from shorter lead times and improved ordering).
- Unwanted stock (avoid ordering duplicate or unnecessary parts).
- Bought-out components (orders placed to bring in parts as required).
- Obsolete stock (identified for disposal).
- Spares stock (achieved through improved spares requirements planning).
- Scrap material (scrap improvements from a range of separate areas).
- Lost stock (improved systems prevent components being either 'lost' or wrongly re-ordered).
- Finished product stock (reduced need to build for stock).
- Component and material standardization (increased ability of designers to reduce variety of raw material and components held in stock).

Direct savings

- Machine running costs (associated with reduction in direct labour).
- Increased capacity reduces need for regular subcontract.
- Reduced load fluctuations reduces need for short-term subcontract to meet delivery dates.

- Capacity created to take on subcontract work.
- Subcontract work taken on (ability created to control such work).
- Lower capital expenditure (improved utilization of machines).
- Reduced stores and production facilities (e.g. fewer lift trucks).
- Reduced floor area (cash flow savings only).
- Reduced scrap and rework caused by making parts to obsolete specifications.
- Reduced scrap from making unwanted components.
- Reduced scrap and rework associated with having fewer split batches and 'panic' jobs.
- Reduced cost of late dispatch (e.g. air freight and express delivery).
- Reduced payment on penalty orders.
- Reduced warranty and service costs by despatching correct specification.
- Products made to customer specification rather than a universal design which has unnecessary features.
- More accurate parts lists avoid despatching unnecessary components.
- Reduced production costs from component standardization.
- Avoidance of planned expenditure needed to maintain existing systems.
- Reduced cost of annual stock check.

Purchasing savings

- Bulk orders with call-off can be established.
- Forward planning of purchase requirements can avoid premium payments for quick delivery.
- Orders can be geared to quantity/price optimization.
- Staff can concentrate efforts on competitive buying, vendor appraisal, etc.

Cost management

- Better cash flow management, achieved by controlling stocks and deliveries, reduces bank overdraft costs.
- More accurate quotations reduces unprofitable orders.
- Feedback control relates production costs to sales estimates.
- Improved variance analysis enables corrective action to be taken.
- Reduced internal and external cost of annual audit.

Sales improvement

(That is, either increasing sales or preventing loss of potential sales.)

- From shorter deliveries.
- From more reliable deliveries.
- From lower costs (ability to offer a cheap customized product).
- Increased ability to match product specification to customer's requirements.
- From an improved reputation for quality (fewer incorrect or missing parts).
- Increased sales of spares, achieved by improved delivery and stocking policy.
- From more frequent introduction of new product designs and design changes.
- Higher initial sales, achieved by earlier launch of new products.
- Increased market penetration over product life due to earlier launch.

A DCF evaluation considers cash flow changes over a project's life, thus an estimate is needed of this life. While it may be assumed that MRPII will be a permanent company feature, with periodic replacements of computer hardware, it should be remembered that MRPII itself may be replacing a 'first-generation' computer system installed ten to fifteen years ago for stock control and costing:

In the same way, MRPII may in turn be replaced in another ten or fifteen years by some advanced integrated system which directly links design with machine operation. Fortunately, variation in product life beyond ten years have very little effect on the DCF return, so that little error is introduced into the evaluation by assuming a ten-year project life.

Many of the problems faced by companies when installing MRPII in the past may be a result of their not having established clearly defined, quantified and measurable objectives and timetable for introduction. Investment appraisal has got to be carried out as an integral part of the process of producing the technical specification and comparing vendors, as well as establishing the objectives and timetable for implementation.

The ability to carry out a financial evaluation, which includes all the factors identified as relevant, prior to the introduction of MRPII has important implications for a company considering such a system, namely:

- The financial analysis enables management to view MRPII in understandable terms and can show that it will be a very profitable investment, thereby increasing management support and ensuring allocation of adequate resources.
- Quantified and measurable objectives can be set which enables progress to be monitored and, when necessary, corrective action can be taken.
- A system can be selected which allows the major potential benefits to be obtained.
- Implementation can be planned to ensure that the greatest financial benefits are achieved at the earliest date.

- Because the benefits of MRPII are company-wide, the evaluation must involve managers from non-production departments, thus leading to a much wider understanding of the system.

Because of the complexity of MRPII, and the long timespan of its introduction, carrying out periodic re-evaluations during implementation as experience is gained of MRPII operation can help to identify any factors which were not foreseen during the initial selection and evalution. In addition, because it may take several years to install a complete system, the needs of the company's market-place may well change during that period, so that the original priorities will need to be revised.

One of the most expensive things that a company can do is to invest in a MRPII system and start to implement it, only to find that as they gain experience there are major benefits which their system is incapable of achieving.

MRPII CASE STUDY

The company manufactures process plant for the food industry and has an annual turnover of £13 000 000. Sales are dominated by a small number of large contracts, each worth several million pounds. As a result, the workload on the factory suffers from extreme peaks and troughs, with extensive subcontract being used to deal with the peaks. The delivery quoted to customers is always much shorter than manufacturing considers possible, thus increasing the need for subcontract and overtime working.

Although the company has a range of products which it can offer, each contract involves a considerable amount of detail design work to match the customer's required specification, with extra features often being added without their cost being fully charged to the customer. Because of the difficulty of forecasting future orders, the company policy is that they only manufacture to order, and that stockholding is limited to raw material and low value standard components (e.g. nuts and bolts).

The company has installed several microcomputer-based systems in recent years, such as for Stock Control and Accounts, and a minicomputer-based CAD system. Unfortunately, these are all incompatible, so that data cannot be transferred between systems, for example, the Drawing Office (DO) produce a handwritten Bill of Materials for each order which then has to be entered into both the Stock Control and Job Costing computer systems.

All the existing systems, except CAD, are very limited in the functions they can perform, so that the intention is to replace them all with a single MRPII system. This will comprose the following modules:

- Estimating.
- Sales Order Processing.
- Nominal Ledger.
- Sales Ledger.
- Purchase Ledger.
- Payroll and Pensions.
- Stock Control.
- Bill of Materials and Master Part File.
- Purchase Order Processing.
- Works Order Processing.
- Routing and Operations.
- Material Requirements Planning.
- Capacity Planning.
- Job Costing.
- Quality Control.

In order to install the system and obtain the benefits from its use, there will have to be several major changes in the company's operation, namely:

- The recording of work done on the shopfloor is very inaccurate and it can take up to two weeks for data to be entered into the existing systems; consequently feedback to Production Control and Costing is poor. At present, when orders are unprofitable there is no way of knowing if this is because of failings in Manufacture, Design or Estimating, or even of knowing with any confidence which orders are profitable. Negotiations are needed to get the shopfloor personnel to record accurately all work done, so that the data in the computer is up to date and reliable.
- The existing Bill of Materials produced by the DO, are very inaccurate and badly structured; therefore a new Bill of Materials has to be designed and the company's product range transferred onto this.
- The stores system is very poor, so that many of the transactions are not being properly recorded; as a result, no one has confidence in stock records. The stores areas have to be made secure and all receipts and issues must be properly recorded.

This means that not only will the company have to install the new MRPII system, with all the changes needed in each department directly using the system, but other major changes in company operation have to be introduced. Because of this, it is assumed that it will take eighteen months before the company starts to obtain the financial benefits of the investment. Although it may take three years to get the new system fully installed, by concentrating on the major savings, these will be achieved first.

Initial costs

	£	
Hardware (capital)	123 800	
Software (capital)	150 000	
Computer Room (capital)	10 000	
Installation and wiring	10 000	year 0
Training	2 300	year 0
Training	6 000	year 1
Customizing software	4 000	year 0
Data entry and Start-up	10 000	year 1
Data entry and Start-up	5 000	year 2

Annual running costs (from year 1)

System Management	20 000
Maintenance	33 000

It is assumed that the running costs (consumables, electricity, etc.) will be paid for by replacing the existing systems.

Savings

The major savings will be as follows:

- At present, the time from the receipt of an order to documentation being issued onto the shopfloor represents nearly 50% of the total delivery time. By speeding up the pre-manufacturing stages, the manufacturing lead time can be increased by at least 50%. This, combined with improved shopfloor scheduling, will increase machine and labour utilization, resulting in a reduction in subcontract. Reducing the present £1 200 000 annual cost of subcontract by 10% (minus the variable cost of producing the work in-house) gives a saving of £42 000 in year 2 and £84 000/year from year 3.
- The present system for estimating prices for quotations is highly imprecise, and because the company will always tend to receive the orders for which they have underquoted, many orders are of marginal profitability. By improving the data available from the Costing System and improving the estimating and quotation procedures, it is estimated that the profitability of orders can be increased by at least 1%, giving a saving of £65 000 in year 2 and £130 000/year from year 3.
- Ensuring that all changes requested by customers, after they have placed an order, are correctly costed and charged to the customer will increase

the profitability of orders by 0.5%, giving a saving of £32 500 in year 2 and £65 000/year from year 3.

- Eliminating transcription errors and improving the accuracy of the Bill of Materials, thereby eliminating the ordering of unwanted components, while at the same time avoiding the present situation where shortages are found in the Assembly Department because some component had not been ordered, will give a saving in production costs of £18 000 in year 2 and £35 000/year from year 3.
- Improved capacity planning will allow the company to quote for additional orders which can be used to fill in some of the troughs in the workload. It is estimated that sales can be increased by 1%, giving a contribution to overhead recovery of £26 000 in year 2 and £52 000/year from year 3.
- Avoiding the manual transfer and re-entry of data between systems will provide a labour-saving, but this may be offset by the additional stores and shopfloor clerical labour needed to improve the accuracy of data. As a result, no allowance is made for labour-saving.
- The increase in manufacturing lead time will increase the amount of Work-in-Progress, but it is thought that this will be offset by a reduction in raw material stocks and improvements in scheduling Purchase orders. Therefore no allowance is made for any changes in inventory.
- The new system will allow departments, such as Purchasing and Quality Control, to become more efficient and thereby reduce costs; however, no allowance has been made for these savings.

Table 17.1 Annual cash flows

	Year 0	Year 1	Year 2	Year 3	Year 4 onwards
Capital cost	−284 500	–	–	–	–
Capital tax	–	+24 894	+18 670	+14 003	Reducing
Installation	−14 000	–	–	–	–
Training	−2 300	−6 000	–	–	–
Start-up	–	−10 000	−5 000	–	–
Running costs	–	−53 000	−53 000	−53 000	−53 000
Less subcontract	–	–	+42 000	+84 000	+84 000
Better estimates	–	–	+65 000	+130 000	+130 000
Customers' changes	–	–	+32 500	+65 000	+65 000
Wrong ordering	–	–	+18 000	+35 000	+35 000
Extra sales	–	–	+26 000	+52 000	+52 000
Revenue tax	–	+5 705	+24 150	−43 925	−109 550
Net cash flows	−300 800	−38 401	+168 320	+283 078	Reducing

Taking a ten-year project life, 35% tax rate and 12% cost of capital, Table 17.1 shows the cash flows used in the evaluation; these give an internal rate of return (IRR) of 43.3% and a net present value (NPV) of +£649 365. In order to find out how sensitive this result is to variations in the estimated savings, some of the factors were altered in turn. If the reduction in subcontract was 5% rather than 10%, the IRR would be 38.4%. If the increase of profitability from improved estimating was 2% rather than 1%, the IRR would be 56.6%. If the increase in sales was 5%, rather than 1%, the IRR would be 63.7%.

18 Computer aided design and manufacture (CAD/CAM)

Any company considering CAD/CAM is faced with a number of decisions. The first is whether to invest in CAD/CAM or to concentrate resources on improving other areas of the company. Assuming that CAD/CAM is identified as the required area of technology, the next decision is the level of sophistication needed.

There are over 200 different CAD systems available, and CAD has expanded from the ability to produce two-dimensional drawing to include facilities such as finite element analysis and three-dimensional, solid modelling. In addition, CAD is being expanded into the production of control tapes for CNC machine tools (CAD/CAM), to produce process plannings (CAPP) and even to directly operate machine tools (DNC). Each of these extra features, when available, will add considerably to the cost both of hardware and software, and therefore must generate additional savings.

Although integrated CAD/CAM is normally portrayed as the objective to aim for, a company has a range of options for producing CNC control tapes:

1. Integrated CAD/CAM.
2. CAD with a separate dedicated CAM system.
3. CAD with separate programming by machine-tool operators.

With process planning, there is also the potential options of either integrated or separate systems. Because integrated systems are only one of the alternative options available, it is necessary for a company to start by identifying its requirements for CAD, and evaluating that investment, before evaluating the additional costs and benefits of the alternative approaches to CAD/CAM and CAPP.

CAD

The early development of CAD was aimed at improving the efficiency of the design process. This trend was reinforced by attempts to justify the investment, concentrating in trying to reduce Design Office (DO) costs. It has now been found, however, that the major financial benefits of CAD come from its use as an integral part of a company's overall management control and information system, rather than an aid to reducing DO costs.

As discussed earlier, the concentration on trying to justify CAD using DO savings led to the use of unrealistic estimates of improvements in the productivity of draughtsmen. Although there will be some tasks where CAD can produce considerable improvements, compared to traditional methods, these tasks may not be representative of the total workload. In addition, allowance has to be made for any extra tasks which the use of CAD may involve.

The need to produce a realistic estimate of the future size of the DO labour-force is not just to calculate the labour-saving for an investment appraisal, but to calculate the size of the required CAD system, both in terms of size of processor and number of terminals. Here the danger is that if productivity improvements are overestimated, the purchased system will be too small.

The objectives for investment in CAD will vary between companies, and this will be reflected in the type and size of system selected. The following checklists have been compiled to help companies identify potential areas of cost and savings; it is not claimed that they are fully comprehensive, but they are designed to help identify the main factors to be considered in an evaluation.

COSTS OF CAD

Initial costs

- Hardware.
- Software.
- Installation (including building alterations, etc.).
- Consultancy costs (may include customizing software).
- In-house project team (may include customizing software).
- Database development.
- Operator training.
- Additional overtime during start-up.
- Subcontract work or use of contract labour during start-up.

Not only will the productivity of draughtsmen be considerably reduced during the initial training period, but the introduction of CAD may mean that a large number of standard components have to be entered into the system, resulting in a considerable increase in workload during the start-up period.

Running costs

- Maintenance contract.
- Insurance.
- Operating costs (i.e. electricity).
- Consumables.
- Software updates.
- Hardware expansion (i.e. additional storage).
- Training updates (i.e. for new staff).
- System management.
- Provision of back-up facilities.
- Shift premium (if shift working is introduced).
- Shift costs (i.e. heating and lighting on second shift).
- Staff upgrading.

Loss of productivity due to system downtime is often quoted as one of the costs of CAD, but in practice the allowance is made not as a running cost, but by ensuring that the size of system (e.g. number of terminals) is sufficiently large to cope with fluctuations in usage. Such fluctuations are more likely to be caused by fluctuations in DO workload than by recovery from system failure, provided that the system is managed efficiently and adequate provision is made for back-up.

Allowance for system downtime and workload fluctuations has to be made in the calculation of future labour requirements, but such an allowance would appear as a reduction in potential labour-saving, rather than as an increase in running costs.

BENEFITS

DO savings

- Reduction in number of existing draughtsmen (may involve retraining or redundancy costs).
- Avoid recruiting additional draughtsmen (including avoidance of recruitment and training costs).
- Reduce DO clerical labour.
- Reduce or avoid subcontract design work.
- Take on subcontract design work.
- Eliminate model making by use of three-dimensional design.
- Reduce outside graphic design work (for Marketing, Service Department, Publicity, etc.).
- Avoids expanding Drawing Office facilities (buildings, etc.).

Increased sales

- Company can quote shorter delivery times (reduced design/documentation time for customers' orders).
- Company can quote more reliable delivery times and improved reputation for delivery (improved control over design/documentation process).
- Improved quality of drawings and documentation reduces production delays (e.g. easier assembly), resulting in more reliable delivery performance.
- Eliminate incorrect ordering of components reducing production delays.
- Faster and better quotations.
- Ability to quote for all potential customer enquiries.
- Company image improved by having CAD.
- Customers would not place orders if company did not have CAD.
- New products can be introduced more frequently in response for need for shorter product life cycles.
- Shorter lead time for new product design gives faster response to changes by competitors.
- Easier and more frequent upgrading of existing products.
- Ability to quote for more orders because of increased ability to match design specification to customers' requirements.
- Ability to quote cheaper product because of ability to match design to customers' requirements, rather than quote more expensive standard design product.
- Increased ability to reduce product cost and improve design to make products more competitive.

Reduced stock levels

- Improved and faster paperwork reduces production lead times, hence reducing WIP.
- Component standardization allows a reduction in finished stocks.
- Standardization reduces variety of raw materials used and stocked.
- Improved documentation avoids ordering unwanted components.

Reduced production costs

- Improved drawings and documentation reduces production costs (e.g. easier assembly).
- Reduced scrap and rework.
- Increased ability to despatch correct product specification reduces service and warranty costs.

- Component standardization enables larger batches to be produced.
- Increased ability to optimize design reduces production and material costs.
- Faster issue of parts lists increases the time for production (reduces need for subcontract and overtime).
- Ability to supply products which only have those features required by customers, rather than more complex and expensive standard products.

Cost control

- Unprofitable orders eliminated by improved estimating.
- In-house cost control improved by better and more detailed estimating and quotations.

SYSTEM SELECTION

Usually in the past, CAD has been portrayed as an investment which will increase the productivity of draughtsmen, and therefore reduce the cost of running a DO which is often regarded as being an unproductive overhead. This emphasis on improved productivity has been reflected in the way that CAD has developed, and has been one of the main reasons for the development of CAD systems based on micro-computers, which has been seen as the most cost-effective way of replacing draughtsmen.

However, the major financial benefits which can be obtained from using CAD are not normally the savings in the DO but come from the effect which CAD can have on the rest of the company, such as Marketing and Production. It is the use of CAD for producing quotations and parts lists, introducing new products and standardizing designs, and for providing Production with improved drawings and documentation, which can make investment in it very attractive.

CAD should be regarded as an integral part of a company's information system, rather than as an electronic drawing-board, and therefore the need is for a machine with a considerable data-processing capability. The need to perform tasks such as producing general arrangement, assembly or site installation drawings for customers, or to select and compare standard components, normally requires on-line access to a database containing all standard components. The need is both to interrogate the database and transfer the selected component design to the CAD workstation.

To obtain full, company-wide potential of CAD the need, then, is either for a large, dedicated mini- or main-frame system or a series of intelligent workstations which are networked into a central file handling and storage computer in such a way that the networking is virtually transparent to the user.

As the power and versatility of intelligent workstations increases, so their use will increase because they help to overcome the problem experienced with the use of central processors. As systems using a central processor start to become fully utilized, the screen response time for all users can become extremely slow, especially if anyone is using the system for, say, finite element analysis, which requires a lot of processing power.

One of the problems faced by companies when selecting systems and calculating costs is in estimating the future size of storage capacity. To obtain the major benefits of CAD, in most companies, means that all users should have fast, on-line access to a large store of drawings. In addition, many companies will need to store on CAD both original and modification versions of all drawings which have been altered in any way. The result is that for CAD to be managed efficiently, the system will need a large and constantly expanding drawing database.

It may be easier to justify complex and expensive CAD systems which enable the company-wide benefits to be obtained, rather than cheaper microcomputer-based ones. The larger systems can provide a better investment than simple ones which only make sense in the context of DO labour-saving. However, with well over 200 CAD systems available, vendors are able to offer systems which can perform a wide variety of tasks, in addition to producing two-dimensional drawings such as finite element analysis and three-dimensional modelling; but buying CAD is rather like buying a car, in that all the extra features cost a lot of extra money!

In specifying the company's requirements, each of these extras needs to be examined not from the view point of 'can we use it', but 'is it really essential?' Several features, such as finite element analysis, may only be needed occasionally, and as such it may make sense to have the work done by a specialist contractor as and when required. The added advantage is that such contractors will have the specialist expertise required for the work.

CAD/CAM

Although CAD/CAM, which by implication means an integrated system, is portrayed always as being 'a good thing', in practice, an integrated system may not be the most economical way of programming CNC machine tools. As we have stated earlier, there are a number of ways of producing CNC control tapes and it is important that a company selects the most economical method, even if it not the most 'fashionable' thing to do.

Many companies evaluate investment in CAD/CAM as an alternative to their existing DO without CAD, and as such find the investment attractive. This, however, is incorrect because the cheaper alternative of a separate CAD system must be evaluated first. The danger is that for some companies the potential benefits of CAD will be reduced by investing in a more complex system, without at the same time producing significant extra benefits from CAM.

In evaluating integrated CAD/CAM it is necessary to identify all the additional costs and benefits involved, when compared with the alternative of having CAD separate from CNC programming. The following are some of the items that need to be considered:

Additional costs of CAD/CAM

- Increased computer size (DO response time should not suffer).
- More complex software as CAD interface is required.
- More expensive CAD-compatible terminals.
- CAD system to give CAD/CAM compatibility may not be optimum for DO needs.
- Programs produced may not be the most efficient for operating CNC machine tools.

Additional benefits of CAD/CAM

- May avoid transcription errors.
- Reduced programmer's time by eliminating need to re-enter component geometry.
- May reduce lead time from design to manufacture.

Companies that make components with highly complex geometry, or where tape preparation is on the critical path for product delivery, may obtain significant benefits from an integrated system. As component geometry becomes more complex, the benefits of avoiding data re-entry increase, but at the same time the complexity of the machine tools involved and their programming also increases, so that the efficiency to the programs produced by some CAD/CAM systems will decrease.

Although an integrated system will avoid data re-entry, the proportion of a programmer's time which is spent on data entry is for most components very small. As a result, many companies will find that the additional benefits of integrated systems will also be very small in relation to the extra costs involved.

In considering the economics of CAD/CAM the most important factor is not the efficiency of CNC programming, but the efficiency with which the programs will run the CNC machine tools. Whereas programming is a one-off cost, running machine tools is ongoing and also represents a much higher cost per hour. An additional danger is that a system selected to provide CAD/CAM capability may reduce the benefits which could be obtained from using CAD in the DO.

While companies selling CAD may claim to be able to offer CAD/CAM, there are, in practice, major technical problems in converting the geometric data within CAD into the format required for CNC programming. Unfortunately, there appears to be no factual information available which compares how efficiently programs produced by alternative methods will run machine tools. Subjective opinion is that programs produced using a special-purpose CAM system, with dedicated post-processors for each machine/control system configuration, will result in programs which make more efficient use of machine facilities.

Several machine-tool manufacturers are now producing machines which can be programmed by the operator while that machine is producing a batch of other components. Provided that the operators are suitably trained and motivated (and because they are highly conversant with all the capabilities of their machine tool), it is likely that the best investment for many companies will be a CAD system for use in the DO, with the CNC programming being done by machine operators. The data link between CAD and the machine tool is the conventional drawing.

PROCESS PLANNING (CAPP)

A logical progression from integrated CAD/CAM is to use the component geometry in a CAD system to produce automatically a process planning which gives a routing and operation times for components and can calculate component cost. The normal distinction which is made between different types of CAPP is 'variant', 'generative' and 'constructive' types. However, in considering the economics of CAPP, a more meaningful distinction is between 'intelligent' and 'non-intelligent' systems.

With 'intelligent' systems, the computer uses the component geometry to make decisions automatically about the sequence of operations. With 'non-intelligent' ones, the human planner makes the decisions and the computer only helps with the clerical functions in order to improve planning efficiency. Several commercial 'non-intelligent' packages are now available and these have been shown to provide considerable improvement in planning and estimating efficiency, as well as providing benefits such as tool standardization. Although 'non-intelligent' systems do not make decisions about routings, the time taken by planners in deciding routings represents a very small part of the total planning process. As a result, such systems can improve the efficiency of most of the work done by planners. Although the scope and operating efficiency of the commercial systems is still being improved, most of the current research into CAPP is directed towards trying to develop 'intelligent' systems.

However, as with CAD/CAM, the most important factor in considering the economics of CAPP is not the planning function, but rather the efficiency with which components are produced. Thus the question is not whether the planning is produced in a shorter time, but whether the cost of manufacture is reduced.

One of the problems encountered in trying to develop a CAPP system which will improve the quality of plannings is that, in most companies, the planning is used only as a general guide. The actual manufacturing method is decided by shopfloor personnel, such as foremen, who will vary it from batch to batch depending on day-to-day conditions, such as machine tool and operator availability, as well as the current production load.

Companies which produce a small number of different components in large volume will spend a considerable amount of time using *value engineering* techniques to try to optimize the design and manufacturing process of each component. Because of this, they will not rely on a CAPP program to determine component routing; therefore it is only companies producing a wide range of components in relatively small batches, using a large number of different manufacturing processes, which would consider using 'intelligent' CAPP.

One of the main criticisms made about conventional planning, and one of the main justifications given for the need to develop 'intelligent' systems, is that different planners will always plan the same component in different ways. The aim with CAPP therefore is not merely to be able to produce a routing, rather to determine the optimum routing. In trying to decide such an optimum routing the system needs not only to consider those manufacturing processes available within the company, it needs also to consider using processes which are only available by subcontracting.

A major problem in trying to develop 'intelligent' CAPP is that the potential number of permutations which have to be considered by the program can become so great that it may be beyond the capacity of any computer to run it. The danger is that, while trying to develop 'intelligent' CAPP is academically stimulating, it may become a similar problem to that of scheduling in Production Control. Although the logic of scheduling seems very simple, no one has yet been able to write a program which can calculate the *optimum* sequence for scheduling ten jobs through ten machines because of the astronomically large number of permutations which have to be considered.

Another reason put forward for the need to develop 'intelligent' CAPP is that it would enable a designer to find out the cost of making the component he was drawing, in order that he could change the design to make it cheaper. However, even if a CAPP system could be developed which automatically planned and costed a drawing, it would unlike a human planner be completely incapable of identifying which features made the component expensive to produce such that it could suggest to the designer how he could alter the design to make it cheaper. All the designer would be able to do would be to keep producing alternatives in the hope that one would be cheaper!

The third reason put forward to justify the need for 'intelligent' CAPP is that the average age of planners is about 55, and so in a few years time there will therefore be a major shortage of planners. This ignores the fact that, in most companies, people only become planners after they have gained many years' shopfloor experience. Although the average age of planners may be 55 now, it was probably still 55 ten years ago.

Most of the potential benefits of CAPP can be obtained today, using packages which are currently available. However, in considering how such packages can be integrated into a company's information system, they use little information from CAD, except the drawing which for operating efficiency needs to be on paper rather than on a computer screen. Most of the information produced by CAPP, such as routings and operation times, is used by MRPII and accounting systems, rather than by CAD; therefore the need is for CAPP to be linked to these systems for data transfer.

CAD CASE STUDY 1

The figures used in the case studies here are based on estimates used by individual companies and are not intended to suggest the correct level of expenditure on items such as training, nor the appropriate system cost for any size of company. Further, the figures should not be used to suggest that any company could have the same costs and savings, rather to show the types of benefit which companies may achieve.

The company makes capital plant in low volume, it has a turnover of approx. £20 million, and although its products have a standard basic design, each order is customized to suit the requirements of that particular customer. The design department has twelve draughtsmen whose work is divided between basic design and customer application. It is estimated that this work could be done in future by eight draughtsmen using CAD; however, there will be additional non-design work, including administration of the CAD system, so that the reduction in staff will only be three people.

The initial costs of the chosen CAD system are:

Capital cost	£240 000 in year 0
Initial training	£2 000 in year 0
Initial training	£2 000 in year 1
Overtime during start-up	£8 000 in year 1

There will be a system update in year three costing £10 000

. The annual costs from year 1 will be:

Maintenance and insurance   £24 000
Consumables and running cost   £2 000

The cost of system administration is not included as a cost factor, but is reflected in the value for labour-saving being lower (i.e. a saving of three not four people).

The major benefits which have been identified are:

1. The reduction in Drawing Office (DO) labour of three draughtsmen; the basic annual salary of £9500 is increased by 33% to £12 635, to include National Insurance, welfare costs, etc. The reduction is assumed to be two people in year 2 and three people in year three and onwards.
2. The current cost of scrap and rework in the company is £95 000, and it is assumed that with better-quality and more consistent drawings, and with more accurate documentation, this would be reduced by at least 5%, giving an annual saving of £4750 starting in year 3.
3. The total book value of all inventory is £4 600 000, and it is estimated that by standardizing designs, this could be reduced by 5%. Of the £230 000 reduction in book value, the cash flow reduction would be £138 000 in year 3 and the tax advantage of stock reduction would be £32 200 in year 4.
4. Faster throughput of paperwork would give manufacturing more time to meet delivery dates, thus reducing the current £40 000 cost of overtime by 10%, and reducing the current £80 000 cost of subcontract also by 10% giving a saving of £12 000 starting in year 2.
5. The increased ability to customize quickly the product to suit customers' required specification, including the ability to quote for more potential enquiries, would help marketing. A very conservative estimate was 1% extra sales (£200 000), giving a contribution to overhead recovery of £70 000 a year from year 2.

Tax is calculated on the basis of a 35% rate and capital allowances on the basis of a 25% first-year allowance, the allowance in subsequent years being 25% of the remaining reducing balance.

Table 18.1 shows the annual cash-flows used in the evaluation taking the life of the investment to be ten years. This gives a net present value (NPV) of +£219 532 and an internal rate of return (IRR) of 30.9%. Compared with the company's 12% cost of capital, the investment appears attractive. However, if the value of extra sales is taken as 5% rather than 1%, the return goes up to +£1 135 325 NPV and 78.5% IRR.

Table 18.1 Annual cash flows

	Year 0	Year 1	Year 2	Year 3	Year 4	Year 5 onwards
Capital cost	−240 000	−	−	−	−	−
Capital tax	−	21 000	15 750	11 812	8 859	Reducing
Start-up costs	−2 000	−10 000	−	−	−	−
Running costs	−	−26 000	−26 000	−26 000	−26 000	−26 000
System update	−	−	−	−10 000	−	−
Labour-saving	−	−	25 270	37 905	37 905	37 905
Production-saving	−	−	12 000	16 750	16 750	16 750
Stock reduction	−	−	−	138 000	−	−
1% extra sales	−	−	70 000	70 000	70 000	70 000
Revenue tax	−	700	12 600	−28 444	1 171	−34 529
Net cash flow	−242 000	14 300	109 620	210 023	108 685	Reducing

When evaluating investment in CAD, the estimates given by departments such as Marketing and Production are normally inclined to be conservative. In the company involved in this case study, for example, Marketing suggested verbally that 5% extra sales was realistic, but they would only 'put their names' to 1%. However, as the investment was seen to be very attractive with the estimate given, everybody was happy to leave it at that.

In many companies, estimating savings is often not at all scientifically accurate and managers tend to work in round numbers –i.e. 1%, 5%, 10%, etc. Although this seems rather crude, the estimates are given as 'it will be at least *x*', so that when the project is seen to be viable at that level, nobody thinks it worth trying to be more accurate.

The evaluations done in many companies include the full level of savings starting in year 1, the implication being that as soon as the system was installed, full savings could be achieved. Although some savings may be achieved in the first year of operation, it is probably more realistic to assume, as in the case studies here, that savings only start at the end of the first year of operation.

CAD CASE STUDY 2

The company makes standard products in medium/large volume and it has six different product ranges. Although most of the sales are made from their catalogue, approx. 20% of the £15 million per year turnover requires some customizing. There were eight draughtsmen working on standard designs and customizing, and initially, all eight would use the system. It was expected that there would be an increase in productivity, resulting in an eventual reduction of two people, as well as allowing for additional work to be done which was not feasible without CAD. The reduction in labour would be by natural wastage, so redundancy costs would not be involved. The initial costs are:

Capital cost   £190 000 in year 0
Training   £1 000 in year 0
Training   £1 000 in year 1
Overtime during start-up   £6 000 in year 1

The annual costs from year 1 will be:

Maintenance and insurance   £19 000
Consumables and running costs   £1 000

The savings were forecast as:

1. Labour saving of one person starting in year 2, and one person starting in year 3; the basic wage of £10 000 was increased by 33% to cover employment costs.
2. Introducing new product designs much more frequently than in the past would increase sales. Each product range would be tackled, in turn, over a three-year-period, and it was estimated that this would increase sales by at least 1%. The increase was phased over three years starting with £50 000 additional sales in year 2, going up to £150 000 in year 4, the contribution to overhead recovery being £20 000 and £60 000 respectively.
3. The redesign of products and component standardization was expected to reduce manufacturing costs by at least 1%, again phased over three years. The cost of manufacture, including material, was 55% of sales value, so the saving would be £27 000 in year 2, rising to £82 500 in year 4.
4. Product rationalization and component standardization would give a stock reduction; in addition, the value of stock would fall to reflect the reduced manufacturing costs. The book value of the original stock was £3 500 000, and it was assumed that this would reduce by 5%, half of the reduction being taken in year 3 and half in year 4. Of the £175 000 book value reduction, £113 500 was cash flow reduction and the tax advantage in the following year was £21 525.
5. The company identified other benefits which were included in their evaluation, for example, reduced scrap and rework, improved cost control and reduced clerical work in Production and Material Control resulting from improved documentation. For simplicity, these have been excluded from the case study.

Table 18.2 shows the annual cash flows used in the evaluation, taking the project life to be ten years, the tax rate to be 35% and a 15% cost of capital. This gives an NPV of +£267 091 and an IRR of 39.3%.

Table 18. 2 Annual cash flows

	Year 0	Year 1	Year 2	Year 3	Year 4	Year 5	Year 6 onwards
Capital cost	−190 000	−	−	−	−	−	−
Capital tax	−	+16 625	+12 469	+9 352	+7 014	+5 260	Reducing
Start-up costs	−1 000	−7 000	−	−	−	−	−
Running costs	−	−20 000	−20 000	−20 000	−20 000	−20 000	−20 000
Labour saving	−	−	+13 300	+26 600	+26 600	+26 600	+26 600
Sales increase	−	−	+20 000	+40 000	+60 000	+60 000	+60 000
Reduced costs	−	−	+27 500	+55 000	+82 500	+82 500	+82 500
Reduced stocks	−	−	−	+56 750	+56 750	−	−
Revenue tax	−	+350	+9 450	−14 280	−24 798	−41 422	−52 185
Net cash flow	−191 000	−10 025	+62 719	+153 422	+188 066	+112 938	Reducing

Chapter

19 Robots

Robots are commonly regarded as 'machines that can replace people', and most of the literature about industrial robots emphasizes their ability to replace manual workers. This attitude is reflected in the way that companies try to identify potential applications and the methods used to justify the cost of investment. This view of robots is also reflected in research and development which tends to concentrate on those features, such as vision, sense of touch and positioning speed, which help to make robots more 'competitive' with humans.

Surveys comparing investment in robots in various countries can be misleading, thus the figures which show that there are roughly five times as many robots in Japan as in the USA are normally dismissed on the grounds that different definitions have been used for what constitutes a robot. However, where comparable definitions are used, such as in Europe, it can be seen that some countries (e.g. the UK) are well behind their competitors in the use of robots. These differences are often explained away with suggestions that it is easier to justify robots in countries, that have higher labour costs such as West Germany.

Surveys of robot users show that where financial appraisal has been used, the justification is often entirely based on labour-savings. It has even been suggested that the way to evaluate robots is to calculate an equivalent 'wage' for a robot and for a human and, if the robot's wage is lower, the robot is 'hired'. Not only does this emphasis on labour-saving greatly understate the potential benefits of robots, but it also limits the range of applications for which they are considered.

Financial appraisal is not appropriate for some applications where the decision to invest in robots will be made on the basis of criteria other than financial ones; for example:

1. Some jobs are extremely hazardous (e.g. jobs involving radiation risks), so that company policy may be that robots must be used for safety reasons.

2. Increasingly there are jobs which can only be done by robots because of their complexity and accuracy.
3. Some jobs (e.g. aids for the handicapped) could be performed by humans but the problems and costs are so great that they are not done.

Although these applications for robots are often quoted, they probably represent only a small proportion of potential applications and financial appraisal will be needed in the majority of cases.

COSTS

In any investment it is necessary to identify all the cost factors, as well as the benefits. In the case of robots, this is extremely important because the cost of the robot itself may only be a small part of the total cost of the installation. For example, in the automobile industry the robot may represent only 25% of the total cost.

Robots are potentially highly dangerous machines which have to be fully guarded in such a way that humans cannot approach them when they are switched on. As a result, the required guard rails and safety interlocks can add considerably to the cost of an installation.

Another major area of cost is the equipment required to transport and locate components because, unlike humans, robots need to have all components presented in a predetermined orientation and position.

Installation and start-up costs

- Robot.
- Project design.
- End of arm grippers and tooling.
- Component conveyors and orientation equipment.
- Controls and interfacings.
- Guard rails and safety devices.
- Site preparation and equipment relocation.
- Installation.
- Programming.
- Training of operators, programmers and maintenance personnel.
- Production loss during start-up.
- Redundancy and re-training.

Running costs

- Maintenance.
- Insurance.
- Electricity.
- Consumables, (e.g. hydraulic fluid).

An important factor in any financial evaluation is the life of the project over which cash flows are discounted. For most AMT projects the accuracy of this value is not too critical because, as shown in Fig. 19.1, the change in IRR resulting from changes in working life is not great when the life of the project will be some ten years or more. With robots, however, the potential life may be very short, so that errors in estimating the life can have a significant effect on the IRR.

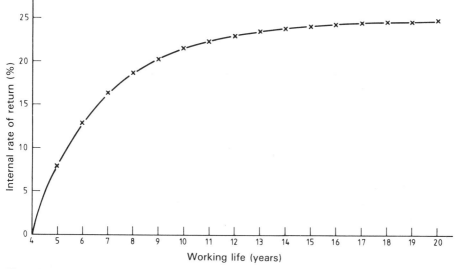

Fig. 19.1 Effect of working life on IRR.

Although the technology of robots is similar to that of CNC machine tools, and is now well proven, the life which is used to evaluate an investment in robots is likely to be determined by the life of the project which incorporates robots, rather than by the physical life of the robot itself. For example, if robots are used for automated assembly, any future change in product design may eliminate the need for robots or mean that robots are no longer economical.

There is a danger that if products have been designed such that they can be built by robots, the ability to re-design the product in future may be constrained by the perceived need to keep on using the robots. Although robots provide much greater flexibility for introducing product changes then does traditional fixed automation, they are much less flexible than humans in dealing with design changes.

Another important factor in a financial evaluation is the expected level of utilization which is used to calculate the magnitude of savings and also to calculate the rate per hour for the company's cost accounting system. When robots are being justified solely on the basis of labour-saving, it is necessary to find applications where the utilization will be high in order to maximize the savings. However, in applications such as the use of robots to deal with fluctuations in sales volume, a low level of utilization can be an advantage because this increases the flexibility of dealing with fluctuations in production.

Human operators unlike robots, cannot be switched on and off as required. In companies where production is intermittent because of fluctuations in sales, trying to respond by short-term hiring and firing can produce industrial relations problems, even assuming that suitable employees could be found when required. Difficulties may also arise with product quality during training.

To cope with sales fluctuations companies can adopt a variety of solutions: they can accept a level of overmanning, carry large buffer stocks or be prepared to lose potential orders. If the current policy is examined, it may be found that robots, with only intermittent operation, are viable without at the same time replacing existing labour.

BENEFITS

Projects aimed at using robots to replace humans in order to reduce costs often start with someone trying to find an application for a robot because 'fashion' suggests that investing in robots is the correct thing to be doing. One of the dangers of this attitude is that alternative conventional solutions may not be evaluated, even if, while a robot may be viable, the less fashionable alternative may prove a more profitable investment.

When applications are selected where the aim is reducing labour costs, they will often result in the installation of a single robot because it is difficult to find jobs which are sufficiently simple and repetitive that they can be performed by robots. At the same time, the task selected must provide sufficient work content to keep high the robot's utilization. The need is to make a sufficient labour-saving to justify the cost.

Alternative types of application, with motivations such as improving product quality or dealing with fluctuating sales, are more likely to involve several robots as an integral part of a major project. In such cases, the evaluation is not of the robots themselves, but the complete project of which robots happen to be part. Thus, in the following checklists of savings, the benefits are not just those obtainable from robots, but also from projects which include robots as an integral part of the project.

Direct savings

- Reduced labour costs.
- Use of robots for unpleasant or hazardous tasks can eliminate costs of absenteeism (e.g. sick pay) and cost of high labour turnover (e.g. recruitment and training).
- Eliminate cost of lost production and poor quality during training of new workers.
- Use of robots to load/unload plant and machinery can improve the utilization of equipment and increase the available hours, thus reducing machine/hour rate and reducing need to purchase additional plant and machinery.
- Reduced scrap.
- Reduced rework.
- Reduced cost of customer service and warranty payments.
- Reduced cost of quality control.
- Reliable and consistent quality eliminates cost of disruption of production.
- Components can be redesigned to reduce material cost.
- Use of robots instead of fixed automation allows for redesign during product life to reduce costs and improve product quality.
- Use of robots instead of fixed automation reduces the future capital cost of new and changed products.
- Reliable and consistent production times eliminates need for safety stocks and long lead times, thus reducing WIP.
- Fluctuating workload can be produced as required, thus eliminating need for buffer stocks.
- Flexibility to produce products to match customers' required specification, thus eliminating cost of supplying unwanted components.

Increased sales (or preventing sales being lost)

- Extra sales resulting from improved product quality.
- Lower production costs gives lower selling prices, resulting in extra sales.
- Increased ouput from existing plant gives more sales.
- Shorter downtime during introduction of new products reduces loss of output and sales.
- Flexibility allows new products to be introduced more often, resulting in extra sales.
- Faster response to changes in competitors' products prevents sales being lost.
- Increased ability to cope with rapid fluctuations in sales volume and product mix.
- Ability to match product specification required by customers increases number of quotations.

- Reduced selling price of products which contain only those components required by each customer increases sales.
- Shorter and more reliable product delivery increases sales.
- Products can be designed which would be impractical or uneconomical without the use of robots.
- Improved company image for sales promotion.

Concentrating on trying to find applications for robots where they can be justified on the basis of labour-saving created a severe restriction on the rate at which robots are being introduced because the number of such applications are very limited. The real potential for the use of robots is in applications such as improving product quality, dealing with fluctuations in sales and improving product design – in other words, increasing a company's ability to supply customers with what they want, when they want it.

The change in objectives, away from labour-saving towards making the company more competitive, means that such applications are likely to be much more profitable but, at the same time, require a change in the type of robots selected. The need is not for fast and complex robots which can be competitive with humans. Machines are required which are reliable, accurate, simple and cheap, in fact fast positioning speed may often be counterproductive.

As well as greatly increasing the range of potential applications, and their profitability, the change in objectives will help to change the view that robots are a threat to jobs. By using robots to help make the company more competitive, the result can be an overall increase in jobs and, as a consequence, the implementation is likely to be carried out with more enthusiasm and prove much more effective.

20 Computer integrated manufacture (CIM)

One aspect of AMT about which a lot has been written in recent years is **computer-integrated manufacture (CIM)**, but this literature has been mainly concerned with technical aspects of the subject; for example, the development of standards such as *open systems interconnection (OSI), manufacturing automation protocol (MAP)* and *initial graphics exchange standard (IGES)*. The financial benefits of CIM are not defined; they are generally assumed to be large, but it is thought that they will be obtained only at some future time when complete integration is possible.

Because the potential benefits have not been identified, there is a danger that CIM will be seen as one more panacea for which a lot of unrealistic claims has been made, and when these claims are not realized and fashion changes, then resources may be transferred away from CIM development.

CIM development is taking place, at present, in a number of different ways, the main ones being:

1. Development of standards such as OSI and IGES.
2. Manufacturers who are extending existing systems, such as CAD, by adding extra features (e.g. CNC programming).
3. Companies integrating computers for specific purposes such as the development of FMS.

Unfortunately, much of this development is random; and it is either aimed at some long-term perceived need where the benefits are not clearly defined or is the result of companies trying to solve short-term problems which are relevant to their own specific needs.

Any company considering its approach to the introduction of CIM must evaluate the costs and benefits of what is available today, and then compare this with any extra benefits which might be obtained by waiting for future developments. To do this, they have to start with the question: 'if full CIM technology existed, what financial benefits could be achieved?', and then consider how much of the benefits can be obtained today. For many companies, the answer is that most of the potential benefits of CIM can be obtained using currently available technology.

THE SCOPE OF CIM

There are two different views about the scope of CIM. Figure 20.1 shows CIM in terms of what is available today, although few manufacturers can offer a system which will perform even these limited functions. Figure 20.2

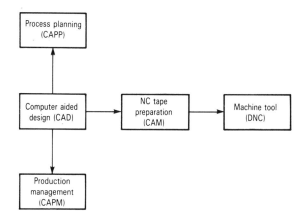

Fig. 20.1 Typical scope of current CIM installations.

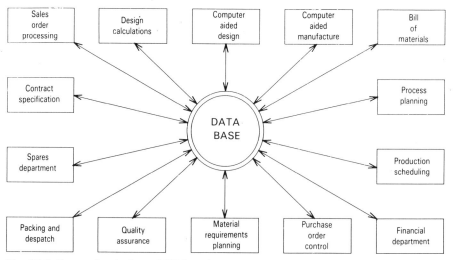

Fig. 20.2 Conventional view of CIM environment.

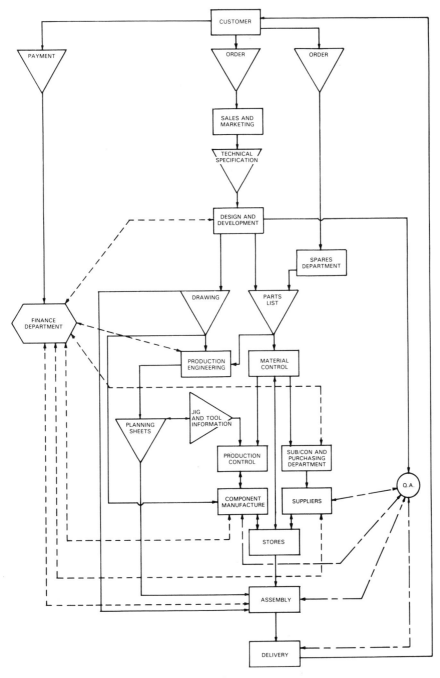

Fig. 20. 3 Simplified view of information flow.

shows the alternative view of CIM as many people expect it to be in the future; however, it is unlikely that such systems will be developed in practice because they make little commercial sense. These concepts of CIM tend to be based either on the limited view of what is currently feasible or a theoretical, and probably unrealistic, view of total integration in the future using a common database. In each case, the ideas are based on what the technology might be able to do, rather than on the financial objectives for which technology may be used.

Figure 20.3 shows a simplified view of the flow of data within a company relating to a customer's order. An equally complex but very different diagram could be drawn for the flow of data relating to other activities such as the design and manufacture of a new product.

What needs to be done is to consider the improvements, as a result of using CIM, that are possible within this type of data flow. However, the aim is not to try to identify areas where integration is technically possible, but rather where the use of CIM can make the company more profitable and competitive.

As discussed in an earlier chapter, two of the most important benefits of investing in AMT are increasing sales volume and increasing the profitability of orders. These are the areas where CIM can make a significant impact. Although a large number of factors can have an effect on sales volume and profitability, here the major factors are:

1. Shorter and more reliable delivery.
2. The ability to offer customers the required product specification.
3. Faster and more frequent introduction of new or redesigned products.
4. Better-quality products.
5. Lower selling price.
6. Faster, more accurate and better-presented quotations.

THE EXTENT OF INTEGRATION

An engineering company, as shown in Fig. 20.3, is likely to be using a variety of computer systems that have been bought at various times to perform specific functions within the company. Most of these will be incompatible in terms of hardware, operating system, programming language and database structure. Fortunately, most of these systems, which were probably installed as self-contained packages, need little or no data from the other computer systems in the company.

Because of the complexity of computer applications in engineering, suppliers tend to concentrate on specific areas of expertise and try to develop programs which provide an optimum solution to a company's needs in that area. Despite the large number of suppliers, very few can offer both CAD and MRP, let alone programs for all the other potential engineering applications. The fact that there are a lot of different ways of trying to provide an optimum program is demonstrated by the large number of packages available. For instance, there are over 200 CAD and 100 MRP systems available, and the suppliers of each would claim to have some advantage over the others.

Even when the seven functional layers of OSI standards are established and incorporated into hardware, it will still not be possible to integrate systems because, as shown in Fig 20.4, integration requires much more than the OSI standards. For most packages the programming languages, application programs, database management systems and databases will still be incompatible. Not only is it in the interest of suppliers to keep it this way because it helps discourage existing customers from changing suppliers, but the nature of programs may require it.

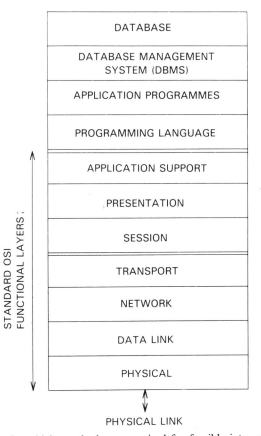

Fig. 20.4 Levels for which standards are required for feasible integration.

Programs such as MRPII and financial systems are designed for data processing and normally use Cobol-type languages, with the hardware configuration and database structure designed to optimize data transfer to and from file storage. CAD systems, on the other hand, tend to use Fortran-type languages, with the hardware and database being designed to optimize screen response and engineering calculation. It is becoming increasingly possible to run packages, such as CAD or MRPII, on several makes of computer, so that it is feasible, in theory, to overcome the problems of OSI standardization by using only one make of computer – i.e. IBM, DEC or Prime – for all packages within a company. In practice, there are major problems in so doing, for there are not only considerable technical difficulties, but may also be large differences in operating speeds. Because the hardware configuration will not be optimal for all the applications, packages may have to be selected which are not the best that are available for the company.

LINKING OR INTEGRATION

A major distinction has to be made between *linking* and *integration*; linking requires only the ability to transfer data in ASCII code in a predetermined format and in such a way that the systems have no ability to interact with each other. Integration not only provides the ability to transfer data, but also allows the systems to interact with each other such that the user of one system can access, interrogate and alter data on another. With some applications, such as FMS, integration is essential because considerable interaction is required between the various computers; in such cases, manufacturers are able to overcome the problems of integration by using compatible computers.

Fortunately, such as in the example shown in Fig. 20.3, most of the data which has to be transferred between computer systems within a company is for management control. As such, it is of a standard nature which can be in a predetermined format, and it does not require any interaction between the systems. This means that the majority of computer systems in a company (which were probably bought as self-contained packages) do not need to be integrated with other systems because the data that is required to be transferred can be transmitted by linking computers.

In some cases, the need is to transfer information rather than data, which requires neither linking nor integration; for example, where the user of one system needs to interrogate another system to obtain information which is to be used indirectly. Thus a designer using a CAD system will need to find out the current stock and WIP status of components which are to be modified. Such information, then, is needed by the designer for decision-making, not for direct use in the CAD system. Transfer of such information can be achieved by providing the designer access to a terminal of the MRPII system, with the designer acting as the link between CAD and MRPII. Other examples of this use of dual systems to obtain information, rather than transfer data are:

1. *Marketing*, when using CAD to produce quotations, need to be able to interrogate the MRPII system to check on possible delivery dates.
2. *Production engineers* faced with a material shortage need to be able to check the CAD system to find out if any alternative can be used and then MRPII to check on the stock availability.
3. *Quality Control*, when trying to find and inspect suspect components, need to be able to interrogate the MRPII system to find the location of all WIP batches and finished stocks.

TRANSFER OF DATA

Potentially, there are three major computer systems in most companies (i.e. CAD, MRPII and Accounting), and each of these needs to be linked to the other two for the transfer of data. In some cases, MRPII and Accounting may be incorporated into one system, while in some companies Financial Accounting and Cost Accounting may be separate systems.

Most of the literature about CAD is concerned with its use in the design function; however, as discussed earlier, the main financial benefits obtainable from the use of CAD can come from elsewhere in the company (e.g. Marketing and Production). In a similar way, the literature about the transfer of CAD data has concentrated on the transfer of geometric data, such as with the use of IGES, but it is not the transfer of geometric data which can provide the major financial benefits.

Where there is highly complex design data, such as the aerospace or nuclear industries, and where quality assurance is of primary importance, it can make sense for companies to have CAD systems which are compatible with those used by their major suppliers in order to avoid transcription errors. The majority of companies, however, would gain little or no real benefit from this and most would find it irrelevant.

Most companies obtain components and materials from a large number of suppliers while at the same time suppliers have a large number of customers, each of which potentially may use a different make of CAD system. However, the only time geometric data may have to be transferred is during the design of new of modified products. Even then, the saving in time by eliminating data re-entry will normally be insignificant.

For internal use, the majority of companies do not need to transfer geometric data between different CAD systems, their need is to transfer alpha-numeric data between CAD and the other main systems in the company (e.g. MRPII and Accounting).

For external use, the data which is regularly transferred between customers and suppliers is concerned with orders, delivery, invoicing, etc., so that although linking systems to transfer this type of data between companies could be beneficial, there is no need for companies to have the same CAD system.

The traditional approach to dealing with customers' orders is the same as used in batch manufacture, whereby an order passes through a series of departments (e.g. Marketing, Design, Stock Control, Process Planning and Production Conrol), and at each stage where work has to be done the order enters a queue of other orders. The result is that, while the time taken from receipt of order to the start of manufacture may be measured in weeks, the actual work content may only be measured in hours.

A survey of eight engineering companies, carried out by UMIST, looked at the time taken for customers' orders to pass through the company. Figure 20.5 shows the time spent in various departments; on average 45% of the delivery time quoted to customers was taken up by the production

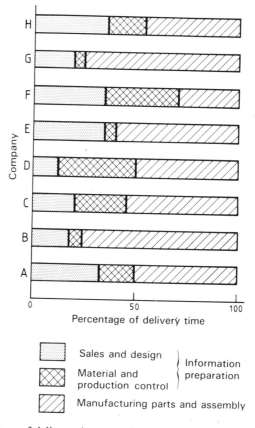

Fig. 20.5 Percentage of delivery time spent in departments

of paperwork before manufacturing was started. Despite the fact that all eight companies said that delivery was important in obtaining orders, most seemed to have concentrated all their efforts in the past on reducing manufacturing lead times. This seemed to be because orders normally only became overdue once they were in production, and although delays occurred in the pre-manufacturing stages, late delivery was usually seen as being a production problem.

It was estimated that by using CAD to deal with customers' enquiries and orders, and by linking CAD to MRPII for the transfer of parts lists, most of the companies in the survey could reduce their delivery time by a third as well as improving the reliability of delivery. Here the use of CAD includes:

1. Converting customers' enquiries into a technical specification.
2. Producing quotations for Marketing to send to customers.
3. Converting orders, based on these quotations, into parts lists and packing lists.
4. Automatically transferring parts lists to Production, indictating any components where new drawings still have to be produced.

In order to improve the speed, accuracy and quality of quotations, it is necessary to improve the accuracy of the cost information available. To do this, the Cost Accounting computer should be linked to the MRPII system to receive data about operation times and methods. At the same time it should be linked to the CAD system to transfer cost data for use in the estimating module within the CAD package.

Transferring parts lists between computer systems using manual data entry is both time-consuming and prone to error. As a result, it is quite common for Engineering, Production and Finance departments to be using a different set of parts lists. By linking CAD to the systems used in other departments, it is possible to ensure that only one set of parts lists, initially produced on CAD, is used throughout the company.

Linking systems for the transfer and updating of parts lists can speed up the introduction of design changes, as well as helping to ensure that all departments are using the same parts lists. In addition, linking rather than integration may help to improve the procedures for dealing with design modifications.

If the CAD, MRPII and Financial systems are integrated such that the user of one system may alter the data on another system, there is a danger that designers may start to modify parts lists in other departments without investigating the full implications, and without adhering to a formal design change procedure. Transferring changes between linked systems means that the users of each system are aware of, and must implement, all changes.

To be able to transfer data between linked systems, the data must be in a format which is usable in both the linked computers. The need therefore is for the development of a standard format for data such as parts lists. All CAD systems could then contain a module in the application program which converts the required data into this format ready for transfer to linked MRPII and Financial systems. These, in turn, would have a corresponding module to convert the standard format data back into the form needed by the application program.

Even without the development of such standard modules, companies can still link existing systems for data transfer. Although this may require a considerable amount of work, because the software within each system will need to be modified, the potential benefits can make the expenditure a most attractive investment.

The potential financial benefits of CIM are extremely large, but most will come from the transfer of data for management control between computer systems. This can be done using existing technology. Because most of the benefits of CIM do not require full integration, the need is for the development of ways which make it easier for companies to identify and obtain the benefits which are currently available, rather than simply developing standards, such as OSI, where the benefits will only be achieved at some date in the future.

CIM CASE STUDY

The company is investing in new machinery and facilities in a purpose-built factory in order to manufacture their latest range of products for the computer industry. The decision they now have to make is whether to operate these facilities with conventional control systems, using manual work-moving and storage techniques, or to invest in completely automated material storage and handling, thereby turning the factory into a CIM environment.

Marketing have estimated that if traditional batch-manufacturing techniques are used, with the consequent long lead times and inflexibility associated with the manual operation of the factories used for the company's other products, sales of the new product will be 400 000 a year at a selling price of £18.50 each, giving an annual turnover of £7 400 000.

The investment which has to be evaluated is not the new factory and machinery because the decision has already been made to invest in these, but the computer control systems and the automatic material transport and storage system. What has to be identified therefore are the additional costs and benefits of CIM when compared with conventional control systems and manual material-handling equipment.

The technology that is being considered is currently available without further development and has been demonstrated in a similar environment. The technology as such is not perceived to represent a high risk, the uncertainty being in the company's ability to change the attitudes and way of working of the people who will move from the existing factory.

The investment includes automatic guided vehicles (AGV) and a fully automatic storage system, and these will be directly integrated with the new MRPII system which the company is installing. This means that all material movement from goods received to final despatch will be completely computer-controlled on a real-time, on-line basis. The on-line control will allow rapid and accurate purging and replacement of stock at all workstations, so that it will be possible to change production between models with considerably less delay than with a manual system and therefore allow for shorter production runs.

Faster changeover and reduced throughput times will enable production to be much more closely related to customers' requirements, leading to both a reduction in the level of finished product stock and an increase in sales volume. The assumption is made that the whole factory can be operated on a flow-line basis rather than as a batch-production unit, which would be required if manual handling and control was used. This would result in shorter product lead times and a lower level of WIP.

The reduced penalty in time and cost of changing between models will enable product variants to be produced in relatively small quantities to suit the needs of specific customers. Using traditional batch manufacture, the orders for these would either have been lost or found to be unprofitable because the product cost would have been too high.

Because all material transactions will be directly controlled by computer, the level of data accuracy will be much higher. This will help provide the confidence in the MRPII system which is needed for the purchasing department to operate on a *Just in Time* (JIT) material supply basis, thus reducing the level of raw material stock which is carried.

Prolonged storage of electronic components leads to deterioration and contamination, creating problems with solderability. The on-line control of all stocks can ensure that material is used on a *first in first out* (FIFO) basis, rather than the *last in first out* (LIFO) stock usage normally associated with manual systems. This can reduce the need for cleaning and washing components as a rework operation and improve the quality of the finished product.

The computer control of all stock movements means that the system can provide the automatic traceability required for BS 5750 quality standard. Trying to meet the requirements using manual systems would be much more difficult and require perpetual stock audit by the Quality Control department. In addition, the much lower stock levels and FIFO usage will mean that any problems of faulty components can be identified more quickly and any resultant corrective action will involve less scrap and rework.

Costs

* The cost of the automatic stores, AGVs, work-handling equipment and

- computer system will be £725 000 in year 0, of this £545 000 would be capital and £180 000 revenue.
- The additional cost of maintenance will be £10 000 a year from year 1.
- An additional person will be needed to monitor the computer system at a cost of £8 500 a year basic salary, plus 33% labour on-cost (National Insurance, etc.).

Savings

- Expenditure of £70 000 on manual storage and handling equipment will be avoided in year 0.
- The need for stores and work-moving personnel will be avoided, saving three people at £7 000 basic wage + 33% from year 1.
- The need for having a progress chaser (@ £8 000 + 33%) and a VDU operator to enter data into the MRPII system (@ £7 000 + 33%) will be avoided, the savings starting in year 1.
- Avoiding the need for the manual perpetual audit required for BS 5750 quality standard will save one person (@ £7 000 + 33%) from year 1.
- In the existing factories stock represents thirteen weeks production on average:
    Finished stock = 5 weeks output. WIP = 5 weeks. Raw material = 3 weeks. It is estimated that in the new factory the stock levels will be: Finished stock = 3 weeks. WIP = 2 week. Raw material = 2 weeks. Inventory is valued on the basis of the cost of manufacture, so relating the reduced stock levels to the forecast output of 400 000 units a year gives a total book value saving of £542 500 in year 1, of which the cash flow element is £355 200, the tax advantage in year 2 being £65 555.
- Based on the cost of scrap and rework in the existing factories, the saving is estimated to be £9 000 a year from year 1.
- Because the factory can run with much lower levels of inventory, the space required for storage will be much smaller; however, the factory has already been built, so no cash flow saving will result.
- Using traditional controls would have meant that manufacturing lead time would be five weeks, but the inflexibility of the factory ordering and control system would mean sales having to quote at least ten weeks. Marketing estimated that if they were able to quote four weeks, and this was achieved consistently, they would be able to increase sales by at least 5%. The contribution to overhead recovery, fom year 1, would be £148 000 a year.
- Given the ability to produce product variants in relatively small quantities, without cost penalty, would allow Marketing to quote for more orders and result in an increase in sales of 2% from year 1. Because Marketing could quote a higher premium price for these orders, the contribution to overhead recovery would be £70 000 a year.

Although the decision to invest would result in a permanent change in the way that the factory will operate, the life of the project in the evaluation is based on the expected life of some of the equipment, such as the AGVs, and is taken to be seven years. The tax rate is 35% and the cost of capital 15%.

In estimating the savings the values for labour, scrap and rework and stock reduction were calculated on the basis of the expected values, but the estimates for additional sales were made on the basis of 'it will be at least as much as this', because there was not such a direct relationship between cause and effect as there was with inventory.

Table 20.1 gives the cash flows used in the evaluation which shows a 61.5% IRR and a +£622,027 NPV. To show how sensitive the result is to the accuracy of the estimates, the following changes were tried.

If the effect on sales is excluded from the evaluation, the return would be 14.1% IRR and −£8,909 NPV, but if, instead of 5% and 2%, the additional sales were taken as 10% and 4% respectively, the return would increase to 99.4% IRR and +£1 252 964 NPV. If the inventory reduction is only 50% of the estimated value, the return will be 44.5% IRR, even if stock reduction is excluded completely the return will be 30.5% IRR. If the labour-saving is completely excluded, the return will be 50.7% IRR.

Table 20.1 Annual cash flows

	Year 0	Year 1	Year 2	Year3	Years 4–7	Year 8
Capital	−545 000	–	–	–	–	–
Capital avoided	+70 000	–	–	–	–	–
Capital tax	–	+41 563	+31 172	+23 379	Reducing	+5 548
Installation	−180 000	–	–	–	–	–
Running costs	–	−21 305	−21 305	−21 305	−21 305	–
Labour-savings	–	+57 190	+57 190	+57 190	+57 190	–
Scrap and rework	–	+9 000	+9 000	+9 000	+9 000	–
Extra sales	–	+218 000	+218 000	+218 000	+218 000	–
Stock reduction	–	+355 200	–	–	–	–
Revenue tax	–	+63 000	−26 455	−92 010	−92 010	−92 010
Net cash flows	−655 000	+722 648	+267 602	+194 254	Reducing	−86 462

Chapter

21 Information technology (IT)

While systems such as MRPII are often known as **information technology (IT)**, the use of the term IT is taken here as applying to those systems, such as *Management Information Systems* (MIS), whose scope and application are not yet clearly defined and understood. Although managers have had difficulty in trying to justify AMT systems, such as CAD and MRPII, there have always been significant direct savings (e.g. labour and operating expenses) which could be attributed to the investment.

Where computers have been used for applications that could not be directly related to the cost of manufacture, or where the potential for direct savings was very limited, such as in marketing, it has seemed that financial justification was impossible. Whereas making substantial reductions in the Drawing Office (DO) labourforce may have seemed to be a realistic objective, planning to do the same with marketing labour would be seen as unrealistic.

Most of the computer systems in manufacturing companies are given generic names such as CAD/CAM, MRPII, CAPP, and so on, whereas in non-manufacturing organizations (e.g. banks, retailers, hospitals, government departments, etc.) most of the systems are simply referred to as IT. The difficulty experienced by these organizations in justifying expenditure, often amounting to several hundred million pounds, has helped reinforce the belief that the introduction of IT, whether it is just a word processor or a complex MIS, could not be evaluated in financial terms.

In trying to show how IT can be evaluated, it is necessary to look at the problems faced by non-manufacturing organizations in order to show that even in such applications IT can be evaluated in the same way as AMT. There is a widespread belief that there is something new or special about IT which somehow makes it different from any other investment, and it is often said that the techniques used to evaluate traditional investments such as machine tools are not appropriate. At the same time, engineers who are faced with exactly the same problems think that there is something different and special about AMT.

Twenty years ago computer systems were being developed to automate existing labour-intensive functions, such as payroll, book-keeping, stock control, invoicing, and so on, and their justification was largely based on labour-saving. At the same time, computer control was being applied to machine tools and the resultant increase in productivity meant that they too could be justified using labour-saving.

As IT developed, its complexity and range of potential applications has increased enormously but, at the same time, the earlier concentration on labour-saving application has meant that the scope for justifying investments on the basis of direct savings has greatly reduced. However, IT is not unique in this: exactly the same thing has been happening as machine tools have evolved into FMS, and the lessons that have been learnt in evaluating FMS can be used to show how the same can be done for IT.

In the early days of computers, companies often employed technical experts, who while they understood computers, did not understand company management. Additionally, the technical jargon they used meant that other managers could not understand computers! The result was that development of systems was normally done on the basis of automating existing procedures, and their justification was on the basis of trying to perform the existing function in a more cost-effective way. This has meant that the aim of IT investment is often seen as being to reduce the cost of computer transactions, and attempts to measure the benefits of IT have concentrated on trying to somehow measure the 'cost of information'.

This has been done by comparing the cost of computer transactions with that of manual transactions, or measuring the time to carry out tasks, such as 'budgets now take a day to prepare rather than a week'. Other approaches, such as putting in mechanisms for charging for IT services, are not really trying to justify the cost, only controlling costs for IT users. As with AMT, the complexity of IT systems has increased to the stage that they can be used to improve the total organization by changing the way it functions, rather than simply trying to improve the efficiency of running the existing procedures.

In fact the 'cost of information' is not the important factor, what matters is the effect that improving the availability of information can have on the organization, and this is the area where the benefits were normally thought to be intangible. The problem with IT has been that people have attempted to measure the wrong things, such as labour productivity, management effectiveness or the quality of information. As a result, investment is aimed at the wrong goals, such as improving the quality of information or increasing managers' productivity, rather than specific financial objectives relating to improvements in the organization.

In trying to measure the quality of information several factors have to be considered. Here it is not merely that the information may be wrong or inaccurate, but there may be a lack of information, or too much of it, or it may be in the wrong form, so that it is difficult to use without error. However, improving the quality of information is not in itself a financial benefit. Measuring the quality of information and trying to define the required quality is part of the process of establishing the technical specification. The financial benefits which have to be quantified are the effects which improved information will have on the organization.

With FMS investment, one has to start by defining the improvements that are needed in the company's ability to meet customers' requirements, and then go on to define the improvement in manufacturing flexibility needed to achieve this. The same principle applies to IT, where the financial objectives have to be defined before any consideration is given to what changes are needed in information, and what technology is required to achieve this change. Unfortunately, at present, managers often start by defining the technology before they attempt to identify the benefits, which is the wrong way round.

In trying to rationalize this, managers often quote examples of how organizations have found that there were major unforeseen benefits which became apparent only once an IT investment had been made. Of course, like most apocryphal stories, the examples quoted tend to have happened in other organizations!

The belief that 'we won't know all the benefits until we have made the investment' is widespread. But it assumes that the senior managers within an organization do not understand the business they are in, and that they cannot predict what changes will be needed to ensure the organization has a viable, long-term future.

As has happened with AMT, the ability to evaluate any IT project and include all the potential benefits shows up here the need for change in both the nature of projects chosen and the required technology. Examples of this change of objective are:

1. A retailer using IT to increase turnover by increasing the ability to supply customers, rather than just using IT to try to control inventory levels, where the ongoing benefit of increased turnover can be much greater than the benefits from reduced inventory costs.
2. An estate agency using IT to provide a better service for potential customers, thus increasing fees and also the number of properties handled, rather than trying to reduce operating costs.
3. A bank using IT to provide a better service to customers with the aim of increasing the number of customers and turnover, rather than just reducing staff costs.

With companies, the reason for IT investment is to increase profitablity and competitive ability and to ensure a viable long-term future, but non-commercial organizations, such as hospitals, police forces or government departments, have a different set of objectives, for their aim is to provide a better and more cost-effective service for their customers, the general public.

The aim, with companies, is to maximize benefits, while with non-commercial organizations, the aim is to minimize the cost of providing the required service; for example:

1. Investment in IT by a police force has to be compared with alternative methods. In order to achieve the required level of policing, is it better to invest in IT to improve the efficiency of the existing police officers, or to invest in providing additional officers.?
2. In hospitals, rather than just trying to reduce clerical costs, the aim of IT is to provide a better-quality and more cost-effective service for patients.
3. A government department responsible for tax collection can use IT to increase the percentage of tax which is collected, rather than merely reducing the cost of collection.

There is nothing special about IT projects which somehow marks them out as different from any other investment, and the evaluation techniques used for AMT can be used for IT. The need is for managers to have a better understanding of the nature of their company's business, and the way that IT can be used to change and improve the organization. As with AMT, most IT projects will make financial sense only when their objective is to achieve those benefits previously excluded as intangible.

22 The future development of AMT

In the past, the development of AMT has been a highly random process, but with the benefit of hindsight, it can be seen that many of the bright ideas of the past were trapped in a blind alley, or were employed to attempt to solve non-existent or unimportant problems. Even when the basic ideas themselves have been correct, their application has not been effective because the potential benefits of the technology have not been clearly defined. Nor have any of the limitations of the application of technology been identified.

As a result, new technology and management systems have tended to be seized on by people looking for new concepts to promote. This has led to many unrealistic claims being made for what becomes the fashion or latest 'flavour of the month'. It has also resulted in the original concept being used for applications for which it was never intended . When these claims do not materialize, the technology loses all credibility and it sinks into obscurity and, as a result, the original good idea fails to achieve realization.

In any field, not just manufacturing, it is only by having clearly defined objectives that research and development can be effective. The problem with developing AMT has been the inability of anyone to define the objectives in analytical terms. When the expected benefits are described in general terms, such as 'increased flexibility of production', 'better-quality products' or 'increased management control', it is difficult to decide on the nature of the technology required to achieve the benefits, let alone decide how these objectives can be achieved in a cost-effective manner.

The first stage in selecting any investment should be to define the financial objectives in such a way that they can be used to define the technical specification. In the same way, the first stage of developing new technology must be to define the financial benefits which the technology is intended to achieve.

In order that the development of AMT can be as rapid as possible, and that once the technology has been developed it is applied in the most appropriate applications, the starting-point must be to define the potential benefits of AMT in quantifiable terms. The development of AMT should not merely be aimed at trying to achieve those benefits which will become available at some undefined date in the future as has tended to happen with CIM. Nor should development be directed only at trying to achieve the maximum benefits which can be obtained in the short term.

It is necessary to start by defining the long-term changes which are needed in manufacturing, and then go on to identify the detailed steps which have to be taken to achieve these long-term goals. By doing this, the development of AMT can be planned such that the major potential benefits are achieved at the earliest possible date. While people believed that there was something special about AMT which meant that conventional investment appraisal and costing principles could not be applied to it, ideas about the way in which AMT should develop were highly subjective.

It now appears that the problems encountered in evaluating and costing AMT have been caused by a combination of the use of outdated procedures and a lack of understanding about the way that AMT can affect a company. In fact there does not appear to be anything wrong with basic accountancy principles, the problem has been their incorrect application.

The ability now exists of considering a company as a total economic entity, of which manufacturing is an integral part, and this means that it is possible to define the way that manufacturing must change in future. This can be done in such a way that the objectives for manufacturing are defined in quantifiable terms.

By concentrating development on solving major problems, rather than on short-lived 'flavour of the month' fashions, the cost of AMT development should be considerably reduced. In addition, the technology which is developed in future need no longer be seen as 'a solution looking for a problem to solve', and the rate at which the efficiency of industry improves can now be much faster than it has been in the past.

Index

Absorption costing *see* Costing
Accountancy procedures 4–5
Accounting rate of return 9, 10, 20–1
Advanced manufacturing technology
    see under individual
    technologies

Batch quantities 79, 139–43
Batch manufacture 121–2
Better quality products *see* Product
    quality

Capacity constraints 88–9
Capital
    cost of 8, 107–12
    intensive 22
    non-capital expenditure 84–5
Cash flows 8, 27–46, 51
Component complexity 141–2, 163
Component selection 147–9
Compound interest 11
Computer aided design 7, 17–18, 38,
    136, 195–208, 219–20
    savings 53, 62, 132
Computer aided manufacture 195,
    200–2
Computer integrated manufacture
    215–27
Computer numerical control 19–20,
    24–6, 36, 95, 138–52
Cost accounting *see* Costing
Costing 80–99
    standard costs 81–3, 121
    systems 2–4, 8, 27–9, 80–1,
    113–14

operating variance 91, 113
Cost of capital *see* Capital
Cost reduction 4

Delayed projects 42–4
Delivery performance 173–4
Depreciation 10, 20, 27–8, 29–31,
    94, 138
    life 36
Discounted cash flow 9, 10–13,
    21–2
Do nothing alternative 23, 24

Family planning *see* Group
    technology
Flexible manufacturing 153–82
    control systems 168, 172,
    177
    factory 171–2
    module 24–6, 158–63
    systems 3, 52–3, 92–3, 133,
    163–8
    tooling systems 161–2
    transfer line 96, 168–71
    utilization 155–8, 164–6
    see also Increased flexibility of
    production
Floor space 55–6

Grants 10, 46
Group technology 94, 122, 125, 129,
    173

Increased flexibility of production
    47–8, 50–1, 154

Industrial relations 4, 130–4
Inflation 111–12
Information technology 228–31
Intangible benefits 2–3, 47–64,
    90–1, 118–19
Interest rates *see* Capital cost of
Internal rate of return 13, 21–2
Inventory 65–79
    reduction 56–7, 59, 76–9, 123,
        187, 198
    valuation 66–76
Investment strategy 2, 127–9
Ivan 21, 33

Just In Time 2, 4, 20, 59, 121–6,
    129

Labour
    hour rate 57–8, 81–3, 85–6, 131
    intensive 22
    savings 4, 78–9, 166, 196, 209
Lead times 121–2

Machine hour rate 83
Magnitude of benefits 58–64
Make or buy 86–7
Manufacturing resources planning 7,
    37–8, 51, 183–94, 219–20
Material requirement planning 37–8,
    78, 136
Monitoring performance *see*
    Post-audits
Mutually exclusive projects 21

Net present value 12–13, 21–2
New technology 57, 104–6
Non-existent benefits 55–8

Opportunity cost 11
Overhead allocation 8, 31–3, 131,
    138

Payback 9–10, 15–20, 35
Plant life 95–6
Post-audits 3, 113–14
Probability analysis 102
Process planning 202–4
Production bottlenecks 88

Product
    cost 88, 96–9
    quality 3–4, 50, 115–20, 214
    life 95–6
    selling price 59–60, 81, 88
Profit and loss account 20

Quality *see* Product quality
Quality circles 117–18, 128

Replacement decisions 22–6
    machines 35–6
Resale value 38–40, 45
Rework *see* Scrap
Risk 3, 100–6, 111
    perceived 12, 176
Robots 209–14
Running costs 6, 10, 14

Sales
    forecasts 87, 124
    increased volume 61, 62–3,
        188–9, 198, 213–14
Scrap 145–6
Selecting technology 135–7
Selling price *see* Product selling
    price
Sensitivity analysis 98, 103–4
Set-up times 139
Simulation 172–3, 175–8
Social costs 53–5
Spreadsheets 32–3
Stage payments 10
Standard cost *see* Costing
Start-up time 146–7
Subcontracting 28–9, 86–7
Subsequent projects 40–2

Taxation 10, 34, 44–6, 108, 112
Training costs 58

Utilization 89, 91–5, 121, 124–5,
    143–5
Value analysis 117, 131, 155
Value engineering *see* Value analysis

Working capital 42
Working life 33–8, 110, 189, 211
Work in progress *see* Inventory